"Some books are packed with useful content. *Stack The Logs!* is JAM-PACKED with useful content. Each chapter provided me with small, bite-sized truths that brought home an important aspect of success. Great reading with time-tested wisdom. Read it slowly and apply it daily!"

—Chris Widener, President
Made for Success and Extraordinary Leaders

"*Stack The Logs!* is a GREAT book which inspires, helps and encourages the reader in every part of life. I recommend purchasing a case of them so that you can have them ready as precious gifts for your friends, family and business associates."

—Dottie Walters CSP, International Speaker,
Author, Consultant
Publisher/Editor: SHARING IDEAS MAGAZINE
Author *Speak & Grow Rich*
President, Walters International Speakers Bureau

"This book is a powerful wake up call for who we can become and how to get the most out of life. Frank Lunn's words will touch your heart, strengthen your courage, and stoke your enthusiasm."

—Rich Fettke
Success Coach and Author of *EXTREME SUCCESS*

"I salute all those behind this worthy project and encourage everyone to buy *Stack The Logs!* Everyone wins from this initiative; especially the children in need of a cure."

—Dr. Walter Doyle Staples
Best-selling author of *Think Like A Winner!*

"*Stack The Logs!* reveals compelling and simple lessons to apply to everyday life. Frank has shown a true grasp for what it takes to be successful. You need to read this as a manual for life success!"

—James A. Winkelmann, President
Longrow Holdings, Inc.

"A great read for anyone looking for success. Makes you sit back and think, 'you know, he's right'. I can't wait to share the book with my staff to use as a framework for achieving an outcome(s), short and long term, through the **STACK™** strategy."

—Ron Schuldt, President
Columbus Data Services

"Read *Stack The Logs!* yourself. Give it to your spouse, your son, your daughter, your business partners, employees, the people you are mentoring and anyone else you truly, deeply care about. This is more than a business book ...*Stack The Logs!* will help you live a better, more productive and successful business and personal life. Frank's practical, thoughtful approach and ability to distill meaningful truths into incredibly powerful lessons makes this book one of the most powerful I have ever read. Pray your competitors don't read this book before you do!"

—Rick Galbreath, SPHR
President, Human Resources Growth
Partners, Inc.

"Learning from Frank's insight and wisdom through *Stack The Logs!* will greatly improve your life! I have benefited for years from knowing Frank and the power of his advice."

—David Breuer, CFP
Financial Planner, Compass Financial
Advisors, LLC

"*Stack The Logs!* is written from the heart by someone who has lived the principles he teaches us. Frank's **STACK™** Action Plan Strategy is an easy-to-use winning formula for success in any circumstance, despite any obstacles. Read it. Use it. Live it."

—Vic Johnson
Founder, www.AsAManThinketh.net

STACK THE LOGS!

Frank F. Lunn was living a normal busy life when he received a phone call that stopped time: His eight-year-old son had just been diagnosed with leukemia. The next six months were a struggle for the entire Lunn family, as they battled with Frankie against a cancer of the blood and bone marrow, a cancer very similar to what had ironically defeated Lunn's father four years earlier.

At the time of his son's illness, the premise for this book was still in its infancy. It is based on his father's homespun advice to "stack the logs," one decision and choice stacked on top of another, until success is acheived.

It took Lunn a while to realize just how simple yet profound his father's wisdom was. He eventually realized that success, whatever your definition, is an accumulation over time rather than a single event. It is about incremental achievement.

As he reflected on a note from his father's birthday card, Lunn realized there were seven essential components to success: (1) plan well, (2) keep an excellent forward thrust to objectives, (3) deal with disappointments and setbacks, (4) create a positive support structure, (5) stay positive and focused, (6) maintain moral character, and (7) keep on "Stacking The Logs!"

Divided into twenty chapters, this powerful text expands on these basic principles, including planning for guaranteed success, and the power of Applied Incremental Advantage, which Lunn calls the "compound interest of success." It also tells the number one reason people fail, and how to overcome it, as well as programming yourself to become a champion with the techiques used by Olympic athletes and astronauts.

Additionally, the book details the history of St. Jude Children's Research Hospital, where Frankie Lunn was treated. Lunn credits his "new family at St. Jude" for teaching him the gift of optimism in the face of adversity and how to weather personal storms and come back stronger.

Frank F. Lunn is an expert in leadership, marketing, and small business entrepreneurship with a proven record of success. He has a diverse background and a wide range of life experiences allowing for greater perspective in sharing and teaching others.

Lunn attended Illinois State University, majoring in economics with a minor in military science. Commissioned in 1987 as an officer in the U.S. Army, he received specialized training in many facets of advanced leadership, logistics, resource management, and strategic planning. He served in the Persian Gulf during Operation Desert Storm and received a Bronze Star for meritorious service. After six years of military service, he retired to the inactive reserves as a captain.

In 1995, he founded CMS Inc./Kahuna Business Group. His unique experience is vital to his role in facilitating and leading Kahuna Business Group through continued growth.

Lunn is a devoted husband to his wife Lisa and father to their three children Frankie, Matthew, and Rachel.

Testimonials and Advanced Praise for

STACK THE LOGS!
Building a Success Framework to Reach Your Dreams

. . . .

"This is a wonderful book, loaded with ideas and inspiration for success and achievement in every part of life."

—Brian Tracy
Best-selling author of over 26 books including *Goals!: How to Get Everything You Want— Faster Than You Ever Thought Possible*

. . . .

"This book is a shot in the arm! Frank Lunn has written a genuine, must-have book that is page after page of timeless wisdom. The aggressive path to success lies within these pages."

—Michael A. Janke
Best-selling author of *Power Living* (Mastering the Art of Self Discipline)
Decorated Navy SEAL, and founder of Special Operations Consulting

. . . .

"Informative and lovingly written, *'Stack The Logs!'* is a treasure for every family. I had the pleasure of meeting Frank and his son, Frankie, and will forever be moved by their sweet spirits. The mission of *'Stack The Logs!'* is clear and powerful: succeed on your own terms with hope, knowledge and a positive attitude!"

—Wynonna Judd
Grammy Award-Winning Country Music Artist

. . . .

"An absolutely heartwarming and life-changing work that will remind you of the greatness inside of us all. A book you want to read 3 times a year!"

—Mike Litman
Co-Author, #1 Best-Seller *Conversations with Millionaires*

. . . .

"This warm and inspiring book is a testament to courage, tenacity and determination."

–Dan Poynter
Best Selling Author, Publisher, Speaker

*"**Stack The Logs!** is a wonderful, illuminating, and inspiring book. Through laughter and tears, you will re-think how you are living your life, and discover how we all have the capacity to contribute and make a difference in the world."*

–Stacy Allison
First American woman to reach the summit of Mt. Everest, Author of *Beyond The Limits* and *Many Mountains to Climb*

"As a father who has spent many months in hospitals with a seriously ill son...I can fully understand why you felt compelled to share your story in order to highlight how it *IS* possible to keep a positive view on life when it all seems to be falling apart. The seven staggeringly simple steps to success defined so clearly in **Stack The Logs!** are a wake up call for anybody who is interested in having a more positive, successful...and above all, happy life."

–Gary Vurnum
Author and Publisher of *Our Success Partnership*
www.oursuccesspartnership.com

"One word... '**Outstanding!**' Not only is **Stack The Logs!** a great business enhancing book but more importantly it's a life enhancing book. Thanks Frank for the timeless wisdom and inspiration!"

–Vance Rowland, President
Alliance ATM

Although the author and publisher have made every effort to ensure the accuracy and completeness of information contained in this book, we assume no responsibility for errors, inaccuracies, omissions, or any inconsistency herein. Any slights of people, places, or organizations are unintentional.

First printing 2004

ISBN 0-9728300-5-7
LCCN 2003101717

The following terms are the trademarked property of
Frank F. Lunn and Kahuna Business Group:
  ICE™ (Incremental Cumulative Effect)
  STACK™
  Incremental Advantage™
  PLF™ (Perspective Learning Forward)

ATTENTION CORPORATIONS, UNIVERSITIES, COLLEGES, AND PROFESSIONAL ORGANIZATIONS: Quantity discounts are available on bulk purchases of this book for educational, gift purposes, or as premiums for increasing magazine subscriptions or renewals. Special books or book excerpts can also be created to fit specific needs. For information, please contact Kahuna Business Group, 801 W. Chestnut Street, Suite C, Bloomington, IL 61701; 309-828-8396.

www.stackthelogs.com

Kahuna Empowerment Series™

STACK THE LOGS!™

The Best Is Yet to Come.
Just Keep Stacking the Logs!

Building a Success Framework to Reach Your Dreams

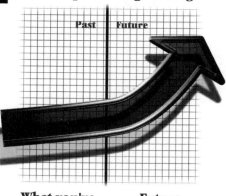

What you've accomplished...   Future potential...

FRANK F. LUNN

Foreword by MARK VICTOR HANSEN

Co-Author of the New York Times bestsellers: *Chicken Soup for the Soul*® series, *The One Minute Millionaire*, *The Power of Focus*

Kahuna Business Group
BLOOMINGTON, ILLINOIS

Table of Contents

Special Acknowledgment to St. Jude Children's Research Hospital

February 2003

. . . .

"No child should die in the dawn of life."
–Danny Thomas, entertainer and founder of St. Jude Children's Research Hospital

. . . .

What could ever be said or what gift could ever be given to appropriately show your full appreciation for saving the life of your child?

To the entire dedicated team of doctors, nurses, technicians, child life, security, scientists, administrators, marketers, photographers, researchers and everyone else associated with this fine institution: *Thank you!*

You saved the life of our son and showed us a face of compassion combined with a purpose for continuing the mission started by Danny Thomas more than 40 years ago. Danny's dream, which you all carry out on a daily basis, could not be more personal for me or my family.

We witnessed miracles and came away from our St. Jude experience better than when we arrived. You have come a long way and yet there is still more work to be done.

With heartfelt gratitude, and motivation to see your excellent work continued, we pledge 10 percent of all of the proceeds from this book to the continuing work of St. Jude Children's Research Hospital.

The wonderful success stories and the incredible improvements made by St. Jude in the last 40 plus years are one of the best practical examples of "Stack The Logs" and exemplary in demonstrating the basic theme of this book.

We wish you tremendous continued success and progress!

Sincerely,
the family of Frankie Lunn,
leukemia survivor

To find out more about the lifesaving work giving birth to modern-day miracles for countless children today and tomorrow, please look up St. Jude on the web at www.stjude.org or contact them at: 332 North Lauderdale St., Memphis, TN 38105-2794; 901-495-3300.

St. Jude Children's Research Hospital

ALSAC • Danny Thomas, Founder

Finding cures. Saving children.

This book is dedicated to my father, Frank F. Lunn III, who passed away on May 8, 1998. We didn't always agree and I didn't always understand, but he instilled much in me that I benefit from every day. I love him and miss him, and hope to continue to learn by his words and example even though he is gone from me.

Dad,

In the memory of your words that echo in my mind every day, this is my attempt to share your words of wisdom and encouragement with others. I didn't realize the awesome power of the simple instructions you gave me at the time, but they prove truer every day!

I sincerely hope that I can instill in my children and those I care about the same practical sense of what success really entails and how to get there.

I miss you and I love you. I am proud to be your son and carry your name.

Your son,
Frank Frederick Lunn IV

This book is also dedicated to my loving family, who mean the whole world to me. To my wife Lisa and our awesome children, Frankie, Matthew and Rachel—I thank you for your love and support.

Foreword by Mark Victor Hansen
Co-Author of the New York Times bestsellers:
Chicken Soup for the Soul® series
The One Minute Millionaire
The Power of Focus

. . . .

"Success is creating a state of mind that allows you to achieve whatever it is you want."
—Mark Victor Hansen

. . . .

You may know me better as the "Chicken Soup for the Soul®" guy. For over 26 years, I have focused solely on helping people in all walks of life reshape their personal vision of what's possible. When Robert Allen and I wrote *The One Minute Millionaire: The Enlightened Way to Wealth*, our mission was to inspire the creation of one million new millionaires this decade. *I believe you can create the life you desire and the one you deserve.* After reading *Stack The Logs!™*, I was both encouraged and inspired by Frank's approach of distilling timeless truths into an easy-to-read and easy-to-apply book. The principles found within are absolutely foundational and universal to success. Combine this with the heartwarming way in which Frank and his family took the horrible storm of childhood cancer and weathered through to come up with something beneficial to others and you have a winning book that should be read by everyone.

I resonate with Frank's personal story as well as with his philosophies and beliefs. Just over two decades ago, I was bankrupt from a failed business, no money and even fewer resources. I knew that my own success would come out of the course I set for myself and I knew the outcome I wanted to achieve. It was not always easy and it was not always fun, but today I am thrilled with my life's journey and my outcome. *Stack The Logs!*™ is a wonderful metaphor for success, one log at a time. You will be amazed at how easily you can apply this text to literally change your own future.

This book is foundational and inspiring. I do not feel it would have the unique and rich texture were it not for the struggle of the Lunn family in one of the scariest things a parent can imagine, a childhood catastrophic disease. Their story and the St. Jude story are both inspiring and insightful to the true nature of success. Success has many measures and is valued differently by each one of us. This success hits many levels.

My philosophy on tithing and philanthropy is widely known. I believe in giving back. Enrich to be enriched; inspire to be inspired. This book gives and receives. Frank told me he wrote *Stack The Logs!*™ with two distinct purposes in mind. His goal with the book is to: *Inspire, Educate and Empower People to Take Bold Action to Achieve Their Dreams!* His other goal is to increase awareness and raise money to assist St. Jude Children's Research Hospital in the ongoing mission of: *"Finding cures. Saving children."* When you purchase and read this book, your outcome is simple: You will definitely benefit yourself. You will also further the work of St. Jude Children's Hospital.

You will thoroughly enjoy *Stack The Logs!*™ and your life will be enriched through the journey.

—*Mark Victor Hansen*
February 2003

Introduction

August 2002

A little less than four years before I started this manuscript, my father died of a rare cancer of the bone marrow and blood. A little less than four months after I began this project in earnest, my eight-year-old son Frankie was diagnosed with leukemia, a cancer of the bone marrow and blood. This book is not about cancer or death. Rather it is about life and living it to the fullest. It is about learning to take control of your life and discovering success on your own terms.

Stack The Logs! is a project inspired by the words of my late father. The courage to continue this book was provided by my son in his example of positive attitude, courage and determination through his battle with cancer. It is about practical application into your life, uncovering and applying simple truths for success in whatever measure you desire.

What does, "Stack The Logs!" mean?

"Stack The Logs!" began as my father's homespun encouragement phrase to me. This book was sparked by an inspiring note he wrote to me the year before his death. Like the character Dorothy from the *Wizard of Oz*, who goes on a journey only to find she already had what she was looking for before she left, my father's words were a stark reminder of lessons learned through study and through life. He knew I was on the right course, although I could not see it at that time. His words were absolutely the right words at the right time. He penned the following in a birthday card:

. . . .

Both Mom and I are very proud of your accomplishments. You have planned well, kept on an excellent forward thrust to your objectives and handled your disappointments well. If you plan to succeed and implement that positive plan, you will still have disappointments. You have a great supportive family and Lisa and Frankie will help carry you through these times. Stay positive, stay focused, maintain your great moral character and...KEEP ON STACKING THOSE LOGS!

. . . .

My wife took the card and had it framed for my office. For three months, I looked at this and thought about his words daily. As I reflected, I noticed seven main components:

1. Plan well
2. Keep an excellent forward thrust to objectives
3. Deal with your disappointments and setbacks
4. Create a positive support structure
5. Stay positive and focused
6. Maintain moral character
7. Keep on "Stacking the Logs!"

In a quick note on a birthday card, my father gifted me with a seven-part blueprint for a successful life. No magic or shortcuts. There is wisdom within the simplicity and a roadmap for success.

When I look back on my relationship with my father, there were certainly periods of conflict. In my early years, I was always trying to swing for the fences to hit a home run. I would start business after business with my sights set on glory and fame. Without a doubt, I was looking to get rich quick. Like the inborn instinct for salmon swimming upstream, sons feel the need to prove to their dads they are better than they are. I did not recognize it at the time, but I certainly was in competition with my father. What I did not realize then, was that my father wished for my success as much as I did. He cringed at every shortcut I tried to take. He was disappointed at times in my decision making and was personally hurt with every mistake I made. I had my share of victories as well as setbacks. In the midst of my ups and downs, he did one thing for which I will be eternally grateful: He forced me to take personal responsibility for my actions. Not always a welcome gift, but it proved to be helpful in my character development.

My father's wisdom was simple and profound, yet I could not grasp it until nearly four years after his death. Success, no matter what your definition, is an accumulation over time rather than a singular event. It is about incremental achievement. His advice was to hit singles with the goal to get on base rather than swing for the fences. Pure home run hitters in baseball and in life are very rare. They occur as the exception rather than the rule, certainly appearing to make it look easy. The hard truth is that life is not easy. Saying life is not easy, however, does not necessarily mean life has to be hard. We tend to make life harder than it has to be. We tend to focus on the wrong things and fail to take deliberate actions toward a meaningful destiny. Unfortunately, the result for most people is an accumulation of random and unplanned events chained together into a destination of chance and uncertainty.

Stack The Logs! is a construction project, as we are all building our lives. Each chapter is designed to be a building block log to be stacked on all the previous chapters. When applied, the principles will unlock the success you desire in your life and enrich those around you. It is my hope to pass on the secrets I uncovered from my father's simple words of encouragement. You have at your disposal a tool to help you achieve success in every area of your life *as you define it!*

Lessons from My Son

On the morning of March 28, 2002, I had a completely full schedule with many things to do. I awoke early to work out and to get to the office so I could start on the outline of this book. I had a series of trips scheduled to various parts of the United States as well as to Korea within six weeks. I was very focused on all these things.

My life, however, was changed forever on that afternoon. My wife took our eight-year-old son Frankie to the doctor to have a pesky rash resembling chicken pox looked at. He had already had chicken pox, so his pediatrician prudently ordered a blood test. The doctor called me at my office shortly after 1:00 P.M. and gave me news that seemed to stop time. The diagnosis came back that Frankie had leukemia. He would have to be admitted to the hospital immediately and then transported to St. Jude Children's Research Hospital in Memphis, Tennessee. My dad died on May 8th four years earlier of a very similar cancer of the blood and bone marrow. Now I am watching my son, who shares my father's name, fighting with a cancer of the blood and bone marrow.

This book was still very much in the planning stage when Frankie's illness occurred. It was a challenging initial six-month fight for Frankie and one in which the final chapter is not yet written. At this time, thankfully, his prognosis is excellent. While it was tempting to put this project aside, I felt compelled to continue to write this book with my family and Frankie's blessing. In addition to the information presented, our hope is to add an additional dimension we experienced and witnessed in others during his battle with cancer.

One of the first things we realized is that you may not always understand why or what God's meaning for you is in a certain situation. With that said, if you look for them, God's blessings are abundant. Although we would not wish this experience on any family, we still feel blessed for so many things it has brought us. I hope to add some texture to the subjects covered in this book. Many of the words were written for my own benefit to help me through a very difficult time. I feel confident they will benefit you as well. Thank you for taking this journey with me. Together we will Stack The Logs!

Part I

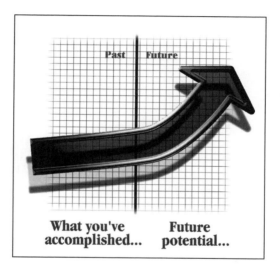

Past | Future

What you've accomplished... Future potential...

PLAN WELL

CHAPTER 1

Secret Principle of Success

. . . .

"Destiny is not a matter of chance, it is a matter of choice; it is not a thing to be waited for, it is a thing to be achieved."
—William Jennings Bryan

. . . .

Like you, I am both ordinary and extraordinary. I have some awesome as well as some less than stellar experiences in my life. I have had great triumphs and victories as well as great losses and heartaches. They have all taught me. I have achieved and succeeded and I have fallen short. I have been a wise man and I have been a fool. I have been smart and well read and I have been ignorant and complacent. I do not claim to have all the answers, but I do have some valuable lessons learned I would like to share to enhance your perspective. Stack The Logs! is symbolism for success, one log at a time. One log at a time is not sexy, but it works. Success is the result of your cumulative decisions and actions combined with your persistence.

Success Revealed

Success is much talked about yet not really understood. Everyone has a different definition and a different path to get to their destination. This book is about basic concepts and a realization that there is no new and undiscovered magic formula. The secret to success is one that is hiding in plain view. Success is a process that must be started and continued through individual actions to its conclusion. Success is a cumulative achievement. Although many may say otherwise in their attempt to sell you something, there are no real shortcuts. There are, however, direct paths with clear guiding principles to create the most efficient and direct routes to our intended destinations.

One of the first concepts of success I learned was taught to me by a man named Paul J. Meyer, a great motivational writer and trainer and the founder of several companies including Success Motivation Institute. His definition explains, "Success is the progressive realization of a worthwhile predetermined personal goal." What this concept boils down to is that success is personal to everyone and is an individual choice. Success for me might be the exact opposite of how another would define it. In addition to the individuality, there needs to be a "progressive realization, as Mr. Meyer points out."

Stack The Logs! was born of a simple phrase repeated to me by my father in the times he wanted to reassure me that I was on the right track and only needed to keep on. He knew from his own life education that success is an incremental accumulation over time; one decision and choice stacked on top of another. Stack The Logs! is about progressively realizing your dreams. It is about finding your way to them through the obstacles now keeping you apart. There is no quantum travel to the destination of success, nor is there any way to bypass the journey to end up directly at the destination. The road must be traveled. Success by practical definition is a process or a journey.

Incremental Cumulative Effect (ICE)

The concept of ICE is an explanation of why you are where you are today or why you achieve the results you currently do. Where you are today is the result of small yet compound decisions added up together to create the sum of your life. If you are well educated, it is the result of many compound decisions in the past that when combined form your current education. If you are overweight, it is the result of thousands of incremental and cumulative decisions about eating and exercise habits. You are the sum of the decisions, actions and habits of the past. Your future lies in those same factors as your life progresses.

The concept of ICE is simple and mirrors the nature of real ice. When cooled to 32-degrees Fahrenheit, water will start to crystallize and form connections to eventually give water structure and hold it together as a solid. Like water turning to ice, defining small or incremental choices made over time compound to give form to your current result (good or bad). In short, we are a product of the many choices we have made previously. Our future then is based on the choices we make today. These choices shape us and provide a cumulative effect.

Saying where you are today is a result of your cumulative decisions is simple. Making changes based on that simple understanding is much easier said than done. This is akin to the understanding that golf is basically a simple sport yet one that can keep mastery forever elusive. Each decision you make adds to and plays off the one before. If you want to change your result in an area of life, you must make a series of changes and then allow those changes to accumulate over time to give birth to a new result.

If your current result is not what you want, you need to make small changes and improvements to get to where you need to be. You will learn as this book progresses how to harness the incredible power of incremental improvements in your life that will over time allow you to absolutely achieve your own definition of success.

The Power of the J-Shaped Curve

The J-shaped curve is both a visualization tool and a real effect. The principle of the J- shaped curve is that your applied effort and output to get a result take far more in the short-term, but that over time your results improve and compound to where the compounding effect creates a greater yield.

The J-shaped curve is mostly flat for a period of time until results catch up with the input and then a dramatic rise of the curve begins to happen. Imagine you are learning a new skill to juggle and you graphed your attempt to do this as you practiced over time. Initially your progress is very slow and filled with failure. Your graph is very flat at this point. Over time and with practice, your skill begins to come around. The results begin to increase and your graph begins its journey upward. Eventually with enough time and practice, you are proficient at the skill and your result graph is now very high, giving your chart the J shape.

Compound Interest as a Working Metaphor

Probably the best example to show the incredible power of the J-shaped curve is the principle of compound interest.

"The most powerful force in the universe is compound interest."
—Albert Einstein

Compound interest is interest that is calculated not only on the initial principal but also on the accumulated interest of prior periods. Let's start with a simple concept and build from there. If you started with a single penny and doubled it every day for a month, how much money do you think you would accumulate? Ask other people what they think. Most people will guess somewhere between $100 and $1,000. It only makes sense since you are talking about starting with a penny and you are only doubling it 30 times, right? The astonishing fact is that if you doubled a penny every day for 30 days, your total would be a mind-boggling amount: $5,368,709.12! The simple arithmetic is illustrated here:

DAY #	MONEY	DAY #	MONEY	DAY #	MONEY
1	$ 0.01	11	$ 10.24	21	$ 10,485.76
2	$ 0.02	12	$ 20.48	22	$ 20,971.52
3	$ 0.04	13	$ 40.96	23	$ 41,943.04
4	$ 0.08	14	$ 81.92	24	$ 83,886.08
5	$ 0.16	15	$ 163.84	25	$ 167,772.16
6	$ 0.32	16	$ 327.68	26	$ 335,544.32
7	$ 0.64	17	$ 655.36	27	$ 671,088.64
8	$ 1.28	18	$ 1,310.72	28	$ 1,342,177.28
9	$ 2.56	19	$ 2,621.44	29	$ 2,684,354.56
10	$ 5.12	20	$ 5,242.88	30	$ 5,368,709.12

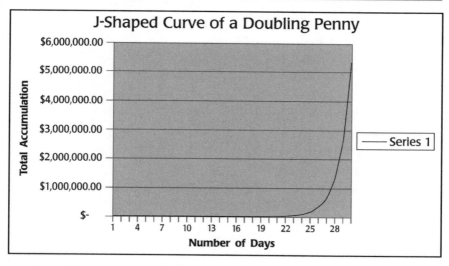

How Compound Interest Works

Compound interest is interest earned on interest. For example: If you invest $100 at 5 percent interest, at the end of one year you end up with $105. But with compound interest, at the end of two years you don't have $110. You end up with $110.25, because you earned interest not only on the principal (the original $100) but also on the interest from year one.

A result of $110.25 versus $110 doesn't sound like much of a difference, but over time it certainly adds up. If you invest $100 for 45 years *without* compounded interest, you would end up with $325 ($100 + $5 + $5). If, however, the interest were compounded, you would finish with $855, because each year interest is earned on the $100 principal plus all the interest earned in previous years.

Look at the incredible difference if you take the same amount and compare the massive acceleration difference with 10 percent interest compounded annually instead of 5 percent.

NUMBER OF YEARS	10% WITHOUT COMPOUNDING	10% WITH COMPOUNDING
1	110.00	110.00
2	120.00	121.00
3	130.00	133.10
4	140.00	146.41
5	150.00	161.05
10	200.00	259.37
15	250.00	417.72
20	300.00	672.75
25	350.00	1,083.47
30	400.00	1,744.94
35	450.00	2,810.24
40	500.00	4,525.93
45	550.00	7,289.05

When you graph this information, you see that as time progresses, the accumulation grows significantly with compounding.

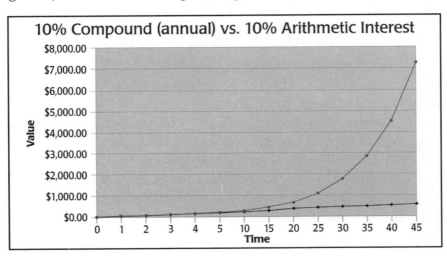

With the principle of compound interest, you have a sum of money invested over time, earning interest. The interest is added to the initial principal where it is also compounded and added to the original sum and the cycle continues. Compound interest starts out slowly but builds over time as your interest earns interest, resulting in a snowball effect.

When compared to your own life and the concept of "Stacking the Logs," it is important to make the comparison and application clear. Look at your applied efforts as principal contribution. Your additional efforts and reinvested gains are comparable to the compound interest effect. As with compound interest, the actual interest rate determines how quickly and how steeply the J shape of the graph will be. Your applied efforts are the equivalent of your interest rate as a multiplier of your initial efforts. It requires patience and consistency, making and reinvesting small gains and improvements over time back into your growing success bank account. In my own case, I did not discover until much later that the shortcuts I had been taking were actually depleting my success bank account and putting me further behind.

Success certainly does not happen overnight; it is incremental—one log at a time. Like the beauty of a sunny summer day that is sometimes hidden in plain sight when we take it for granted, so also are the principles and foundations of success. They are hidden in plain sight, available for everyone, but used by relatively few.

Suppose you are learning to juggle. Practice (frequency, intensity and duration) determines your results. If you practice once a month for 10 minutes, you may eventually see some results. Imagine, however, that you worked daily for 30 minutes of intense and concentrated practice. If you were to graph both cases for a year, the second would have significantly higher proficiency at the skill of juggling by the end of the period.

Unfortunately for all of us who live in a very impatient society, we cannot microwave our results or take shortcuts. Even with the principle of compound interest, we still must wait for a period of time to allow the initial results and our reinvested gains to fully produce. Just as the penny doubled daily for the first 10 days only produced a result of a measly $5.12, by the end of the second 10 days, the result was over $5,200 and the result at the end of the third 10 days over 5.3 million.

Most people fail to achieve great success in an endeavor because they quit before they really see the gains and results improve. History is filled with stories of people who failed simply because they quit too soon. We will discuss this further, plus strategies for overcoming it, later in Chapter 10.

Applied Incremental Advantage

We have already learned of the concept of ICE and how our decisions shape us. When we put all the building blocks together, we finally have a finished principle to apply. Applied Incremental Advantage is the compound interest of success. It is the small gains reinvested and magnified to create a successful result in your ICE.

When understood and *applied* over time, the principle of Incremental Advantage will be a dramatic accelerator to your dreams as compound interest is a massive accelerator to your savings. We will be applying the principle of Incremental Advantage to all that we discuss in this book. Look at the example of technology and human achievement. We have come further in progress in the last 25 years through the application of Incremental Advantage in these areas than in all of previous history combined. This understanding is the magnification of the compound cumulative effect. Every new advancement brings forth compound advancement in other areas. Look at what computers alone have done for the world and technology in the past 10 to 20 years.

The Stack The Logs! principle of Applied Incremental Advantage very simply is compound and reinvested incremental improvement applied back into your life. This is an awesome and incredible power that can absolutely change your life. Ensure that you are doing the right things in your life to get the results you want to make gains and improvements by reinvesting your gains and improvements. As you continue to "stack your logs," your personal success graph begins to resemble a J-shaped curve and your results are magnified.

Remember, success is not an event or a one-time destination. Success is an accumulation of actions in the right direction toward what is meaningful to you. Like the principle of compound interest, compound incremental improvement takes time before dramatic results are evident. My father used to advise me to "keep Stacking the Logs! and eventually the pile will be so high people couldn't help but see it."

Breaking the Chains of Average

I heard Paul J. Meyer ask a question in a seminar. His simple yet profound question was, "What is average? Is it the best of the worst or the worst of the best?" Unfortunately, in our comfortable society, we are spoon-fed what people want us to know, comfortable in our routines and live a treadmill existence of one day repeating into another. Henry David Thoreau once said, "The mass of men lead lives of quiet desperation." Average is certainly not the ideal plateau for us to strive for.

Average is very much the enemy of excellent. Most people, as addressed in this context, are the hoards of decent average people who do not seek to be better than they are. They flow in a current of a status quo river trapped into a destination they will not know until they arrive. These people will be carried by the current of life. They suffer the fate of giving up control and giving up any real say about the journey, choosing instead to release their authority over their own lives to fate, circumstances and the momentum of their present condition. This is sad but true. This is average.

The goal of this book is to assist you to make changes in your life—to seize the great opportunity and abundance available for the asking. We have power to break free from the momentum of our current life path and make changes. The aim above all is to take you out of the "most people" class and give you a greater measure of control over your life.

Sir Isaac Newton's first law of motion basically says: *An object at rest tends to stay at rest, and an object in motion tends to stay in motion unless the object in either case is acted upon by an outside force.* What this means when applied to success is that people tend to remain the same or on the same path. It takes an outside force to act upon an object to get it to change. Hopefully this book will provide some insights and techniques to assist you to find a way to change and start "Stacking the Logs" for a brighter future. In the upcoming chapters, you will learn principles and techniques designed to apply Incremental Advantage to your current situation to accelerate your journey. In the next chapter you will learn the STACK Strategy that when applied will guarantee your success in all your endeavors.

"The best way to predict the future is to create it."
—Peter F. Drucker

CHAPTER 2

STACK™
Strategy for Guaranteed Success

. . . .

"Concerning all acts of initiative and creation, there is one elementary truth—that the moment one definitely commits oneself, then Providence moves, too."
—**Goethe** (1749–1832)

. . . .

The Principle of Incremental Advantage

Do you think you have to be twice as effective as you are now to double your income? Do you think someone who earns 10 times what you currently earn is 10 times smarter or 10 times more efficient or 10 times more talented? Of course not! The secret of the increased result is found in the principle of Incremental Advantage. It is the key to unlocking the rewards you are seeking.

There is an old story about two campers in the woods who begin to hear the telltale signs of the feared grizzly bear approaching. One of the campers immediately sits down and slips on his running shoes. Exasperated with the apparent futility of the situation, the other camper begins to scream. "Are you crazy?

What are you doing? Don't you know it is impossible to outrun a bear?" To which the other camper replied, "I don't have to outrun the bear...*I just have to outrun you!*"

The moral of the story dramatizes the slight edge or Incremental Advantage one camper had over the other to save his own life. The true nature of the principle of Incremental Advantage is not about competition with others, but rather a process to improve yourself and your capabilities. Slight improvements over time will yield larger results over time.

Example: Assume you decide that you can save $50 a month for the future. Simple enough. At a decent rate of 8 percent compound interest over 10 years, you will have saved $9,147.30. If you kept at it for 20 years, you would have an even greater total of $29,451.02. Notice that the time period doubled, yet the result was nearly tripled due to compound interest.

What if you kept everything else constant and employed the principle of Incremental Advantage? Assume that each month you could add just one additional dollar for a little incremental boost. Month two would add $51, month three would be $52 and so on until the end of the same 10-year period. With your Incremental Advantage, you would more than double the amount with $18,713.14 after 10 years. If you maintained your resolve and kept at it for the entire 20-year period, amazingly your incremental accumulation would be $82,349.44. Can you visualize the J-shaped curve?

Incremental improvement involves action and small growth or extra input. Over time and compounded this produces a dramatically enhanced result. This result is your personal Incremental Advantage.

Incremental Advantage in Action

Nowhere is Incremental Advantage more apparent than in the world of sports. The difference between victory and defeat lies in the blink of an eye. Athletes earning millions of dollars are separated only slightly in performance from athletes barely surviving. The batting averages of the greats are less than one hit out of ten better than the also-rans.

On July 25, 1999, Lance Armstrong, the outstanding American cyclist and cancer survivor, crossed the finish line in the world's foremost long-distance bicycle race, the grueling 2,292 mile Tour de France. Three years after successfully battling testicular cancer, Lance fought through hardships, competitors and fatigue, yet pushed on to win four stages of the 20-stage race. Armstrong received glory and the spotlight winning in 91 hours, 32 minutes and 16 seconds. First place and remembered for generations to come.

Yet behind him in the same 2,292 journey was second-place finisher Alex Zulle from Switzerland. The difference in time between the record books and obscurity: 7 minutes and 37 seconds. Armstrong, the victor, was only a little faster (about 1/10 of 1 percent) than his nearest competitor, Zulle. Overall, the top 10 finishers were within a microscopic percentage (around 4/10 of 1 percent). Ultimately, Armstrong carried himself to victory with only an Incremental Advantage yet his rewards were tremendously greater than the next person. Success in our lives, first place versus second, achieving and falling short, many times is determined only by the smallest of margins. The basis of applied Incremental Advantage is that small yet directed actions repeated over and over again will generate massive results. The principle of applied Incremental Advantage is the foundation of success. It is true that luck and other factors sometimes play a role, but applied Incremental Advantage is often the underlying basis.

Another Incremental Advantage sports illustration comes from the 1994 Winter Olympics and the stunning victory for American speed-skater Dan Jansen. Pushing forward after a fall in the previous race. Pushing forward after years of near victory—yet rewarded only with disappointment and heartache. Pushing forward after the tragic loss of his sister. Pushing forward in 1994 finally to achieve a gold medal in the 1000 meters with a stunning time of 1:12:43. One minute, 12 seconds and 43/100 of a second to a new world record. Dan Jansen's Incremental Advantage between a glorious moment in history etched in the minds of millions and an insignificant footnote in the record books was 29/100 of a second. In a race for the gold, first place by even 1/100 of a second makes all the difference in the world.

The difference between being a great athlete and an average one is usually found in the Incremental Advantage…just a little better applied over time. In sports, it doesn't matter whether you win by a mile or an inch. Second place is considered the first place loser. Life may not prove quite as dramatic. In life, not all of our actions are in competition with others. Not every measurement is definitive. However, the cumulative effect of the Incremental Advantage in our lives can be the difference between happy and productive lives and ones filled with grief and despair.

STACK Strategy for Guaranteed Success

Understanding that the theme of Stack The Logs! is one where success is a compound Incremental Advantage over time is important, but only the beginning. A great concept will not carry you to your destination without a strategy and applied action to make it happen. The STACK Strategy for guaranteed success is a simple process. It is the applied "how-to" aspect to put the concept to work. The principle of Incremental Advantage is very powerful, but must be applied into a strategy or it is meaningless. The STACK Strategy is in essence five easy steps to an Incremental Advantaged outcome. This formula can be used for any area of life or any course of endeavor. Again, simple doesn't necessarily mean easy. The concept of losing weight is simple: Expend more calories than you take in and for every 3,500 calories more that you do this, a pound of fat will be used in the process. Very simple concept and yet there are so many diet and fitness books, pills, shakes, gimmicks and shortcuts sold in the United States to where it is now a multibillion dollar industry.

At its core, the STACK Strategy is a goal-setting and goal-achieving process. I have been a student of goal setting and similar topics in earnest for almost two decades and I can say with certainty that although there are some differences with wording and structure, if you boil it down to its bare essence, you would find that the process is virtually the same. It is timeless and also proven.

The STACK Strategy will give you a practical framework to allow you to fully realize your dreams and ambitions.

STACK Strategy: Five Steps to an Outcome

S – Set your destination and course
T – Take immediate action
A – Accept results simply as feedback
C – Correct your course based on feedback
K – Keep on Stacking the Logs!

. . . .

"I respect the man who knows distinctly what he wishes. The greater part of all mischief in the world arises from the fact that men do not sufficiently understand their own aims. They have undertaken to build a tower, and spend no more labor on the foundation than would be necessary to erect a hut."
—Goethe (1749–1832) German Philosopher

. . . .

S: Set Your Destination and Course

It is easy to dream. It is easy to wish and hope. Many times people think passing thoughts and open their minds to new and different ideas they would like to accomplish. It's an easy step for most people and also where it ends for them. Most sparks of goal setting are usually stopped considerably short, ending life as a wish or a hope or possibly even a dream, but never a true goal.

As in traveling, in order to achieve an outcome, you must have a destination. Aimless travel is merely wandering and aimless ambition is success squandering. You would never think to take a trip without having an idea of where you wanted to end up. It is so simple and yet so few people take the time and effort to create a destination for their lives.

Choose a target destination and then figure out the best way to get there. This is certainly a dramatic oversimplification, but no less valid. If you follow this step and clearly figure out what you want, you begin to gain leverage over your circumstances.

Knowing your intended destination provides an understanding of the route you must travel and plan accordingly. If you plan to drive to a destination, you plot it on a map, estimate time, plan for fuel and other related contingencies. With a goal, you need a plan of action to factor in the same types of things. A clear goal in mind as your destination and a clear action plan of your course puts you well on your way to achieving your desired outcome.

T: Take Immediate Action

Once you have an intended destination, the only thing that will transform your dreams into realities is *action!* I cannot stress this enough. Having a destination and a course without action is like sitting at your kitchen table with a map highlighted from your town to Disney World and just continuing to look at the map. Nothing happens without action. If you wait two weeks, study the map further but take no action, you will still be at your kitchen table. *Nothing happens without action.*

Results follow action. Until you take action and as Tony Robbins would assert, "Massive Action!" to your plan, your plan will never turn into the reality of a goal achieved. Many times it is difficult to start and taking action is certainly a defining choice. When a rocket like the space shuttle launches, more than 90 percent of all energy is used just to get the craft out of earth's orbit. As we discussed in Chapter 1, Newton's first law of motion explains a body at rest tends to stay at rest unless acted upon by an outside force. Without action your dreams, goals and ambitions will never materialize. When you start to ride a bike, the most effort required is the first pedal action off dead stop. It is the same with action toward your desired result. The hardest steps are the ones at the beginning.

When you know where you want to go and have a plan to get there, action is just starting on the journey. Taking action doesn't even have to be the most appropriate action, just movement in the right direction. Even poor or bad results from action are better than the lack of results from inaction. In physics as mentioned above, the most difficult time is at the beginning. Any action is better than no action because with any luck, you will learn and adapt. Follow-up action can then be more practical. Additional action can be taken and your path to your destination is lessened.

Amazing Action Secret of Success

This may surprise you, but here is a little-known secret that when applied will dramatically improve your success rate: *Action begets action!*

Yes, this is real. This realization when applied will help you to gain a slight edge or Incremental Advantage in all your other steps. Action starts forces in motion and allows for momentum to begin. Newton's first law of motion adapted to goal setting might be restated as, *a dormant goal will remain a wish, hope or dream until or unless acted upon by an outside force with action.* Action creates opportunities. Action allows for learning and adapting along the path of achievement. Action creates movement and momentum to carry you forward.

Practical Example

I had a dream of writing a book for many years. Up until December of 2001, all I had were a bunch of notes in a binder and ambition in my heart. As I was working on my goals for the upcoming year, I firmly decided that I would take the time and effort and set my goal to write my book. I now had a destination. I thought everything through and created a plan of action with what I knew at the time and what I thought would need to be accomplished to successfully have a book in print.

I had many questions and absolutely no experience in book writing; but I knew how to take action. With so little real knowledge or experience, I determined that for success in this project

I would need to take immediate and abundant action. As I began to take extreme action, I found some amazing things.

I found that the principle of the J-shaped curve was alive and well with this project. I had to expend time and effort and money into learning as well as doing. I bought books, watched tapes, researched on the internet and gradually gained confidence that I could successfully undertake and deliver on this project.

Sometimes there are skills or subject matters you know, understand and ultimately have a good handle on. Sometimes you know very little or even find out later that you did not know as much as you once thought. As you begin to take action, you learn what you did not know and you develop gains on many fronts. Action begets action and success soon follows. Synergy in nature is used to describe situations where the whole is greater than the sum of the parts. Two boards each able to bear a load of 20 pounds when stacked together can withstand not just 40 pounds, but 50 pounds or more. This is synergy in action. Action begets action and you develop synergy with your own activity.

People who successfully lose weight usually start with small eating changes. Those changes lead to the beginning of a little exercise. With some positive results, more action is applied to eating habits. Stairs instead of the elevator, half a can of pop, light on the snacks and many additional small action steps begin to appear. Results improve and action steps increase. Action begets action and results follow.

A: Accept Results Simply as Feedback

This is a difficult concept for some people to get over. The fear of failure is like the stinging fear of rejection. It is embarrassing and it can cause doubts. When we don't get the desired results we seek or the instant gratification we crave, it is too easy to draw back and quit. We question our motives. We question our abilities. Sometimes we even question our worthiness. It is sad, but many times we use feedback as validation for our failure rather than see it for what it is…feedback.

Feedback by definition is only information. Feedback is neutral; it is neither positive nor negative. We are the ones who attach meaning to it. Feedback is there to give us indications of our surroundings and our situation. If you accidentally touch a hot stove, your instant feedback is that it is very hot and your hand should find an alternative resting place. Results should not invalidate the goal nor should they discourage us from what we seek. Results should be accepted as feedback to help us know if we are on the right track.

Imagine this test. You are placed in a very large but completely dark room with four tables. On one of the tables is a magnificent prize of a box filled with money and rare coins. The other three tables are empty. Also in the room are obstacles such as chairs, stools and toys. Your task is to find the treasure chest. What do you do? Well, this seems pretty simple. You would feel your way around in the dark until you found your treasure.

Think about this a little. As you start to move, you end up kicking a stool. Do you quit? You kick a stool, trip over a chair and run into a table. Are you discouraged? You continue trying and after getting past the labyrinth of obstacles you find a table, but it is without the treasure you seek. You do this several times and find nothing. Are you discouraged now? Actually in a test like this, you would probably move systematically and as you bumped into obstacles remember where they were. In this controlled experiment, you would most likely accept the results as feedback and change your approach slightly until you found your treasure even if you got some bumps and false starts at the beginning.

Why is it that as soon as we are on a path to our destination and we run into some resistance, we get discouraged and quit? Why do people take negative or less than positive results as an indication that they have failed or as a reason to give up? As adult humans we are a paradox. In our youth, we failed hundreds of times in our initial quest to walk. We routinely failed in almost everything we attempted to do as we were first learning. Look at children and how much they fail versus succeed when first starting out. Eventually they get and even master the skills.

Why then as adults have we lost our resiliency and our ability to accept our results as only feedback for change? The truth is that there are many reasons from social conditioning to lack of continued teaching beyond formal education (who was your last formal teacher and how long ago?) and reassurances as we grow older. The other truth is that it really doesn't matter, because we can learn to adapt and overcome that part of our adult nature.

C—Correct Your Course Based on Feedback

If you are on a road to go from one city to the next and you hear on the radio the bridge is out or that there was a big accident and traffic is at a standstill, what do you do? Quite naturally you would accept that feedback and then look to alter your course.

Pilots flying planes are said to be off course far more than they are on course with wind and other factors moving the plane. Pilots are trained to gather feedback from maps, instruments and visual clues and then to correct course or other aspects of the flight based on this new knowledge.

If your current activity is not producing the desired result, change your activity based on the feedback provided. If Oreo cookies, mint chocolate chip ice cream, pop and potato chips don't provide the result you seek, make a change based on the feedback. If you are driving and find yourself a bit lost and then finally see a landmark that you recognize, you course correct based on the feedback.

Every step you take when you walk is a miracle of feedback, neuro-communication, muscle control and course correction. You take action and stimulus goes to your brain. Your brain is given feedback from your feet, legs and eyes, as well as other parts of your body. When you walk and an obstacle appears in front of you, your brain automatically analyzes the feedback from all inputs and then sends out a course correction based on that feedback. If it is a curb, you lift your foot a little higher and extend your stride. If there is a pole in your path with other people approaching, your brain guesses the best maneuver for you to get past your obstacle without running into anyone. On your way to achieving your goals, you will hit snags and there will be feedback provided to you from your actions. Take your feedback and course correct based on the new information.

K—Keep on Stacking the Logs!

As we have seen with the principle of Incremental Advantage, your results will be small at first. In fact, your results at the beginning will be far smaller than the effort used to that point. When I began writing this book, I took more than 50 hours of action without writing a single word of manuscript. I took action not only in research and understanding the subjects I would write about, but also the writing process itself. I expended many hours of effort yet had no written words to show for it. After more time, I finally had an outline that started to take shape and a concept that worked. As I progressed further, my results began to show themselves and some of them were tangible. As my outline turned into chapters and text began to look like what I initially envisioned in my head, I was encouraged to keep going. Now I was producing the results I desired. My J-shaped curve finally began to magnify and turn dramatically upward until I had a finished product—a manuscript.

Cumulative, compound and incremental are adjectives relating to and describing the subject of improvement. As you progress along your journey and your objective, you will begin to see small successes and gains. Keep on! Keep progressing and making gains and then add those gains to what you have done so far. It takes time and it takes persistence. If you are on a drive to Disney World and you are in the middle of nowhere, but you know you are on the right road, you just have to have the patience and persistence and possibly even tenacity to see it through till you arrive at your destination.

The phrase, "keep on Stacking the Logs," is both encouragement as well as an action step in its own right. When you have yet to arrive at your goal but know you are taking the right action and doing what's necessary, there is a period where your action step is just continuing to take the action you need. Soon enough, your results graph will begin to rise and your goal will be realized.

"You must follow through with your plan with dogged determination and the trenchant zeal of a crusader." I first heard this quotation as a student of Paul J. Meyer, a master of metaphors. I have personalized and repeated those words many thousands of times to myself in an affirmation, to continue on when I knew I was on the right track, though still plodding.

It is very difficult to keep on when we look to our left and right and see supposed examples of others succeeding while we toil on with our dreams. Today's society is a tradeoff of monthly payments and mortgaged tomorrows for a little fun right now. Most people refuse to delay gratification. They want what they want when they want it. It takes guts to stick with your plan even when it is not easy. We live in a world full of wants disguised as needs to distract us and pull us off course. If you have or know any children, you will understand that wants are sometimes cleverly packaged through advertising to appear as needs, as your children argue like skilled trial lawyers for what they think they "need."

The STACK Strategy will serve you well if you use it to keep yourself grounded in the basics. The strategy will always work if you use it. As we continue, we will add other dimensions and look at additional areas to gain Incremental Advantage in your life and your endeavors.

Stack The Logs! Recap

S—Set Your Destination and Course
- Know your destination and motivation.
- Know where you are in relation to your objective.
- Plot a course to get from where you are to where you desire to be.

T—Take Immediate Action
- Know what action you need to take to get to your objective.
- Take action.
- Keep taking action.

A—Accept Results Simply as Feedback

- Know where you are in relation to your goals.
- Allow results to be a neutral feedback mechanism for your progress.
- Maintain your motivation to progress to your destination.

C—Correct Your Course Based on Feedback

- Change or adapt your approach until you are making the progress you want.
- After you make changes, go back to your feedback mechanism for an update.
- If you are on right course, add more fuel to the fire and maintain your heading.

K—Keep on *Stacking the Logs!*

- Sustain patience, persistence and determination to reach your destination.
- Repeat any previous steps as needed, but maintain action until your goal is achieved.

When you know where you want to go and why and are making progress through action taken, receiving feedback and making minor course corrections as needed to stay on track, persistence to achieving your goal or arriving at your destination is the final component. It is challenging to just keep going when it seems like you are barely moving. Patience and persistence are always rewarded. Remember, success is not an event, but rather a process of building over time. Success is a cumulative effect. Oddly enough, so is failure.

. . . .

"There are no secrets to success. It is the result of preparation, hard work, learning from failure."
—General Colin L. Powell

. . . .

CHAPTER 3

The Key to the Journey— A Compelling and Dynamic Destination

- -

"Make no little plans, they have no magic to stir man's blood and probably will not be realized. Make big plans, aim high in hope and in work, remembering that a noble and logical diagram will not die."
—Daniel H. Burnham

- -

Implementing a tool like the STACK Strategy is important in developing a framework for success. Unfortunately, a strategy alone is not enough. As we learned previously, we need to take action, action and more action to give wings to our dreams. Action is the engine that will move us from wish to where we want to go. A vital part of action is motivation. The root word of motivation is "motive." Our motive for doing something is our reason why.

Compelling and Dynamic Destination Overview

What separates goal achievers and the dreamers who never get out of neutral? What allows some people to accomplish fantastic endeavors even through tremendous struggle while over-coming terrible adversity? What attributes or skills are in place that people of great accomplishment possess? In the study of successful men and women throughout the ages, one theme is constant. From Joan of Arc to Sir Edmund Hillary; Benjamin Franklin, Margaret Thatcher and Gandhi to modern-day sports icons like Lance Armstrong, Michael Jordan, Tiger Woods and the late Walter Payton—they all had one thing in common. Each possessed from their earliest childhood recollection a great desire coupled with a clearly envisioned destination for their life. The list mentioned demonstrates the diversity of the different individuals' dreams. The constant is that each held a clear view of their life's purpose—their compelling destiny. Destiny at first blush may seem like a fancy power word. At the core, the destination is where you want to go. Setting a destination for your life is working to predetermine your destiny.

Compelling "Why?"

One of the most important success factors is to ensure you have a strong enough "why?" to initially create and then sustain the action. It is critical to have a compelling and dynamic destination. Your "whys" need to answer compelling questions to sustain your activities. Is this really important to me? Am I willing to make the sacrifices for this destination? What kind of investment in time, money and frustration am I willing to expend? Am I really serious about this endeavor or is this just a wish? Without a compelling enough why, the first resistance en route to your destination shuts you down and forces you to reassess the initial desire for your goal. This is why so many people set and fail on their New Year's resolution. It sounds great and even compelling when the words leave your mouth announcing the intent to quit smoking, lose weight, work less, exercise more, etc. Yet when the first real challenge comes and the first test of motive arrives, the exclamation point of the goal withers into a period and then ultimately dies as a question mark. Do I really want to get up early and exercise? Do I really even need to give up my food desires? Does it really matter if I smoke?

Most people have a low resolve and lack the strength to carry them through the difficult periods. Successful people find a bridge to cross the chasm of difficulties and challenges and span the gap with the realization that their dreams on the other side are worth the efforts. It is important to assess your own motivation. Strong motivation can produce astounding results. Men and women have climbed the highest mountains, we have explored space, people go to school for years for their professional endeavors, businesses are started, etc., all with enough motivation. Lack of motivation has left countless people living lackluster lives of average mediocrity short of their true desires.

There are always tradeoffs. Action steps toward your goals are tradeoffs from other activities. Without a strong enough "why?" you get discouraged and quit before you ever taste the fruit of your rewards. I have witnessed many people who have dreams, but those dreams are obviously not compelling enough to get the people to take action. Instead of the skills needed to harness the great potential within them, many people become skilled at the art of mediocrity. They get great at skills such as learning to live below what they are capable of achieving and adapting to average. They can rationalize away nearly any situation. They can justify their lack of achievement and, most prized among the skills of the underachievers, they can deflect blame and responsibility and attribute it to other people, circumstances and the most hapless of adversaries, luck. Of course I am being sarcastic, but I can guarantee that right now you can think of at least a handful of people who are skilled in the art of mediocrity.

You need a why as well as a where. Without both, you are a boat adrift. The main reason most people fail is they do not have a plan. Amazing, but how sad it is the aimless life that some people lead.

The Other Side of "Why?"

"Why?" as a motivational force and understanding is only half of the equation. Like the yin yang that form a circle, there are other facets of the same question that need to be addressed to understand the full measure of motivation. The first part of the "why?" is why you want something. Understanding this helps you understand and fuel your motivation. It is vital to question, assess and understand why you want to achieve something.

In addition you must understand why you are where you are and why you have achieved the results you have achieved. The other "why?" is about understanding why you are where you are in your life. If your relationships are all in turmoil, you need to ask and understand, "why?" If you are in poor financial condition, it is important to have a strong and compelling "why?" to be debt free, but you must also understand why you are where you are. With a complete understanding of why you want to achieve as well as why you are in your situation, you have better tools to create a compelling future.

Start asking yourself "why?" Ask it about everything, like a five-year-old with a desire to know more. Why do you do the work you do? Why are you in the situation you are in? Are you where you chose to be or have you been swept away with the current of momentum? Days turn into weeks, weeks into months then years and suddenly you are where you are. Why do certain people not seem to like you? Why do you have a difficult time staying focused on one task at a time? This is not psychobabble. This is a rational approach to understanding fully where you are and gaining a complete accounting of your assets and liabilities.

Lesson from Old Man River

The Stack The Logs! metaphor of persistence and taking action one action step at a time toward your goals is only part of the process. Without a compelling and dynamic destination, your persistence is merely plodding. While in Memphis with my son, we had many opportunities to view the mighty Mississippi River, or "Old Man River." One day in mid-June after much rain, the great river was swollen up her banks and moving with a tremendous current. We watched the commerce as large barges moved quickly downstream toward their destination. We also witnessed other large vessels struggling mightily against the extraordinary current. These barges seemed to barely move as they inched their way up the river. Certainly it would have been easier to move with the current, but as in life, with the current is not always where our destination lies. It takes a great deal of effort to go upriver. But with a compelling and dynamic destination, the applied effort will take you there.

Without a very strong and powerful engine, the barges would easily have been swept downstream. Many people find themselves on a river with a strong current and they simply allow the river to carry them rather than direct their own destination. If you let the current of the river carry you, your final destination will be washed out to sea. Without a strong personal engine and a compelling force to drive you in your intended destination, you will be a prisoner of the current. How many people sadly allow their lives to be washed out to sea because they allowed the prevailing current to carry them?

Compelling Destination

Destiny and destination are virtually the same word. It may take a strong motor of force to move up through the current, but the alternative is being adrift and going where the river takes you rather than where you decide to go. A raft adrift on the river with a mighty current has few options with regard to destination.

You must have a compelling enough "why?" or motivation, or your goal will not have fuel to carry you. For you to succeed in reaching your goal it is imperative that you not only know *where* you are going, but also have a *why* you are going. Going upstream and against the current takes tremendous effort. Without a compelling underlying motivation, the attempt against the natural flow will give way to the will of the river.

Vision

Vision creates a picture in your mind or in the minds of others to assist in the compelling aspect of your destination. All great leaders have the proven ability to create a vision of the future and to share that with others as a compelling motivation for action. People with vision do not have the ability to see the future, but rather the ability to accurately assess the current situation and set conditions or changes to make their own path to the future. Successful people are not hampered by their condition and situation; rather they take full advantage of it and create a path from where they are now to where they want to be. Vision is about being sensitive and alert to opportunities, especially those disguised as difficulties.

Vision is also about being adaptable and relating the normally unrelated. Successful people are innovators with their current situation. Many times genius is not so much about creating something completely new as it is adapting something existing for current benefit. No where is this more prevalent than in the growing convenience convergence. Look at the success of convenience stores today. They barely resemble gas stations of 20 years ago. They are a successful adaptation of existing ideas blended to create a new future. Twenty-five years ago, most people changed their own oil in their cars. Today you see this as the great exception to the mass convenience and proliferation of oil change shops.

This innovation is available in your life as well. Vision is an instrumental tool for creating and sustaining motivation. Without the ability to imagine your future in vivid detail you lack the necessary underlying drive to maintain focus on your goals. Without this determination, your objectives seem to diminish in desire and your journey is stifled. All of this is part of planning and setting your own course for your life.

Imagination

If you were anything like my kids when you were young, you played with imaginary friends and were able to amuse yourself more with the boxes the toys came in than the toys themselves. As kids we are allowed to imagine and practice skills. As we grow, having an active imagination is usually applied to people, with a hint of disdain. It is not a characteristic we value unless you are involved in art or drama. Having an overactive imagination is not to be prized, but rather is said to discount a person's opinion or thought. In truth, imagination is the enemy of the dull, consistent and routine existence that often plagues us. How many people do you know or know of who gave up their powers of imagination and now lead a life that is devoid of true happiness with the exception of escapist pursuits?

Imagination is a tool you can use to stimulate and create your vision not for what is or what will be, but rather for what is possible and for what can be. There is so much available to know, to do and to be, but only when you can envision it in your mind first. We need to go against convention and be people with active imaginations, and daydream of what we want in such inspiring detail as to lift us off dead center and push us compellingly toward our future. God has given us a great imagination and yet how often we stifle our impulses and dull our creativity to conform to an artificial society. Do not be constrained by convention. *Dream!* Allow yourself to imagine destinations and journeys far beyond the complacent harbors where your vessel now sits. A very apt quote by Admiral Grace Murray Hopper says, "A ship in port is safe, but that's not what ships are built for."

Dynamic Destination

To be successful in whatever your definition of success is requires a destination that not only is compelling, but also recognizable. Imagine going on vacation and just driving along day after day. Cries of "Are we there yet?" come as a constant reminder that you are nowhere close to your destination. As the driver of this hapless journey you think to yourself, "I don't know where I am going or where I want to go, but I know this ain't it!"

I have always liked the word dynamic. It carries a notion of force and it has change and adaptability within its character. Powerful words like dynamite and dynamo are derived from the Greek root word of *dunamis* meaning energy or power. A person of charm and charisma is said to be dynamic in their personality. Dynamic as a word relates to energy, change, activity, force. In relating to a destination, it may at first seem to not relate at all. After all, isn't a destination static or nonmoving?

Actually in real life, our objectives are constantly moving and changing. Look at the previously mentioned sports figures— Lance Armstrong, Michael Jordan, Tiger Woods and Walter Payton. They all achieved greatly in their endeavors and in many cases beyond what everyone else even thought possible. Yet as tribute to their competitive and compelling drives, success pushed them even further. The nature of their challenges continued to evolve and escalate. What was once a mighty peak becomes merely a plateau to envision the next great challenge. Successful people are constantly challenging themselves and retooling the framework of their goals and desires with force and energy. This allows their dreams and goals to remain dynamic.

Definiteness of Purpose!

A course set for a dynamic and compelling destination is the precursor for a life of purpose. Have you ever had the opportunity to know or observe a person who was very driven and had a distinct definiteness of purpose? When properly in balance, a definiteness of purpose is marked by clarity and directed activity toward a clear-cut objective. There is a difference between a casual stroll with no particular place to go and a walk with purpose.

When you know where you want to go or what you want to achieve and move directly on that path, the feeling is exciting and liberating. There is power in the direct route, in the shortest and most pragmatic route to your destination. So few people know what they really want that they find themselves on the meandering path rather than the fast track.

Planning—The Blueprint of Your Life

Right now stop and answer this one question: Do you have an overall blueprint for your life with exquisite detail and a complete list of goals with the action steps necessary to achieve? Chances are you are not completely able to answer this in the affirmative. You may have a decent idea of what your life is about and might be able to name off some wants and desires, but most likely you do not have a blueprint for your life. Why am I so sure? Statistically over the past 50 years and proven in survey after survey, less than ten percent even have written goals. Some studies show 3 percent and others 5, but the sad truth is that even achievers do not have a true blueprint for their lives. Most people lead uncoordinated efforts with focus shifting from priority to priority without ever designing the blueprint for their life. The ICE (Incremental Cumulative Effect) of their lives are random events tied loosely together with a skill set developed out of necessity, and desires born out of what appears possible only in light of the current circumstances.

Many people are in jobs they hate or careers that don't fit them only because the current of the river of ICE carried them there. Did you choose long ago to do exactly what you have always dreamed of doing and are now in the perfect situation to capture all of your life's goals and ambitions? Or, did you somehow from circumstance after circumstance and event after event wind up in your current situation? Unfortunately, most people are where they are today in all respects of their lives out of a series of sometimes random and tangent happenings in life so that they just kind of wind up where they are. It does not have to be this way! No matter where you are now in any area of life, you have the power to set a new course and make changes to affect your new created and planned future. Where we are today, for better or for worse, is where our thoughts have taken us. With those same thoughts, we are, for better or worse, the architects of our futures.

Creating a Blueprint for Your Future

Before Frankie's illness, we decided we wanted to sell our house and build a new one. We did our research and asked ourselves "why?" regarding all of our assumptions in designing the house. We viewed other successful blueprints and talked with others who have knowledge in our endeavors. We learned a great deal and probably still made our share of mistakes. Before one speck of dirt was lifted from the property or any concrete was poured or any boards nailed, we had one thing firmly in place: our blueprint and design of our new home.

Having the blueprint enabled us to visualize what our house would look like and how our family could utilize and enjoy the home together. This motivation was called into question on a number of occasions as we continued with the entire process of selling our old house four months before the completion of the new house and having to live in a temporary home. We had to move, pack up and undertake the building process during Frankie's treatment in Memphis. The subdivision in which we were building had delays of five months, which backed up our construction timetables. There were a number of obstacles and issues that stood between us and our completed new home. Our compelling vision of Frankie restored to good health and our family reunited in a living space far better suited to accommodate our needs kept us going and provided the vision and motivation we needed to persevere.

No homebuilder of any type would ever consider building without a blueprint. Without a blueprint or design information, you wouldn't know how much or what kind of material you would need. You couldn't estimate the number of workers you would need, the tools required or even the money necessary to undertake the task. Could you imagine the face of the banker after you asked for a loan on a building you would make up as you go?

You would not construct a shed without a plan. Why then do we naturally let our life follow the meandering course of the circumstances around us? Why do we go to work and do today basically what we did yesterday with knowledge that tomorrow will also be virtually identical? With weekends as a diversion, a virtual ocean of distractions all around us and mind-numbing media to dull our brains, is it any wonder that we accomplish so little when our potential is so vast? Is our comfort level so low that we are happy with mediocrity?

There will always be issues and challenges in our lives. We do not have to succumb to the notion of settling with what life has to give us. We have the power, enabled by us in our creator, to rise above our circumstances, educate ourselves out of illiteracy, motivate beyond our complacency, design what we can visualize and ultimately create what we desire to build. Life is a work of art designed by the one who lives it. Control over our blueprint and the resulting construction in our lives truly rests in our own hands.

Faulty Roadmap

Many people start on a process of personal achievement and set goals and objectives only to fall short or give up before ever achieving anything of significance. Unfortunately most carry a faulty roadmap.

I have had many opportunities through army training to practice land navigation. This skill is crucial in successful army operations and was taught and reinforced during all of my training at every level of my army career. The army made it very clear that to lead yourself and others in combat, you must know where you are at all times, where you are going and the skill to find the best route to get there. Within this skill are many other sub-skills and techniques to learn. You have to be able to read a map, identify terrain and determine your position. You learn to figure your position on a map using reverse triangulation. With this technique you take two visible landmarks and plot your relative position to both on the map then draw lines back from the two landmarks. Where the lines cross is the point of intersection and generally where you are.

Although I try hard to stay out of the woods these days, I have found this to remain a relevant skill. In any situation, you have to know where you are, where you are going and the most direct route to get there. If you are deeply in debt, unless you know where you are and where you want to be, your problems will continue. This is so true for many of life's problems. Rather than attack them basically, simply and in a direct manner, we seem to choose any alternate means. Rather than taking stock of where we are and where we need to be and the most direct route to our goal destination, we look for shortcuts that take us off the map we know. Many times this takes us further and further away from our destination. The famous pioneer Daniel Boone said, "Having an exciting destination is like setting a needle in your compass. From then on, the compass knows only one point—its ideal. And it will faithfully guide you there through the darkest nights and fiercest storms."

It seems so simple, yet so many people fail to take the direct path and instead rely on a faulty roadmap. A map of San Francisco, no matter how detailed or current, will do you absolutely no good in Chicago. Faulty roadmaps can take many forms. They can be roadmaps others prepared for you. They can be roadmaps created by yourself that are nowhere close to accurately portraying your real situation. Sometimes the maps are of the right area, but wrong time frame. A map of Chicago from 20 years ago will be of little use today. Being lost in the past is still being lost.

"If you don't know where you are going, you will wind up somewhere else."
—Yogi Berra

Without a compelling future and a good roadmap to your desired future, you are merely on the treadmill of life. Your journey is in response to the day's events and other people's expectations. Your future is limited by necessity and constricted by external forces that seem destined to keep you unhappy. Most of us know about goal setting and have been inundated with it for some time to where we are almost numb to the concept.

Having a clear vision and a compelling destination allow you the feeling of confidence that you know where you are going and you can measure your progress. When you know where you are going, you can establish a route and benchmarks along the way. This sounds so simple and yet so many people miss it. The mass of our society today does not take action daily on their dreams because they have no compelling destination. They lack confidence in their abilities. Without change, they will stay on the treadmill of life until some event outside their control kicks them off.

Creativity and Applied Imagination

Albert Einstein, the most famous and recognized scientist in history, once made a shocking remark reflecting on imagination versus knowledge. Contrary to other people's left-brain-only analytical characterization, Einstein declared, "I am enough of an artist to draw freely upon my imagination. Imagination is more important than knowledge. Knowledge is limited. Imagination encircles the world."

How much money do you think has changed hands in the world because of a little company selling a product whose very essence is nothing but carbonated sugar water? How many people have been affected in one way or another by this little company called Coca-Cola? Billions upon billions of dollars have transacted since this product hit the market. The impact has been felt in every country in the world. From advertisers to concessions to sporting events and concert promoters, supermarkets, gas stations, employees, bottlers, distributors, etc., down to the individual consumer who pays for and enjoys the product. Who has not in some way been affected or had exposure from some aspect of this product? From consumers to investors, there has been an amazing impact.

A $40 investment in 1919 cashed in 74 years later in 1993 would have yielded you a $2 million return. This little product grew up to an adult behemoth multinational corporation. Interestingly enough, however, is that this colossus, this billion-dollar, multinational empire with over 44 percent share of the global market began in the applied creativity and imagination of one man, Asa Candler, a drug clerk who bought a worthless formula for this beverage. It was not the secret ingredient in Coca-Cola that created the success; it was the secret ingredient in Asa Candler.

Ray Kroc, a barely surviving milkshake equipment salesperson, applied his imagination to something the McDonald brothers could not see. In this, Ray Kroc created not only a franchise empire, but an entire new category: fast food. Sam Walton applied his imagination to see what no one else could. In his imagination he created a concept adapted from another industry to create a new industry giant and category creation with Wal-Mart. From the imagination of just these three simple men came *trillions* of dollars in commerce and they have forever changed the world.

No one can define success for you. Only you measure what is important to you and take confident strides toward your intended destination. Make your goals and targets realistic and attainable. Remember incremental achievement. You can perform tremendous accomplishments and climb the highest mountains with a compelling and dynamic destination to motivate you. Big dreams start with small action steps. Start small yet maintain steady progress. No climber starts with Mount Everest as their first climb. Your journey to your compelling and dynamic destination is now only one element away. Now it is time for…*action! The fuel of your dreams.*

"Think like a man of action, act like a man of thought."
—Henri Bergson

CHAPTER 4

Action! The Fuel of Your Dreams

. . . .

"Whatever you can do, or dream you can, begin it. Boldness has genius, power and magic in it."
—Goethe (1749–1832) German Philosopher

. . . .

"Action is the foundational key to all success."
—Anthony Robbins

. . . .

Knowledge Without Action Is Only Potential Power

"Knowledge is power" is a well-used phrase; however, it is really a misconception. The truth in the saying is only half right as knowledge in and of itself is only *potential* power. What good would it be to read the best book in the world about financial wealth-building concepts and yet invest no money? Twenty years later you might be knowledgeable beyond belief yet you would be without wealth. Knowing about the latest, cutting-edge nutrition and exercise techniques will not shed an ounce of fat away without the corresponding action to transform the newly acquired knowledge from potential energy into practical energy.

Much as when we were young and learned about the difference between potential energy and kinetic energy, knowledge without action is the boulder at the top of the cliff or the taut rubber band stretched to the limit. Without action to release the energy, it lies dormant even in the midst of its potential. Potential means you have not done it yet. Potential is only valuable in the conversion to actual. An athlete with tremendous potential who does not take action and apply his or her potential is of no more use than an athlete with low potential. Like the spring coiled, rubber band stretched or rock on the edge of a cliff, nothing happens until there is a force applied to that situation. Nothing happens with any amount of knowledge until there is action applied to it. Without action there is no result. Simply knowing that water will change form at 32 degrees Fahrenheit will not create ice. Without action applied, knowledge is essentially worthless.

Conversion from potential to actual is where the main disconnect for people lies. In the path of personal and professional development, the point of action and application is the moment of truth in conversion to something of potential to something of value. Reading this book or any like it yet not taking action to apply or utilize the knowledge with action is little better than not reading. Knowledge does not become power unless action is applied. If you read this book and do not create an action plan for your life, what benefit does reading serve?

Action Can Overcome Challenges

As action begets action it is also true that success begets success. This is the foundational principle of Compound Cumulative Incremental Improvement. As you make gains in your life and reinvest them, your overall results improve. In addition success in one area creates success in other areas.

For example, imagine a bright and personable salesperson named Bill. In contrast to his intelligence and pleasing personality, Bill is overweight, unkempt and disheveled with an average vocabulary and skill set. Although he has had some decent success recently, Bill has never broken the $50,000 mark with regard to income, a benchmark very important to him. After not fitting into his newest pair of pants, Bill makes a commitment to take charge of his life. He decides to take action first in the area of fitness and physical appearance. He listens to educational and inspirational tapes in his car. He starts an exercise program, although very slowly. At first it is hard for Bill to even get out of bed, but he pushes forward to his desired outcome.

After 90 days of sustained effort, Bill notices an interesting thing: not only is his weight going down, but he has improved his selling and improved his income. After another 90 days, he begins to feel like a different person even though he is still more than 50 pounds from his ideal weight. His exercise habit allows him to get to the office earlier. He is more alert and awake. His attitude improves and his outlook brightens. Bill sees more people and is more effective with them as he has learned and worked hard to improve his skill set. His confidence improves and his outward world begins to mirror his inner world in his new attitudes and actions.

Now fast-forward to the anniversary of Bill's transformation. The action he initially began to change his appearance created a positive ripple effect in every area of Bill's life. He is very close to being his ideal weight. His fitness level and overall health are very good. His family has been the recipient of improvements in his life as his demeanor has changed, allowing him to be more relaxed. Bill's skill set and vocabulary increased as a result of listening to educational tapes in his car while driving to appointments. The other positive outcome for Bill is that his income not only significantly broke the $50,000 barrier, but he also won a sales contest and earned a vacation for his wife and child. The action he took to improve his physical life created action to also improve other areas of his life.

The former story is true, although it is a combination of several people I have observed. This was an example of a "success spiral." Like the fine threads of a screw, the distance from one thread to the next may appear to be very slight. As the screw is turned, the threading creates movement as it pulls itself through the material one small increment at a time. This happens in our life as well and can be either an upward positive spiral or a downward negative spiral. A downward negative spiral is seen in people who allow a single habit to take control of their lives. Whether food, drugs, alcohol, gambling, lethargy or any other negative characteristic, the lead negative habit creates a path for other negative consequences and results to follow.

Conversely, positive results come from positive action. Motivation comes as a result of taking action. Drive yourself to consistently do the small things that lead to success. Learn to compel yourself to take action even when you don't feel like it. After you take some action, you'll be more able and motivated to take additional action. This process creates momentum in the desired upward positive spiral. This, in turn, creates an Incremental Advantage.

You Can't Think Your Way Out of a Hole

Education or knowledge alone is not the key to wealth and success. Knowledge is only the first step. Application is the real key. Imagine putting together all the ingredients necessary to bake a delicious chocolate chip cheesecake. You just purchased the best cookbook on the market for this delectable treat. You can almost smell the rich flavor as you mix the ingredients together in the bowl. You then place the mixture in a pan and put it in the oven…yet never turn on the stove. What happens? Nothing. Without the application of heat, there is no transformation from raw ingredients into what you desire as a finished product.

Take one step. Keep in mind Newton's first law of motion. Take a step and create activity and motion toward your goals. It takes more energy to get a train started than it does to keep it moving. It is like this when you want to accomplish something meaningful. The most difficult time is the contemplation prior to starting. Doubts, second guesses and fear, all work to prevent you from taking action. Have you ever had to push a car? It's most difficult for the first few inches. After you start, momentum acts as an ally to assist your efforts. You must believe that you have control over your own future. Action is empowering and liberating. Even when you are not necessarily doing the most correct activity, do something to propel you forward. Action releases and uncovers future steps and creates opportunities and learning.

In true Stack The Logs! fashion, there are results created that can be incrementally reinvested and improved upon. As I began to take action toward the writing and creation of this book, small successes in learning and doing produced results for me to build on. As I started to show a tangible outline and chapters, my confidence grew and I was able to continue to learn and apply what I was writing about. Some of the action steps I took were not the most direct route to my objective, but in doing, I learned and could apply to other areas of my undertaking. Action and consistent forward progress were my only real goals during several stages of this project. Action leads to confidence then proficiency in whatever you choose to do. Although I read several books for information along this journey, without application those things learned are only ingredients in the pan.

Action Creates Optimism

Rock climbers scaling sheer cliffs look for small toeholds and fingerholds to grab onto and lift them past to the next one. Success in this endeavor takes one movement after another until you arrive at your destination. Small movements, hand over hand, allow for the destination to be reached over time. Take action and look for partial solutions or create small successes. For example, if you start to doubt yourself or lack confidence to move boldly down a path, catalog some or all of your past successes even in unrelated areas. Do not allow yourself to get boxed in with limited options. Seek creative, even partial solutions.

Action sets the basis for the cumulative effect and leads to success. The law of incremental improvement explains that gains made in one area of life tend to transcend and produce effects in other areas as well. Every improvement and advantage gained in one area ads to improvement and gains in other areas. This is akin to the rich get richer concept. Flood your chosen opportunity with activity. As the famous German philosopher Goethe remarked, "Knowing is not enough; we must apply. Willing is not enough; we must do."

Create Your Own Luck

Seize opportunity! Take bold and audacious action. Action creates activity, which creates choices. Choices create opportunities that create more chances for action. Bold and audacious action creates a chain reaction that will lead you to your destination. Other people may call it luck, but you will know what brought about your results.

This is an oversimplification, but nonetheless applicable. Assume your goal is a result of 50 "heads" on a coin toss. To make it interesting, you do not know the results until you are done and so you have to guess how many tosses it will take to accomplish your goal. You know statistically that you have a 50 percent probability of achieving your result on every attempt. While there is a small chance that you could achieve your result with less than 100 tosses, there is a greater probability of success the more tosses you take.

You might attempt to learn a new skill or method of tossing the coin which could increase your percentage of successful head tosses. The reality is that the more you toss, the greater your probability of achieving success.

Concept of "Befriending Sara"

In our company, we like to talk about being bold and audacious. Sometimes this is just a courage builder to get us started. When you take a path and set on a course, you need to embolden yourself to create inner belief and desire. When I first started this writing project, I got off to a quick start and then like most people, I let fear, doubt and worry creep into my thinking. I got a little nervous about my own writing ability, the readership of the book, publishing details. Frankie's illness came and ironically I nearly quit writing a book with a strong theme of perseverance.

Fortunately I received some encouragement from a new friend I made while in Memphis. She provided me with candid feedback to my early work and helped me realize I could make it happen if only I would apply the concepts of my own book. I decided at that point to take action. I boldly declared to some of my close friends and business associates what my goals were and they supported and encouraged me. They also provided a level of accountability, expecting that at some point there would be a manuscript to read.

It is amazing when you take action how nature will open up paths and situations that were not available before will present themselves. At Kahuna Business Group, we call this concept "Sara." We talk about being nice to Sara and try to invite her into all of our plans. The more bold and audacious our vision, the more we look for ways to encourage Sara's participation. Sara is actually our pet name for *serendipity*, which the American Heritage Dictionary defines as, "The faculty of making fortunate discoveries by accident." Some might call it manufactured luck.

Serendipity is the act of finding something valuable or delightful when you are not looking for it. The history of the word "serendipity" dates back to 1754 when it was coined by English writer Horace Walpole. In a letter to a friend, he created the word derived from a Persian fairy tale he once read called *The Three Princes of Serendip*. The story told of three Persian Princes sailing off to discover their fortunes in a land called Serendip (present-day Sri Lanka). In their journeys the princes made many types of astonishing and pleasant discoveries about the island. They had near-magical experiences with luck seeming to guide and direct their fortune as they were presented with opportunities never expected.

Sara does not come out of the blue. She only comes when invited and she is only invited through activity toward your goals. This follows closely with the concept of creating your own luck, which is simple. It is about increasing exposure and your opportunities for success. An actor who puts tremendous effort into exposure, taking all kinds of jobs to create networking relationships and to allow people to see his or her work, suddenly is discovered.

Luck or applied serendipity? A real estate broker makes extra calls and cultivates referrals from everyone with whom she works. She practices her profession, reads books and listens to tapes to improve her skills. She networks in her community. She maintains her fitness. She arrives at the office before her co-workers with her day preplanned from the night before. She has a disciplined and organized approach to her business focusing the majority of her time on the highest payoff activities. She earns more money than anyone in her office and seems to have business come from out of nowhere. Luck? More likely manufactured luck as a byproduct of activity and hard work.

The Magic of 80/20— Applied Incremental Advantage

Around 1895, an Italian economist named Vilfredo Pareto made and wrote about an amazing phenomenon. He observed that in his society, there was a natural division between what he called the "essential few" and the "insignificant many." He noted that the "essential few" were the top 20 percent in wealth and power and that the "insignificant many" made up the remaining 80 percent. Pareto discovered that almost all economic activity was subject to this unequal division as well. Observed and quantified in countless examples over time, the Pareto Principle became the hallmark of time management.

The Pareto Principle, or the 80/20 Rule as it is also called, says that 20 percent of your activities will account for 80 percent of your results. Of course, this is manifest in the J-shaped curves we learned about earlier. Eighty percent of your revenue will come from 20 percent of your customers. Eighty percent of your headaches will come from 20 percent of the people with whom you work.

All Action Is Not Created Equal

When you look at all the action steps needed to achieve a goal or to accomplish your objective, you are likely to find that the Pareto Principle is alive and well within your planning. Most likely if your plan of action was a list of 1 through 20, there would be four items of far greater importance to success than the rest. The key in taking action is not just in activity, but rather smart activity. Undertake the activity that will provide you the greatest gains in your journey.

In your list of 20 items to do, 4 of those items will provide as much or more value or movement to your objective than the other 16 action items put together. Often the most valuable action steps you take are the most difficult and complex. Just as often, however, the payoff for accomplishing these tasks is proportionally far greater than the others to moving you to your destination.

Nothing really happens unless you take some action or do something to make it happen. The most difficult part of any important action step is beginning it in the first place. Once started, motivation to continue is easier. Taking action is the only way to create a bridge between goals and accomplishment.

Victory Over Procrastination— Take Action!

At first blush this might sound overly simplistic. Action creates momentum. Momentum grudgingly breaks loose the bonds of Newton's first law of motion. Let me share an example. I work out regularly 30 minutes, getting up at 5:00 A.M. to do so. I don't always feel like it. If I am really struggling, I tell myself that I only have to go and do 15 to 20 minutes. But once I get started, I almost always find I can easily go the distance to my target. It is impossible to take action while still trying to remain in the state of slumber. It is difficult to break Newton's first law of motion (a body at rest tends to stay at rest...), but once action is taken, the gravitational pull of the pillow is lessened. The further you get away from the bed, the better your chance to maintain your new momentum.

There is a total difference in feeling and attitude when you are 50 pounds overweight and doing nothing but getting worse versus starting at that weight and making true daily progress. Procrastination is the failure to begin, to put off, to delay the start and ultimately leave your potential wasted. We all have difficulties with this at times. We must exert great effort to overcome the gravity pull of the force keeping us from taking action on our journey.

Incremental Dissipation

Probably the worst procrastination offender in the world today has just two initials. Man has yet to invent a more diabolical way to sap the ambition out of people than the nemesis of action—television. The TV and its hundreds of mind-numbing channels seduce us with the promise of leisure, rest and entertainment. What a slippery slope as entertainment turns into habit and the comfort of non-productivity. Have you ever caught yourself flipping through channels hoping something good would be on TV so you would have an excuse to remain in your comfy chair and not tackle any of the tasks before you?

I am not necessarily advocating getting rid of your TV set(s) and fancy entertainment equipment. I need to point out, however, if not kept in check, you may fall short of your dreams and desires because of the complacency and comfort TV provides. The hours the average household spends in front of the "boob tube" are extraordinary.

According to Nielson Media Research 2000™, the average person watches over 30 hours of television per week, which translates into 1,460 hours or the equivalent of 36 40-hour work weeks wasted in escapist activity. Imagine what could be done with just a small percentage of those hours if directed into Incremental Achievement activities.

Stack The Logs! Incremental Advantage Application

Below are some tips to break the barrier and win the battle over procrastination:

10 Incremental Advantage Tips to Win Over Procrastination

1. Identify your list of things to do and write them down. Many times we magnify how much we have to do and it shuts us down or overwhelms us. By writing it down you eliminate this in your imagination and take control over your tasks.

2. Prioritize your tasks so you know which has the highest potential payoff. Strive to do the highest paid work first. It may be tempting to knock off a $2 task that seems less intimidating than the $1,000 one, but keep the payoff potential in mind.

3. Create deadlines for yourself and your tasks. Having a deadline to be accountable to gives you urgency.

4. Break larger projects into smaller parts or action steps. In just a few minutes, you could complete an action step that brings you closer to your goal.

5. Use your mood to your advantage. Contrary to what I said in number 2 about highest payoff, sometimes you are frustrated, tired, angry or in a state not conducive to your best output. This is the time to just continue to work. Even if it is not the highest payoff activity, sustained activity is better than no activity. Too often when we are not feeling like it, that's when we need to push through and maintain momentum for a better day.

6. Clear off your desk and concentrate only on one task. Design your work area productively. Keep all those items you use or need for projects nearby.

7. Develop the habit of "Do it now!"—especially with small tasks before they pile up.

8. Enjoy your time off and allow yourself to stay fresh.

9. Reward yourself along the way. Combined, this refreshes you and continues a motivation cycle to maintain your progress. Delayed gratification for your final results is important, but small and targeted rewards can really help move you down your path. Target your rewards in line with your goals. If your goal is fitness, reward yourself with a new pair of running shoes as you progress.

10. Remember the concept of Incremental Advantage. Add more time to your day for a slight edge. Get up a little earlier or take less of a lunch break and over time you will begin to accomplish more than you thought you could. Not only will you get more done, but you will feel better and more in control of your destiny. Adding 1 hour of productive time a day is 365 hours a year that could be invested in your future. This is the rough equivalent of an extra two weeks a year of productivity.

Successfully getting what you want or achieving a goal boils down to the following components:

STACK
Set your course
   Take action
      Accept results as feedback
         Correct course based on feedback
            Keep on "Stacking the Logs!"

Action is absolutely essential to this strategy. A blueprint without construction does not produce a house, a roadmap without the travel keeps you separated from your destination and a goal without action stagnates your dreams to what might have been rather than what can be.

The Currency of Your Dreams

Look at these two familiar aphorisms: "Talk is cheap" and "Actions speak louder than words." Not only were we raised to believe this about others, but we also generally believe this about ourselves. Hundreds of times we have said what we were going to do and then fell short or quit. Like unborn New Year's resolutions, we are challenged to find a way to increase our currency with ourselves to create credibility with our subconscious mind. Action and small steps and successes in the direction of our dreams enhance our currency with ourselves. When we make a bold statement without commitment or follow-through, we deflate the value of our currency. Dreams transform into reality through one simple manner of transportation: purposeful action. Brian Tracy relates the following wisdom: "One of the marks of superior people is that they are action-oriented. One of the marks of average people is that they are talk-oriented."

Success Is a Result of Resolute Action

Your success will begin to accumulate as soon as you begin to pursue it in earnest. To reach your goal or to attain what you desire, you do not need to know all the answers in advance. Instead, you only need to have a clear idea of what your goal is and a plan working toward that goal. Break your challenges into smaller parts to deal with one at a time in order of priority. Develop tendencies toward taking resolute action. You can make something happen now and take a step in your intended direction. Your opportunity is in taking action where you are right now. It is rightly said that the journey of a thousand miles begins with one step, but that step must be taken. Take a cue from Kramer, the infamous character from the hit series *Seinfeld*, as he likes to exclaim, "Giddyup!"

World War II General Omar N. Bradley observed, "We are given one life, and the decision is ours, whether to wait for circumstances to make up our mind, or whether to act and in acting, to live." To turn our dreams into reality, we must convert potential energy into kinetic or real energy. If you are waiting for your dreams and ambitions to suddenly materialize, you will be waiting for a very long time. Doers almost always outachieve thinkers. It is better to have components of both, but if given the choice, be a doer. The world is filled with smart people with a plan who have never gotten off the mark. If you lack skill, do it anyway and you will learn. If you lack knowledge, do it anyway and you will acquire the knowledge necessary to achieve what you set out to achieve. You have all you need, but in the words of the now famous Nike advertising slogan, "Just do it!"

Part II

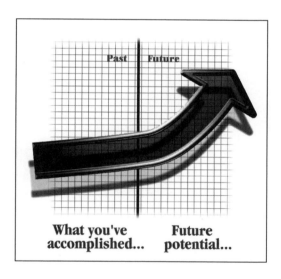

What you've accomplished...   Future potential...

KEEP AN EXCELLENT FORWARD THRUST TO YOUR OBJECTIVES

CHAPTER 5

The Only Limiter
of Your Success... You
(and How to Get Out of the Way)

- -

"Truly, thoughts are things, and powerful things at that, when they are mixed with definiteness of purpose, persistence and a burning desire for their translation into riches, or other material objects."

"Whatever the mind of man can conceive and believe it can achieve."
—Napoleon Hill

- -

Both of these quotes from Napoleon Hill are from his timeless best-selling book, *Think and Grow Rich*. After much reflection, I would have to point to the application of these two passages in this one book as a turning point in my life. My journey into personal and professional development has brought me to hundreds of books, seminars and audiocassettes, yet the essence of that journey is nicely summed up by Napoleon Hill.

To better understand the work, it is important to understand the way the project came about.

Napoleon Hill was born into and lived in poverty around the turn of the 20th century. He later lifted himself out of poverty to become a millionaire, best-selling author, advisor to three U.S. presidents; earn his doctorate; and receive many other accolades and recognition. Dr. Hill spent more than a quarter century researching, studying and then writing about his observations. Like the law of gravity working for us or against us, whether or not we know it, he observed a set of laws that govern success in any field. The study he performed was instigated, yet interestingly not funded by, the wealthiest man alive at that time, steel magnate Andrew Carnegie.

Certainly Carnegie could have funded the entire project without even blinking an eye to help out this poor young reporter from the backwoods with no formal education. A grant from Andrew Carnegie would have clearly made life less stressful for the young Napoleon Hill. Instead, the wily Scotsman introduced the eager student to some of the most successful men in America at that time. Senators, bankers, scholars, captains of industry, pillars of society and the elite of the elite of the day were prepared to share their commonality in the science of success with young Hill. He was given unlimited backstage access to a cast of great renown so he could learn from them, firsthand, and discover the secrets of their success. The entree he received and the doors opened were incredible, proving to be life changing for not only Hill, but also the millions he would later affect through his writings. Carnegie did not fund Napoleon Hill's journey through discovery because he knew the only way Hill was going to really discover the truth of the principles would be to live through them. This would provide him the same advantage every person who succeeds must live through in order to learn the necessary lessons.

I first read *Think and Grow Rich* when I was just beginning my professional selling career. The book planted seeds of awareness and understanding that would later germinate into many wonderful opportunities to learn and grow. To me, the word "opportunities" means both positive and negative experiences. Within each experience was truly opportunity shaped by my own thoughts. Napoleon Hill observed, "You are searching for the magic key that will unlock the door to the source of power; and yet you have the key in your own hands, and you make use of it the moment you learn to control your thoughts."

This concept is so simple and yet it is given so little attention in our life. Our own thoughts create our attitude and feelings, the rudder to direct our ship safely to the port of success or into the perilous rocks of failure. Yes, you are in control. The captain of your ship, pilot of your plane, driver of your vehicle in this journey. You possess a tool that is more potent than any supercomputer on earth and more powerful than even an atomic bomb when properly harnessed. Even those two aforementioned examples were initially created as thoughts in the mind of man.

Look at the sample of quotes below and notice the common theme.

- "A man is what he thinks about all day long…How could he be anything else?" (Ralph Waldo Emerson)
- "As a man thinketh in his heart, so is he." (James Allen)
- "You are not what you think you are; but what you think, you are." (Norman Vincent Peale)
- "Whether you believe you can or believe that you can't; either way you are right." (Henry Ford)
- "Thought is the original source of all wealth, all success, all material gain, all great discoveries and inventions, and of all achievement." (Claude M. Bristol)
- "Remember happiness doesn't depend upon who you are or what you have; it depends solely upon what you think." (Dale Carnegie)
- "The soul attracts that which it secretly harbors; that which it loves, and also that which it fears; it reaches the height of its cherished aspirations; it falls to the level of its unchastened desires. Every thought-seed sown or allowed to fall into the mind, and to take root there, produces its own, blossoming sooner or later into an act, and bearing its own furtive of opportunity and circumstance. Good thoughts bear good fruit; bad thoughts, bad fruit." (James Allen)

- "There is no prosperity, trade, art, city, or great material wealth of any kind, but if you trace it home, you will find it rooted in a thought of some individual man." (Ralph Waldo Emerson)
- "Both poverty and riches are the offspring of thought." (Napoleon Hill)
- "Whatever you vividly imagine, ardently desire, sincerely believe and enthusiastically act upon, must inevitably come to pass." (Paul J. Meyer)

This collection might have easily contained thousands of quotes professing that all human achievement begins in the mind of man as a gift from our creator. This can be used for good as we can point to many thousands of innovations and inventions we take for granted in our comfortable lives today. We have seen examples of selfless people, thinkers and great humanitarians. On the other side of the coin, we have wars and atrocities against humanity and we have the darker side of man's power to create. As men and women, the only attribute that truly separates us from the animals is our ability to think. This gift has been used for both noble as well as evil pursuits since the earliest recorded history.

Your creation of your individual future will come not through your ability to create with your hands nearly as much as your ability to create with your mind. Within the thoughts filling your mind come tomorrow's achievements. Ultimately, it is the destiny you decide firmly for yourself. Or, as we have learned previously, in the absence of your own designed or created destiny, you will become part of someone else's. It has been said that people who lack goals will always work for people who do. I am not saying that everyone needs to quit their job and start their own business to be their own boss. There is nobleness in work and absolutely nothing wrong working for someone else. Truly, even in a job, you have the ability to assert control and affect your future. The diligence of your actions, the focus on the task at hand, the mastery of your skill sets even in the most mundane job will allow you to retain a sense of control over your future.

This concept travels far beyond normal work. It is important to understand that we are either working on our own plan for our lives or we give up control to the circumstances of life and the agendas set for us by other people. The surest route to an unhappy existence is to feel out of control and to feel helpless in an existence that is without destination. How many people do you know who are on a treadmill existence doing the same thing yesterday, today and tomorrow with the only escape being the weekends and pursuits of leisure and entertainment?

Getting Out of Your Own Way

Goals and dreams are individual and unique to each person. Within this there are key principles that allow the process of goal setting to work universally. To be effective, our goals must fill us with a feeling of positive emotion. Without intense emotion, we have difficulty breaking the idea through our subconscious mind. Your subconscious is aware of everything around you and bombarded with millions of images and stimuli. It acts as a filter to separate what is important. Think about the thousands upon thousands of images, conversations and input going on around you. If your subconscious were not working, you would literally go insane with the overload of stimuli. To effectively break through the clutter and the protective barriers nature installed, we must have a steady repetition of the stimuli we want to input with high emotional intensity. The more of our senses we can employ in this the more effective the programming. This is why goals must be clearly defined and positive. It is difficult to imagine a negative goal and it is impossible to visualize a vague undirected goal. You would never visualize a vacation without clearly thinking in terms of your destination. At this moment, can you clearly articulate your major goal in one sentence?

You don't have to set a hundred goals, just set one, follow the process and achieve it. Take that success and invest it back into your next goal and then repeat. Remember, success does not come in one event; it is an accumulation of events over time.

In his groundbreaking book, *Lead the Field*, Earl Nightingale refers to an article written for the *Saturday Review* by Herbert Otto, a prominent psychologist and chairman of the National Center for the Exploration of Human Potential. In this study, famous and world-renowned scientists and thinkers commented on how little of our capacity for thought and creation are ever really utilized. Recognized experts like Margaret Mead and Abraham Maslow agreed that most humans use less than 10 percent of our capacity and ability. Mr. Otto himself remarked, "My own estimate is 5 percent or less." Our goals are in the future. We are where we are. Our mission, should we choose to accept it, is to bridge the gap between where we are now and where we want to be in the future. Earl Nightingale succinctly boils down our results to, "We become what we think about."

Governor of Our Potential

A governor is a device or external component added to an engine to regulate temperature, pressure, air flow or fuel flow. Usually a governor is used to prevent excess speed or pressure to a vehicle. In large multiuse tractors that plow or mow, this can be very beneficial where the load of the engine varies and can prevent damage to the engine from excessive revolutions per minute. In auto racing, sometimes a device called a restrictor plate will be used to prevent speeds above a certain set limit. In this case the goal is to prevent speed for safety or to ensure that the competition is fairly matched. Considering all of the latest technology in racing, without this, there would be speeds far above safety level for the racers.

Many years ago, I had the opportunity to drive halfway across the country in a rental moving truck that had a governor on the engine preventing speeds above 65 miles per hour. With my foot all the way to the floorboard, the speed would not go above 65. This was one of the most frustrating drives of my life—and also most dangerous. While I understand the concept of staying within the speed limit, there are times when increased capacity for speed is important. When you are in the far left with three lanes to cross and traffic steady to your right, sometimes it is necessary to increase speed to take advantage of an opportunity to get in front and pass.

What Are Your Governors?

We are all naturally bound with certain physical limitations that cannot be overcome. Although there is infinite potential within these physical boundaries, we sometimes create our own limitations to further restrict or act as a governor to our potential. You cannot always control circumstances or what happens to you, but these are not limiters to your success. You are the limiter to your success and, as the title of this chapter says, you must learn the vital skill to sometimes get out of the way. Most of the barriers to success and happiness that we see in life are self-imposed and self-created. We are the wardens and guards of our own prisons. We are kept locked up out of conscious, unconscious choices as well as habits and conditioning that we allow to control us.

Baby elephants in the circus are conditioned early by tethering them to the ground with a rope to constrain them. They struggle and pull in vain against the rope and find that the rope will not allow them to move. Over time this struggle and futile result condition the animal that the rope will bind them and they cease the struggle knowing that they cannot break free. The harness creates the limit of the boundary for the small elephants and they are conditioned to the situation. Over time, the elephant grows to a point where its new strength and power could easily rip the restraint from the ground. The full-grown elephant certainly has within its power the ability to escape and yet the early conditioning creates the ongoing limits to the elephant's freedom. An elephant can easily pick up more than a ton with only his trunk. Many people allow themselves to be artificially restrained in thoughts and results. Ultimately we are restrained by our self-imposed boundaries and limitations.

I read of a study where a barracuda and a goldfish were placed in a large fish tank. The barracuda immediately ate the goldfish, as you might expect. Then the researchers placed a glass partition inside the tank to separate the barracuda from its intended prey. The barracuda would swim and run into the glass and the goldfish remained unharmed. After a time the researchers removed the glass partition and found something quite amazing. The goldfish, although no longer physically separated and protected from the barracuda, remained safe. The conditioning of the failed attempts to eat the goldfish when the glass partition was in place created a new self-imposed limit to the barracuda.

Can you think of times in your past where you may have seen failure or had a figurative chain binding you or a glass wall keeping you from something you desired? There are millions of people walking around today with past failures or missteps that have conditioned them to self-imposed limits. It is sad that many people are still living out their fears and self-created limitations from events or situations that happened back in their childhood or early adolescence. A bad social situation with shallow and immature peers creates a reflection decades later that you are awkward and not popular with people. A failure in sports leads to the new belief that you are not athletic and you fail to attempt to be. Less-than-stellar grades lead you to the notion that you are not smart or don't learn well. All of these and similar fears and emotions are self-created, baggage we can choose to carry or let go. As nice as it would be to blame others or circumstances or outside influences for where we are in life and our level of ability to ascend to the heights we choose, the reality is that we alone carry the overwhelming majority of that responsibility. Recognizing this fact is the very first step toward being in control of your own destiny.

Destroy Self-Limiting Beliefs

We are our biggest obstacle to success and need to find out how to get out of our own way. We unknowingly are the biggest millstone around our own necks. We literally sabotage our success and take away our own advantage. How ironic and how cruel that every day we face our staunchest foe in the mirror. We certainly don't knowingly set out to get in our own way; we are programmed and taught how to do it.

Early in my sales career I read a remarkable book by Dr. Maxwell Maltz, who was a world-class plastic surgeon of great renown and author of the 1960 bestseller, *Psycho-Cybernetics*. As a plastic surgeon, Dr. Maltz was intrigued with how he could transform people with severe deformities and cosmetic maladies to look normal, yet the patients still had an exaggerated negative mental picture of themselves and carried with them the same insecurity and unhappiness as before the successful surgery. Dr. Maltz's work has influenced nearly every aspect of human potential.

His ideas and theories regarding the brain's programming have been instrumental in modern-day breakthroughs in business and sports psychology. Current-day marketing genius and entrepreneur Dan Kennedy has worked with and incorporated concepts from Dr. Maltz's writings in his adaptation, *The New Psycho-Cybernetics*. This material can be applied to reprogram your brain, thereby creating permanent changes in your life.

Borrowing from their concept of peak performance, I will use the following example. Imagine you are in a large room that represents your real limits. You can go no further than the exterior walls of the room as they are your complete boundaries. Now imagine you are in a very large elastic box within the room. The box can shrink or grow with effort. Currently the inner box is only taking up a quarter of the space within the outer room of your real limitations. The inner box represents your self-imposed limits. The space between the inner and outer box represents your potential and what is possible. Dr. Maltz describes peak performance as when the walls of the self-imposed limits stretch all the way to the walls of the real limits and fill up all the space of underutilized potential.

Habits of Success
Versus Habits of Failure

Habits of success are the vital few areas with tremendous potential to help you forever add leverage to your life. These are the 20 percent activities to provide the 80 percent results as we learned from Pareto. Our habits are like a conveyor belt taking us to either the finishing floor or the scrap heap. The choice of which conveyor belt to be on, or which habits to carry us through our lives, is one we must make and carries consequences we must live with. Stephen R. Covey, the brilliant author of the phenomenal perennial bestseller and absolute must-read, *The 7 Habits of Highly Effective People*, adds, "Power is the faculty or capacity to act, the strength and potency to accomplish something. It is the vital energy to make choices and decisions. It also includes the capacity to overcome deeply embedded habits and to cultivate higher, more effective ones."

In application to ICE, I take Dr. Covey's words to mean that our habits have brought us to where we are today, but we have a choice as to which habits we want to carry us into the future. What will your Incremental Cumulative Effect be in five years if you keep your current habits? What habits are the vital few or 20 percent you should cultivate and focus on to achieve the 80 percent results improvement in your life? Habits of success allow for improving, learning and stretching beyond what is comfortable.

Invest a little time and some resources into self-planning to discover for yourself the key areas of leverage needed to elevate above the crowd. Identify one habit that if you could waive a magic wand and change, would have the most dramatic impact on your life. Would it be exercise? Mental development? More time with your family? Developing a spiritual life? Take time to contemplate this as it should be your starting point. Once you identify the habit and take immediate action toward your objective, your life will never be the same.

For me, the leverage I lacked was in the area of physical fitness. I needed exercise as a daily part of my life but had several negative habits lined up in opposition. I needed to change my self-image and my belief structure from an overweight, always tired, semi-stressed individual to one of a fit, healthy, vibrant and optimistic person. I realized that if I could change some key habits, I could create positive results and positively affect other areas of my life. The next step for me was determining the specific habits I would need to cultivate to support my new belief structure. I decided I would begin every day at 5:00 A.M., with my day planned the night before. I would be energized and exercise each morning to get into my office early with blood coursing through my veins. I would take time for scripture reading and prayer before I began my work. I then would take an hour for reading, study or writing before my day began.

These were all habits started very slowly and with some frustration. I worked through the start-up resistance to where I could continue my habits of success every morning almost without exception. Success in my morning habits gave leverage to effectiveness habits relating around my values in other areas of my life. My weekends are generally my own, for my family, friends and church-related activities. I leave the office around 5:15 every night so I can focus on time with my family. After my kids are asleep, I then have time to spend with my wife or do additional reading or writing. These new habits were surprisingly easy to follow after I clearly identified my priorities and objectives. It is said it only takes 21 days to change or develop a new habit. I found this to be mostly true, but not completely. In my case, I needed to support my habits with self-talk and asking the right questions.

For instance, you may remember the old Dunkin' Donuts commercial with the older gentleman who ran the store getting up when it was still dark. Shuffling his feet, his head angled down and his eyes looked up glancing past his forehead, he looked pathetic as he muttered lifelessly, "Time to make the donuts."

I concentrated and planned for a different approach as I set my alarm for 5:00 A.M. I go to bed, not counting sheep, but reflecting on my major objective, visualizing it in detail as I drift slowly to sleep. As the alarm goes off, I am awakened refreshed and invigorated and I say to myself in a proud and excited voice (but not so loud as to disturb my wife), "Time to Stack The Logs!" I get out of bed with purpose and begin my daily success habits.

Does this happen every morning? Well, no. Truthfully, I would rather sleep in, but as I do these actions and say these words, it does have an effect on me. Some mornings my tone and body language resemble the Dunkin' Donut's man, but each day the habit gets easier and easier with other benefits carried through my day. After I exercise, my creativity and imagination are definitely enhanced. Most of my work-related problem solving comes from reflections and active thinking post-workout. I now carry a notepad to the gym since some days I get a torrent of ideas as I challenge my aerobic capacity on the exercise equipment.

As we have seen in the pattern of action begets action, success begets success, etc., good habits beget good habits. Continuing on with the wake-up-early and exercise (actually two separate) habits, I found that when I was working out, my circulation increased and my energy improved. The next progression was a closer look at my eating habits. Do I really *need* to clean my plate? Will my leftovers in any way affect starving kids in another country? In the voice of Glenda, the *Wizard of Oz's* Good Witch of the North, "Will eating beyond satisfaction of my hunger lead to good ICE or bad ICE?" Eating habits triggered new activity habits and choices. Each action triggered opportunities for leverage in other areas of my life.

All our habits are interrelated and connected in various ways. How you feel impacts how you act, which reflects in your attitudes and interaction with others. This in turn reflects back to you in their attitude and action, which affects the way you feel, which impacts how you act. This is but one of hundreds of interconnected habits that drive your life. When you begin to elevate one, it impacts others and you will see a rise in your personal results graph. The more habits you can get to work for you rather than against you, the more effective you will be in every area of life. As you exercise, your prospects for increased income develop as well as your looks, fitness, attitudes, stamina, creativity and a host of other factors related to components having to do with opportunities to increase your income and your career.

You Are the Brakeman

In the old steam-powered trains there were, as the conductor's assistant, at least one and sometimes two brakemen to help stop the train as it carried forth with tremendous momentum. Before the train started on its course, the brakeman would test the brakes to ensure they worked properly. The other *very* important task the brakeman had to do was to release the brakes or the engine would fight the force of the brakes causing serious problems for the maintenance of the train and the brake system. A train trying to commence movement, or a car at a red light with the brake on at the same time the accelerator is pressed, produces high RPMs and tremendous potential energy, but no motion. Until the brakes are released and the engine is free to do its work unencumbered, the vehicle or train is at an extreme disadvantage. Perhaps you have been in a car with the emergency brake still on while trying to accelerate. The car lumbers forward depending on the setting of the brake. If the car moves at all, you can feel the strain and the two forces working counter to each other.

One popular misconception is that others keep us from moving forward or put the brakes on our lives. The truth is that we are the brakeman for our lives. Only we can release or hold the brakes on our lives. As the brakeman, it is your sole responsibility and your obligation to your desired future to release your brakes. Get out of your way and allow yourself to become the person you desire to be.

"Successful people have the habit of doing the things failures don't like to do. They don't like doing them either, necessarily, but their disliking is subordinated to the strength of their purpose."
—Albert E. Grey

CHAPTER 6

Personal Initiative!
How to Completely Separate Yourself from the Crowd

. . . .

"Do or do not. There is no try."
—Yoda

. . . .

Achieving Incremental Advantage

We have discussed Incremental Advantage at length in all of the previous chapters. Its application is the bedrock success principle represented by the Stack The Logs! metaphor. Success, as we have learned, is about the little things providing a slight advantage or incremental edge over time. These little successes add up and accumulate into larger successes. In life, you are not competing with others. Your only competition is with yourself and the self-imposed barriers you desire to break through. You may feel like you are in competition with others in our zero sum world. In truth, however, what others think say or do is irrelevant to your long-term situation. You certainly may have some ups and downs in the short run regarding other people. But in the long race of your life, your steady pace and deliberate course run with the end in mind will dramatically separate you from the crowd over time.

Incremental Advantage Master Skill—Applied Knowledge

Aristotle, the famous Greek philosopher, in his essay titled *Metaphysics* asserted, "All people naturally desire knowledge." Information in and of itself is the start of knowledge. A majority of people are complacent to what they have already learned and no longer willing to push the boundaries. Complacency and unwillingness to change the perspective on learning and knowledge trap many people into an existence less than desired and far less than they are capable of achieving.

Knowledge acquisition is a lifelong learning commitment. The acquisition of knowledge is integral to achieving your goals and creating your desired future. Sir Francis Bacon coined the oft quoted phrase, "Knowledge is power." Throughout history, the educated class has always maintained a distinct advantage. In the past education was a rare privilege, sometimes only allowed through "proper birthright." Even today in some areas of the world education and knowledge are limited to countless people. It is not, however, unavailable to you. In fact, there is more available knowledge now than at any other time in history. Knowledge is essentially yours for the asking on any subject you want. Unfortunately, the availability for some diminishes the value. If you are serious about putting in motion events to better your life and create what you desire, you must take advantage of the knowledge available to you. Henry David Thoreau observed, "To know that we know what we know, and that we do not know what we do not know, that is true knowledge."

Everything we need to know and every skill of achieving our dreams can be acquired through knowledge. Knowledge is abundant and available to all who seek it. We are all born into the world ignorant and without knowledge. Whether we chose to remain ignorant or take action to adapt and apply knowledge to our advantage over our environment is a choice. Each choice or series of choices culminates over time in our destiny. The real question is whether we want to end up where fate takes us or take control to whatever degree we can to choose our own destination. Knowledge applied to your life gives you power over your life and leverage to affect your own future. To advance toward your goal, it is necessary to keep your eye on the goal and continue to grow in knowledge as well as application of the knowledge toward your objective.

Acquire and Apply Knowledge

Think about the structure you had while you were a child in school between kindergarten and grade 12. You had teachers, parents and a system designed to move you up and through it. The very design of the American school system is one of incremental learning progression with a promotion to a higher grade eventually leading to a graduation of the system. What if there were no system in place for education, would you have had the inclination or the discipline to get the education you got? Why is it that in school you have the system to get you through this education process, then it leaves you alone without a basic structure or system of success beyond the basics? Why are people going through our school systems not taught about their potential? Why are our children not given the tools to understand their potential and to make the most of it as they grow and develop? The sad truth is that after the education we are forced into, most people stop learning.

If you want to be successful in any endeavor, you must commit to learning. Most people look at learning as what they did in school. After graduation they feel their learning is over. Never at any other time in history has there been so much free knowledge available on any subject. From libraries to the internet, there is enough information available to get your doctorate degree in any chosen field. Why is it then that most people resist learning and a system of learning outside of what we had in formal education? Commencement is a ceremony that most go through at graduation. Both the words "graduation" and "commencement" have meanings that imply continuing. Commencement quite literally means beginning or originating; graduation implies moving to another level.

There are so many things to learn and with that knowledge improve and enrich our lives. Knowledge, education and training could not be a more powerful lever for applying Incremental Advantage to your life. The Japanese have a term for the process of never-ending improvement, *kaizen*. Most people have a built-in resistance to such a commitment and instead place a greater emphasis on entertainment and escape rather than improvement. Improving yourself is a daily and incremental activity. Look for things to pique your curiosity and new things to learn. Adapt your learning into small changes and improvements. Continue to learn and apply knowledge in small ways to further improve. Then build on those improvements. This positive *kaizen* cycle is the bedrock to creating incremental improvement in your life and achieving your goals. The principles we have discussed are known by many yet applied by few. Being part of that group sets you apart and allows you to separate yourself from the crowd.

Knowledge Begets Knowledge

Knowledge increases awareness of opportunities, relationships and things unseen. Knowledge creates new connections and new patterns of thought, it increases your perception of the world around you and the opportunities therewith. Like your vantage point as you climb a large hill, your perspective is clearer the higher you go. Knowledge builds upon itself and raises elevation allowing for increased perspective. The process of adapting information to our use or applying information to our situation begins the cycle of Incremental Advantage. Learning, as a natural counterpart to goal setting, is most effective when you set out to learn with a specific objective in mind. The better educated and informed you are with relation to your objective, the more you will find yourself discovering opportunities you may not have seen before.

Information is more readily available and convenient to access than ever before, yet unless you take action to acquire and apply information, it is of little use. With a computer and internet connection, you can have a virtually unlimited amount of information on any topic you can dream up. But as with all information—verbal, print and other media—you have to filter the information and weigh the source while comparing to other information to make knowledgeable decisions. In school, we learned rote or static information that does us virtually no good unless we are a contestant on a game show. To achieve a sustained improvement in your results, you need to constantly acquire, apply and reacquire in an ongoing cycle of growth. Knowledge plus applied action one time will produce a minimal short-term change at best. This would be like reading a good diet book and changing your habits for one day. Little to no result would happen and certainly no long-term change would take place. What is missing is consistent applied action over a significant period of time.

If your goal is wealth, the way to those riches is not winning the lottery. Instead, it is patient and repetitious accumulation, spending less than you earn, seeking new opportunities to earn, learning about money dynamics and many other small actions that build over time. It is taking the right actions and adding patience and persistence over time to achieve the result you are looking for.

Chris Widener is the founder and president of Made for Success. In his book of the same name, Chris explains the equation for long-term achievement and accomplishment as, "Your short-term actions multiplied by time equals your long-term accomplishments." Knowledge adapted to your goals provides leverage and becomes a significant tool for accelerating your progress. The best investment we can make is learning with a purpose as it improves our production capability.

Learning and development are yin yang counterparts of goal setting. When you connect your learning and acquisition of knowledge to apply it to your goals, your results improve. If you are on a sailboat adrift in the water, applied knowledge of sailing techniques suddenly become invaluable. Knowing your situation in relation to your destination, you can apply knowledge to move you more efficiently toward your destination.

Applied knowledge is the cure for ignorance and the short-est path to our goals. Becoming a Cliff Claven (the know-it-all, king of useless trivia, bar stool warmer from the TV sitcom *Cheers*) will not move you closer to your goals. Applied knowledge in the form of techniques, insights, applications, examples of others on a similar path will provide you with a more direct route to your goals and shorten your learning cycle. All knowledge is interrelated. An educated and knowledgeable mind can make connections and applications beyond the immediate scope of the situation. The genius is not necessarily creating new ideas, but rather the practical adapting of ideas to fit the situation. Famous scientists like Galileo, Newton, Einstein, Edison and Bell derived many of their theories or inventions from observing nature and relating or adapting to the outcome they sought. How you interpret patterns or happenings may seem irrelevant to most. As you train your mind, unrelated information and knowledge leads to insights to create a vision or path to your goals. Some of the best business successes were adaptations of one industry into a completely unrelated industry.

The more you learn, the more you can apply to other situations. Create a desire for knowledge. When you were in school and forced to learn it was dull and laborious. Desire for learning and applying the knowledge to your goals and dreams turns drudgery into an adventure. Information applied turns to knowledge and knowledge applied matures into wisdom.

Return on Investment (ROI) of Self-Improvement

What is the ROI in the acquisition of knowledge or personal or professional development? Is it worth spending $20 on a book versus $20 on a meal? Look at a book's table of contents, then ask yourself whether or not the time, effort and expense of the $20 purchase would be returned to you in the acquisition of the benefits or even one single applied concept. Most high achievers will invest between 3 and 5 percent of their income into development. Imagine taking just 1 percent of your income and investing in personal or professional development as an Incremental Advantage success multiplier.

Assume you start out making $20,000 per year and you invest $200 over that year into directed information to be applied to your life. The $200 investment will produce an incremental increase in your effectiveness that will, over time, yield greater productivity and greater potential to earn. The growth in earnings brings with it a corresponding increase in your investment back to yourself. As your income rises, your development and capacity also rise. Over time, small applied activity done consistently will result in improving results. Imagine, like most achievers, you did invest 3 percent of your income and 3 percent of your time (approximately 5 hours per week or 45 minutes a day) to invest directly into developing your talents, skills, applied knowledge, etc.? Could you imagine the incremental impact? Next time you have a $20 bill in your hand, take a look at it and ask yourself if it would be better invested as food in your belly or in a book related to your chosen field of endeavor?

One of my favorite authors and speakers is Brian Tracy, a leading authority on unlocking human potential and pushing the boundaries of personal effectiveness. He has authored more than 16 books, including such bestsellers as *Focal Point* and *Maximum Achievement*, and recorded over a dozen audio programs. In his best-selling book, *Focal Point*, he suggests, "You are your most valuable asset." He asserts that you should spend at least as much money upgrading your skills and abilities each year as you spend to keep you car on the road. The transformation and your ability to earn more is at your disposal, one action step at a time. Investing in personal and professional development is probably the greatest of all the Incremental Advantage applications.

Many times we are in jobs, roles or professions not because we consciously chose to. Instead we end up where we are because of ICE. The good news is that it is not too late to change or re-choose your targets based on new information. The old paradigm was high school to trade or college then on to a career until retirement. That is no longer the norm. It has been proven time after time: income will rarely exceed personal development. It has been theorized that if you took all of the money in the world and gave it equally to every person in the world, that it would eventually gravitate back to where it currently is. You can't have more until you can become more.

I recently overheard a conversation where someone literally told another person, "My job stinks so I just goof off. If I had a better job, I would work harder." How backward this is, yet how widely held. Jack Welch, the former CEO of General Electric and one of the most famous and recognizable corporate leaders of the late 21st century, is quoted as saying, "Control your destiny—or someone else will."

Time (Choice) Management

There really is no such thing as time control or time management. You do have the ability for time choice and event or activity management within the time allotted. This may seem like a small distinction, but it is quite important. You cannot control time; no one can. Your success in "time management" is to better control your incremental activities within a given time period for success. Instead of spending time in front of the television or in relaxation activities, what if you invested those hours in study toward improving your skill set or increasing your specific knowledge in your industry or exercising, etc. Imagine what that translates to over time. I am not against relaxation and leisure in moderation. Unchecked, however, the tradeoff between what Brian Tracy characterizes as tension relieving versus goal achieving is tremendously steep. Success comes not through the months and years, but through the hours and minutes and the choices within each.

How to Get Promoted in Life

Don't wait for things to happen. Set yourself apart from the crowd and make things happen. Take initiative and take a chance. Most people never will, so if you do, it naturally sets you apart from others. We all have areas of weakness and personal liability. Our strategy should be to determine which areas are improvable to provide us maximum benefit for the investment of our time, effort and energy. Don't spend time and effort dwelling on your limitations or what you can't do. Instead, look to magnify and capitalize on your strengths and potential. Spend energy focusing on finding Incremental Advantages and changing and improving areas you can rather than focusing on what or why you can't.

Assume you have two financial accounts. One is a mutual fund providing you an annual yield consistently in excess of 15 percent per year. The other account is a savings account getting you 3 percent if you are lucky. You just earned a thousand-dollar bonus check and you want to invest all of it. Assume further you have emergency savings covered and you are interested only in future gains with this newfound money; where do you invest it? Unless there were some compelling reason otherwise, you would naturally invest your capital where it could get the highest return on investment. It is no different for your skills, talents and abilities invested in the time increments available and equal to all human beings. Leverage and separating yourself comes from consistently doing the highest payoff and highest leverage activities.

Most people look outward for success. They look for someone else to appreciate them, someone else to promote them, someone else to motivate them. *Success is not external shining in, it is internal radiating out.* If you look for other people to define your success or happiness, you will never find your full measure of either. You are the convening authority for your own life, not others. If you want a promotion, set up the conditions to get promoted. Apply the STACK Strategy and you will find the power and control in yourself, rather than in others.

You, Inc.

When you have your own business, it is clear to see the selling of services or other value in return for money. You may not realize this, but even if you are an employee, you are basically self-employed. You are your own personal services corporation selling to one customer—in this case, your employer. Whether you earn minimum wage or are in the top bracket of income earners, your business entity, You, Inc., is at the heart of your earning. In a job, you package and market your talents, skills, abilities, attitudes and efforts into something traded to your employer for income. This is no different from being self-employed. The quickest route to earning more money is to recognize your situation and to provide more value to your organization. The more you develop your skills, talents, abilities, attitudes and efforts into value for your employer or your clients, the more you earn and are worth.

In working with other business owners, as an employer myself and a former supervisor of over 350 people, I can relate to you the most desirable characteristics for employees. Skill and talent are helpful, but only a basis to start. The most important characteristics revolve around attitude. Employees who have a positive attitude, are willing to learn and grow and take initiative to advance the supervisor's goals or take away headaches are rated the highest. Is this any surprise? Employees provide leverage to a business. The more benefit an employee brings you, the more valuable they are in the leverage they bring to advance the business's objectives. If you want to earn more or move up in an organization, add more value to your supervisor and the organization. If you have your own business, do the same for your customers. It is quite simple, but missed by so many who forget they are hired to serve rather than be served. If you cannot provide value to an organization, why would it employ you? If someone else can provide the same value you do for less money, why would they not look to replace you with that person? If you have scarcity mentality, this might rub you the wrong way or make you scared. I challenge you to look at it in the reverse. Knowing most people look at their jobs as an entitlement, find ways to add more value, learn more and apply your skills to your organization.

Create a personal balance sheet for yourself. List your assets and liabilities in the areas of knowledge, talents, skill set and abilities. Also evaluate your attitude and advantages you have as a benefit. Your liabilities are only what you have yet to learn and apply to improve the items on the asset side. You may think you have more liabilities, but those are only self-limiting beliefs created and enforced by yourself. The key to your potential is to develop and refine the potential of you. The concept of You, Inc., is not new. It has been used by many people to illustrate that your earning power and production capability rest squarely on *you*.

What are you doing to push the boundaries and improve the production capability of You, Inc.? The good news is that you don't have to get all of your education at once. You don't have to quit your job to go back to school or take a sabbatical to learn new things. The best education is the application of knowledge to your goals. Incremental learning is certainly a "log stacking" activity. Learning is like climbing a mountain. The more you climb, the more you see and the better you can improve your perspective of all that is below you.

Application Example

Four years ago, I had the occasion to meet a young man named Jason. He was working two jobs but had not yet settled into a career. As it turned out, our organization had an entry-level opening for a person with his skill set. What really made this young man stand out to me was not only was he self-taught in many areas, but also his attitude and willingness to do whatever it took in his current situation. While working at a convenience store, he developed programs on his own time to create leverage for his boss and value for the store. He took on extra work and found opportunities to be of service in the ugly areas (places no one else wanted to contribute). Sensing in this college-aged young man a strong desire and a willingness to learn and grow, we hired him to be a technical customer service representative.

Jason began his career with us in what may have been seen as the lowliest of jobs. He worked hard and maintained his attitude. In the past four years, Jason has continued to grow and develop taking initiative to not only relieve me of headaches, but to significantly add value to our organization. He has continued to assume more responsibility and take initiative. Any time there was a problem or Jason fell short from his objectives, he took complete responsibility and grew from the experience. Not only is Jason a valuable employee, he literally promoted himself to department head, part of our company's executive team and minority shareholder in the business.

Inversarian Principle

"Inverse" means opposite, contrary or parallel in the other direction. During rush hour in a major city where most people live in the suburbs, most of the traffic is going out. An inversarian strategy would be to live in the city and work in the suburbs to avoid the traffic created by the masses. Inversarian is observing what the crowds and masses are doing and then doing the opposite. We have already determined that most people are average and this is not desired. The masses live in wide open comfort zones of neither total lack nor total plenty. To separate from the crowd, use the inversarian principle to your advantage. Most people do little more than what is expected of them. Doing more than expected and providing more value, sets you significantly apart.

To stand out from a crowd is to be different. Now you could dye your hair purple, pierce all exposed flesh and paint your body with art, but this type of standing out will not likely afford you the results you seek. To achieve any reward is to pay a price. Whether athletic, social or business endeavors, there is service rendered and a price paid. Initiative is a starting point. The human race largely goes forward on a march, not knowing the riches and beauty around them. We assume because millions are doing it that it is okay. This is the largest misconception and fraud pushed on us. I am all for educators and have a tremendous respect for anyone in that profession. I am severely troubled with the education system as a whole, however, as it does not produce the effect of teaching kids to think and achieve. Millions of people live an average existence when there is a world of abundance theirs for the asking if they were only willing and understood how.

Parlay small successes into larger successes and magnify your results. This is compound success, just like compound interest. The gains will at first be small and imperceptible. As you apply and reinvest your gains they become more significant. My father's advice to me to "stack the logs" was encouragement to reinvest my wins and small gains in my situation at work. Eventually the pile grows and others take notice.

If you want to move ahead of your peers you must have better results. You will not get more money or an increase in responsibility until you deserve and earn it. Nothing is given to you. My biggest frustration in all my time in my employer/supervisor role is a person who does less until they make more. On the highly recommended tape series by the late Earl Nightingale, he talks about a man standing in front of a fireless stove complaining that he would not add wood until there was more warmth, not recognizing the fundamental aspect that wood or fuel precedes the heat. Effort precedes rewards. I have heard it is said that the only place where success comes before work is in the dictionary! Have you seen people with this entitlement attitude who feel that showing up or just doing their job entitles them to rise in income and responsibility? You don't rise through an organization or get true rewards unless you demonstrate your efforts and prove your worth.

Do More Than Expected

Take initiative. A person with strong personal initiative is basically a leader of self. A leader should never have to be told what to do, but rather be a person with vision of the future outcome desired and an understanding of the path to get there. A leader takes initiative and action to move themselves and others down that path to the ultimate destination. Most people wait for circumstances. They wait to be led or told what to do. Instead, be a leader, take initiative and take control of your future.

A match can start a forest fire, a single comment can trigger a large argument and a single event can precipitate a chain of events significantly out of proportion to the initiating event. Dr. Stephen Covey remarked, "I am personally convinced that one person can be a change catalyst, a 'transformer' in any situation, any organization. Such an individual is yeast that can leaven an entire loaf. It requires vision, initiative, patience, respect, persistence, courage and faith to be a transforming leader." Leverage your success within the organization. Project the right attitude to others. Take on more work and look for ways to build value in your organization through becoming a problem solver. When you take on projects to challenge and teach you new skills, you grow in value while you increase your potential in your current or future organization.

There are no shortcuts on the path to demonstrating value to others. It cannot be said, it must be shown consistently over time. Sometimes this means coming in early and staying late. It may mean doing what is asked to the best of your ability, then doing more. It is about finding opportunities to do things better and more efficiently than they've been done before. When these things are done with enthusiasm and a positive attitude, it creates separation from the crowd. When you get right down to it, what organization or employer would not be excited about your being on their team? Your goal is to make yourself indispensable within the organization. Little actions consistently over time with the attitude of service will clearly provide you tangible rewards as you progress. Charles Colton observed, "The consequences of things are not always proportionate to the apparent magnitude of those events that have produced them."

Look for Opportunity to Offer Value (Usually Hidden in the Ugly Areas)

Hard work is part of success. The harder the work and more intense the effort, the more "luck" seems to work in your favor. To get paid more, provide more service. Doing more than you are paid for to separate from the crowd is certainly not a new concept. Earl Nightingale sagely expressed, "Always do more than you're paid for or you'll never be paid much more than you're getting now." Increasing value to receive increased value is nothing more than the law of the harvest (sowing and reaping), which is similar to the law of cause and effect. It is also put forth in Newton's third law of motion of every action having an equal and opposite reaction. If you are dissatisfied with a result, you must look first at the output. Rewards come in proportion to service or value rendered. Look for opportunities to exceed the expectations of others and eventually your success will exceed your own expectations.

Attitude makes all the difference, especially in application to the task at hand. There is an old story of two shoe salesmen being sent by their respective companies to Africa to expand each company's worldwide presence. The first salesman, after less than a full week on the continent, called his boss back in America completely distraught and disillusioned. "There is absolutely no reason for me to be here," he said. "Most of the people don't even wear shoes yet." The other salesperson after his first week called his boss absolutely ecstatic. He said, "I can't believe this opportunity, it is incredible and I want to thank you so much. Most of the people here don't even wear shoes…yet."

. . . .

"We are what we repeatedly do. Excellence, then, is not an act, but a habit."
—Aristotle

. . . .

CHAPTER 7

Learn How to Always Fail Forward

. . . .

"Failure should be our teacher, not our undertaker"
—John Maxwell

. . . .

Almost any great accomplishment you can think of has at some moment in its origin a failure or door closed that you can point to as the original seed of success. Robert Collier said, "In every adversity there lies the seed of an equivalent advantage. In every defeat is a lesson showing you how to win the victory next time." An old Chinese proverb relates the theme in the words, "A gem cannot be polished without friction, nor a man perfected without trials."

It is important to cling to this notion that failure and setbacks carry opportunities within their core. Some of these opportunities lie in new paths and new directions. Sometimes it may be in learning or experience to be stored away for future application. Sometimes it may be in rescuing ourselves from a path that would have proved disastrous. I can now look back at many of my experiences that I classified as failures, with the clearer perception of time and see how each has benefitted me.

Failure is a label we attach to an event or a set of circumstances. In and of itself, there is not an intrinsic meaning, but rather the meaning we attach to it. If you think you are about to get fired and waiting for the fateful call, when the phone rings you are filled with apprehension and dread. But if you are expecting your boss to call to inform you of a raise or promotion your emotions are turned the other way. The ringing phone in and of itself provided no meaning. The meaning came from the emotions attached to it.

You will have "learning experiences" others call failures. Embrace this learning and failure as part of the learning process. Failure and setbacks always precede success. Look at the Apollo Space Program for a high-tech example of successes and failures building upon each other for great achievement. For a low-tech analogy, look at learning. As I help my son with third-grade homework, it seems so basic to me, yet for him it is a process of learning. Trial and error are part of how all of us have learned any skill we now possess. From simply walking to any complex skill we have now, we each went through a process of learning through trying, failing, adapting, learning and repeating the cycle all over again.

What most people do after a failure or setback is to feel stung, hurt, embarrassed and refuse to try again. Worse, they dwell on the negative and let it influence future situations and future outcomes.

Pain Precedes Progress

In the sport of bodybuilding and weightlifting, muscle fibers will not grow until pushed to failure. Once the muscle fibers break down, then after a period of healing, they will rebuild larger and stronger. Bodybuilders seeking large muscle gains create and follow through on a systematic plan over time to constantly produce failure. Interestingly enough, they must be creative in finding new ways to induce this failure as the muscles become resistant to breakdown and failure.

The weightlifter's adage of "No pain, no gain!" applies to our lives as well. Without failing, there can be no real growth. Anyone who works out at the gym lifting weights or engages in heavy manual labor understands that growth comes as a byproduct of resistance. The arm of the blacksmith is made strong and powerful by the daily resistance of the hammer.

If you set out to learn a musical instrument, language or skill, you will fail far more than you succeed in the beginning. Failure is a part of the process and needs to be recognized as such. Failure is not bad until we allow permanence. Attempting a new skill and quitting after initial setbacks is failure. Working through the skill and taking feedback from each failed attempt provides progress to your goal. With persistence and applied learning, each failure brings you closer to your desired competence level. Overcome obstacles to get stronger. Pain precedes the gain. Just as within muscles, growth follows failure. Robert Kennedy said, "Only those who dare to fail greatly can ever achieve greatly."

Failure Is Part of the Process

Aristotle, the famous Greek philosopher, said, "For all the things we have to learn before we can do them, we learn by doing them." Try juggling if you don't know how. You can learn, but it will be ugly at first. Can you imagine a baby learning to walk through studying others, yet never crawling, standing or attempting the first awkward steps that result in a topple? From a pure analytical observation, a baby goes through a J-shaped curve to success. A baby crawls, fails, walks poorly and improves slightly. The results graph remains flat until success turns the corner and the curve shoots upward with an improved outcome. Anything worth doing well is worth doing poorly...at first.

The mistakes of the past are your paid-in-advance learning experiences to apply to the future. Without the failures, you would never have the success. Success is sometimes in proportion to the failures you recover and learn from.

Success Through Increased Failure?

"Once burnt, twice shy." "Fool me once, shame on you; fool me twice, shame on me." "Let that be a lesson to you!"

Have you heard these phrases before? Do you know people who had one negative experience and completely shut down in that area? It is unfortunate we are conditioned to try to avoid failure at all costs when really we should be failing more. In sales, the typical ratio is 10-3-1. What this means is that for one sale you have to talk to 10 people, 3 of whom you will go the distance with and ask them to buy, then one will say yes.

Let's say that I earn $100 on every sale. I know that 10-3-1 is my ratio and I know this year I want to earn $30,000. I know I need to make 300 sales this year, which breaks down to about 6 per week. To get 6 sales a week, I know I must see 60 people per week to ask 18 to buy, of whom 6 will say yes. What if I want to increase my success? In my current ratio, I fail 70 percent with the people I initially talk to and then, with the ones I ask to buy, I fail another 66 percent of the time. Why, in aggregate, I fail 90 percent of the time! How do I make more money? Fail more often!

Now this is not nearly as brutal and sadistic as it may seem. Each failure pays off in experience in dealing with people; it brings opportunities to demonstrate my integrity and character, sowing future seeds of opportunities and referrals. My skills increase as does my effectiveness. Every failure brings me closer to my next success. Any sales trainer will share with you that success and failure in selling are connected. The law of probability says that your success rate will rise correspondingly to your failure rate. With a good attitude and learning mentality, each failure creates an improvement and increases your overall success probability.

Imagine you are given a pile of 10,000 envelopes and the knowledge that one contained a check for $10,000. You know there is a reward and all you have to do is open them up until you find the prize. How many times would you be willing to fail? In this case wouldn't you be willing to fail as often as you could (as many as 9,999 times), knowing each failure brought you that much closer to the big payoff?

Anything Worth Doing Is Worth Doing Badly

Skill development happens through practice, trial and error. Whether you are attempting to learn a new language or a new computer program, when you begin you will fail more than you will succeed. Your skill acquisition will start off ugly. Over time and with applied Incremental Advantage, your skill will grow and your results will improve. Everyone learns this at the beginning of life until we are taught and conditioned to forget it. Can you name four people you know who decided they were not cut out to walk and quit after a few falls? Facetious yes, but we are conditioned to this behavior of quitting after a few attempts rather than seeing it for the growth experience it is.

PLF

While I was still in college and part of the Army ROTC program, I was presented with an unbelievable opportunity. I was sent to Fort Benning, Georgia, home of the "Airborne!" I was very excited because I really wanted to go to Airborne school and learn how to successfully jump from a perfectly good aircraft. Airborne school was an exhilarating experience and a military right of passage for many. The course itself is three weeks long, which doesn't sound like much, but it is very intense. Filled with rigorous physical training, the Georgia summer and an Airborne instructor in your face most of the time; the course is challenging. We had to master how to rig our chutes, how to load and exit the aircraft, how to maneuver our parachutes while in the air, how to clear the landing zone and many other facets. What we spent the most time on was the skill of controlled crashing.

Certainly a parachute slows you down so you do not crash into the earth at terminal velocity; however, there is still considerable speed when you land. Perhaps you have witnessed sport parachuting and how fast their approach is. In the last few seconds, the sport parachutist pulls down on chords to collapse the chute and slow it down. With the exception of elite units, most of the army parachutes do not have this feature and there is little you can do to slow your descent rate. Even with a parachute your impact is about the same as jumping from 10 to 15 feet with no parachute.

Over time, the army learned and perfected a method of landing to absorb and spread out the impact of the fall and lessen the overall effect of the crash. This technique, known as a parachute landing fall, or PLF, allows the body to collapse in a way that spreads the impact out over several points of contact rather than landing on your feet and doing severe damage to yourself. The essence of the PLF is about position upon impact. Each point of contact must come in the right order and with the correct form to allow the body to act as a collapsible spring. The correct position is feet and knees together. The correct order points of contact are (1) feet, (2) side of lower leg, (3) side of quadriceps, (4) buttocks and (5) back. All this happens quickly in a fluid, collapsing motion.

We spent literally days practicing this from every imaginable angle and in every painful way you can think of. Because you are a passenger of the wind and do not control your direction, you might have to PLF in any direction. Front PLF, left PLF, side PLF—again and again we would practice falling. We slid down cables and did PLFs in the sawdust. They had a sadistic device called a swing landing trainer that started you on platform about 6 feet high. Wearing a harness attached to a pulley system, you were swung into motion by an instructor. Then at the instructor's whim, he would let go forcing you to do a perfect PLF…or do it again and again and again….(Did I mention the intense Georgia summer sun and the people in your face?)

We would drill and drill and drill on how to fall, culminating in a drop from a parachute hooked up to a 250-foot tower that pulled you up and then dropped you. Like an amusement park ride on steroids, this tower exercise was both exhilarating and terrifying and the last step before "jump week." Drills, training, practice every day for almost two weeks did one thing above all else: It took the conscious thinking out of the equation and allowed the reaction essential to the skill to be forever imbedded in our subconscious. During the next phase we would jump five times in different situations to qualify as "Airborne" and earn our jump wings. I will always remember my jumps and I will never forget learning how to fall. That has helped me significantly in my life as I have found myself hurtling toward the ground out of control in more than a few situations.

Just as the army uses a PLF to teach soldiers how to fall, we need to practice PLF in our lives when we have failures or feel like our life is crashing in around us. In the army everything has an acronym, so I adapted PLF for use in my life. My new PLF is Perspective Learning Forward. I use this when I feel like I'm crashing back into earth with a failure, setback or disappointment. Henry David Thoreau said, "It's not what you look at that matters, it's what you see…"

Perspective allows us to look fully at the situation in evaluating what went right as well as what went wrong. Perspective helps to put things in proper place. "Sure, losing money on this deal hurts, but I have great friends and a family who love me." Learning is about moving on and learning forward is about positioning so that even if you fail, you lessen the impact and don't remain on your fourth point of contact (your bottom) for long. When you act with integrity, especially in difficult times, you sow seeds for future success. When you fail and look for ways to adapt and do better next time or find in yourself a hidden strength lying dormant until rightly challenged, you are learning forward.

Stacy Allison, author of the book *Many Mountains to Climb*, holds the rare distinction of being the first American woman to reach the summit of Mount Everest. I had the pleasure of meeting Stacy in person and hearing her speak about her amazing adventure. Stacy talks about examining your experiences. She asserts that, "Whether we succeed or fail at it, the most challenging climb in the world will not help us grow unless we take the time for reflection. Unexamined experiences don't produce insights. Insights and wisdom come with reflection and analysis."

PLF is a simple strategy when trained and drilled into your subconscious, allowing you to make the most out of every situation and even more out of the ones others might classify as bad situations. Put into practice the habit of PLF to maintain a positive approach to your life and a winning attitude despite what comes your way and you may still find yourself on your fourth point of contact (buttocks)—but not for long.

After Action Analysis

In the army, after a mission, we are taught to painstakingly review the preceding mission as to what went right as well as what went wrong. The military calls this review process an After Action Report. We were taught this skill, not to criticize or berate others, but to use focused reflection backward to have better results going forward. This is difficult to do and we are conditioned to want to forget and get past issues, especially when they're painful. As a young officer in Desert Storm, I made plenty of mistakes, but I had a commanding officer who allowed me to grow from my mistakes rather than to be broken by them.

When you go through an event, perform an after action report for yourself. If in this situation again, what should I do differently? What factors should I have given greater priority? What components were the greatest leverage in the situation? What would I not do again? What did I do better than expected? These kinds of questions can be asked honestly of yourself without blame or humiliation. Remember, the goal as part of the STACK Strategy is to accept feedback for information to make a course correction. Without the introspective look back, it is hard to gain perspective to apply going forward.

It is important to distinguish between failure and temporary defeat. Most of what people sometimes feel is failure is really only a setback. Sometimes this setback is a pause to keep you from running off the cliff. After the healing power of time many situations we initially see as failures are really blessings in disguise. Reality is brought back into focus. We learn or are forced to redirect our energies down a more desirable or prudent path. The crushing blow of rejection and failure you might have experienced in the eighth-grade dating scene gave way to better relationships and opportunities. At the time it was the end of the world. The perspective of time and your current situation puts that emotion into a new context.

Looking at setbacks and failures as valuable lessons does not happen naturally. You have to develop the habit of reflection. Being able to face yourself head-on in times of testing and difficulty is the only way to really profit from the experience. When you face the facts, analyze the situation and learn from it, you ensure that you don't repeat the problem or have to suffer it again. I have had many setbacks, defeats and failures in my life. I can't say with certainty that I always profited from the experience. After some time and reflection, I can look back and gain a better understanding of what happened, what I learned and how that benefits me now. In reflecting backward on some of my setbacks and defeats, I can now clearly see the value of each. In some cases what was at one time a demoralizing defeat was actually a turning point in my life.

This exercise in active reflection will be very revealing. It may offer you much needed answers to some burning questions in your life. There is an old saying, "Those who don't know history are bound to repeat it." Initially intended in a more global and political realm, it is tremendously applicable to personal situations. Another saying is, "If you continue to do what you have always done, you will continue to get what you have always got." If you run up your credit cards and then get a home equity loan to repay your credit cards only to later rerun your cards, you have not learned or profited from your experience. The profit in the adversity or setback is applying it to your future. I would challenge you to take a little time out to dwell on some of the setbacks, failures or adversity you may have encountered in a mini–after action review. See now with the perspective of time what value you can create from the situation. See if you can recognize the lessons you were being exposed to and if you learned from them.

Take Risks

Without risk there would be no achievement and no great endeavors. All successful people take chances. Meeting new people is a risk. Learning and growing is a risk. Risk precedes reward. Risk is not nor should it be reckless. The reason most people do not take risks and stay in a comfort zone is that they fear the unknown. Preparation, knowledge and past experience soften the landing for risk and any potential downside. We need to enable ourselves to make mistakes. There is no better instructor than failure. Yes, it is a rude awakening and at times we find ourselves on our fourth point of contact.

Failure and success are like the Chinese symbol for the yin and yang. It is indistinguishable where failure stops and success begins. No person who sustains success does so without failure. Most successful people have a far greater share of failures in their lives than people who are unsuccessful. Babe Ruth is an oft cited example of success through failure in that he could never have achieved the pinnacle of his successful home runs (741) without the corresponding high number of strikeouts (1,330). Failure is a stepping stone and many times the precursor to success.

There is an old story of a boy talking to his grandfather about success. The boy asks, "Grandpa, how do you achieve success?"

Sagely, the grandfather replies, "Good decisions."

With this the young man asks, "Where do good decisions come from?"

"Experience."

With that, the grandson asks, "Where does experience come from?"

Sagely again, but with a sly grin, the grandfather replies, "Bad decisions."

"When a person with experience meets a person with money, the person with experience will get the money. And the person with the money will get experience."
—Leonard Lauder, president of Estee Lauder

Failure with redirected energy seeks out possibilities and creates new opportunities. Failing and accepting responsibility and learning from the failure, is the essence of failing forward. We all fall down. Failing and then not putting that to use is a waste of the learning resource.

President John F. Kennedy's highest level of popularity came after one of his most public failures. After the infamous Bay of Pigs incident, President Kennedy took responsibility and bore the weight of the loss with dignity and character. This failure was not remarkable of itself, but the fact that his popularity soared after the incident was. His humble and forthright approach to his short-term failure turned it into a longer-term success. The conclusion drawn by millions of people was that President Kennedy was a better man through how he failed.

To Get Out of a Hole, You Must Stop Digging!

Failures are really only lessons to be learned. Every outcome produces either the desired result or not. The result that misses the target still provides information to assist in the next attempt. While in the army, I spent a small amount of time learning about the artillery. When you fire and miss your intended target, you make a slight adjustment in the angle to bring the round in closer or make it go farther. In the same way, if you are off to the right or left, you can also make those minute corrections. After a miss, you analyze, adjust and refire. This is not failure, but is part of the process. Once you hit your target, you know your range and direction and can direct all the firepower, "steel on target," you need to accomplish your mission. Henry Ford remarked, "Failure is the opportunity to begin again more intelligently."

"Just because something doesn't do what you planned it to do in the first place doesn't mean its useless....Surprises and reverses should be an incentive to great accomplishment. Results? Why, man, I have gotten lots of results! If I find 10,000 ways something won't work, I haven't failed. I am not discouraged, because every wrong attempt discarded is just one more step forward...There are no rules here; we're just trying to accomplish something."
—Thomas Alva Edison

Part III

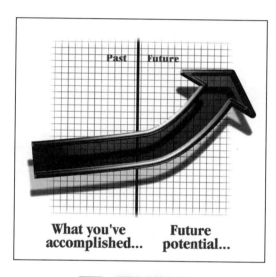

Past | Future

What you've
accomplished...

Future
potential...

DEAL
WITH YOUR
DISAPPOINTMENTS
AND SETBACKS

CHAPTER 8

Dominate Fear and Make It Your Servant

. . . .

"C130 rolling down the strip, Airborne daddy gonna take a little trip.
Stand up, hook up, shuffle to the door, Jump right out and count to four.
If my chute don't open wide, I've got another one by my side.
And if that one should fail me too, look out ground I'm coming through.
If I die on the old drop zone, box me up and send me home
Tell my son I did my best, and bury me in the leaning rest."
—Army Airborne running cadence

. . . .

What in the world was I thinking? As I looked over the shoulder of the man in front of me, I could see the ground and trees more than a thousand feet below. As we got closer to the jump zone, I felt the fear welling up in my stomach and looked around to see if anyone else was scared. It wasn't a paralyzing fear or one that would prevent me from doing what I'd just spent the past many days preparing for. I knew I was ready; I had been trained and drilled thoroughly. There was no question I would exit this aircraft of my own free will when the command to "Jump!" was given.

Fear; what is it that prevents so many of us from achieving or even taking steps in that direction? Why do so many people allow fear to shut them down and prevent them from trying something that is a precursor to succeeding?

Fear Is a Tool

Think about entering into a completely new situation. To effectively deal with and meet it head-on, imagine that your senses heighten, your energy is amplified, your blood pressure is elevated, your awareness increases, you feel an excitement in your entire body as you become completely aware of your surroundings while your brain is in overdrive with neurons firing so fast, they react nearly instantaneously with the stimulus provided. Sounds pretty neat doesn't it? It appears logically to be the very best tool in order to maximize the new situation. We call this state "fear" and usually look upon it as a negative thing.

Upon entering a new situation, we naturally want to take in all the information we can to best help us respond to what is in our environment. This is why all of our senses have heightened awareness and our physical capacity is increased to its fullest. It helps process the new information for the action necessary in "fight or flight." Fear also forces us to let go of what is not essential at the moment. We automatically focus on what is critical for our survival.

A large component of doing our best in a new situation or environment involves learning and adapting. Fear provides much to learn about the situation and more importantly about ourselves. Fear is positive primarily in three cases:

1. When you allow it to work in your favor as an automatic response or reflex as it has been used in nature since the very beginning.
2. When you utilize it as feedback to channel constructive forward action.
3. When you use it as feedback to reassess the situation and take an alternate action.

Fear is not the enemy. All people, great and small, have fear. The difference comes back to how we respond and what actions we take. I felt great fear staring out the door of the big military cargo jet, before my first jump (okay, on all the jumps!). My fear was taken into consideration as it mixed with exhilaration and my body responded to the situation to allow me to take action. Fear becomes negative when it becomes magnified or when it is nonspecific leading to paralysis or a shutdown mode. Fear in the present state based on real issues or events leads to positive benefits. Fear created from doubt and worry about things not yet come to pass or extrapolated worrying about the future is unproductive. This is the cause of a significant amount of stress and unhappiness in many people's lives.

FEAR—False Evidence Appearing Real

I am not sure where I first heard this acronym for fear. Most of what we experience as fear is not real; it is false evidence appearing real. Fear was initially an instinct used for survival in the "fight or flight" response mechanism. Outside of those engaged in life-or-death situations, most of us are rarely in the zone of life-or-death fear. Even those in law enforcement, military and firefighting are rarely in extreme fear situations. Most of what we fear, we imagine, projecting ourselves into future situations or living out future consequences.

At its core, fear is really being afraid of something in the future. This means that it has not happened yet. I certainly don't want to minimize or trivialize real fear and its purpose in "fight or flight," but it is important to recognize that fear is a response to a stimulus. We give meaning to the stimulus and are much more in control than we sometimes seem. If you are afraid of roller coasters it is because you can imagine the worst thing happening and it paralyzes you.

The antidote to fear is simple: *action!* The secret the U.S. Army uses to get soldiers to jump out of perfectly good airplanes is amazingly fundamental. The army trains and trains until the actions become automatic and all thinking is out of the equation. By the time you are in the door and waiting for the jump command, everything is automatic. Action produces new conditioning and creates a new response to the stimulus. Over time, action allows a reprogramming to the natural stimulus and response. In essence, training and new conditioning is the same as reprogramming your natural instinct. Confidence is built and can be applied into new situations.

Most people think, contemplate and dwell on the negative possible outcome of a given situation and then use that as a reason to shut down or to not take further action in this direction. When you have a goal or target in mind that is beyond the normal reach, the natural tendency is to first be excited thinking you can do it. This is followed by a period of small doubts followed by larger doubts and worries. Ultimately, you begin to question your thinking, finally give up your goal then rationalize why it wasn't even a very good goal to begin with.

Here is just one example, but I am sure you will recognize the pattern and be able to see how it happens numerous times in our lives. Say you have a dream. You imagine how great it could be and what the benefits to doing it are. You are pretty sure you could do this, you start to dip your toe in the water and then you let a few people know your idea. The people you share with are excited for you and encourage you, followed by ominous negatives that they innocently inject into your dream. This negative feeling bonds with the dormant negative you may have already had and starts to give you some nagging doubts. Eventually the nagging doubts grow and you eventually give up your dream somehow convincing yourself that you didn't really want it anyway.

Fear can be a repeating pattern and a conditioner to force us to shut down anytime we try to rise above where we currently are.

Distract Your Fear

Recently I worked with my five-year-old son Matthew on a goal he set for himself to jump off the diving board. He was doing very well on his swimming and had no problem jumping into the pool. But the deep end had him scared and he continued to back away from the challenge even though a lifeguard was right off the end. On the final day of his swimming lessons, we tried a new approach. Matthew and I discussed his fear and what he wanted to do. I told him about my experience jumping out of airplanes in the army and how I was scared. I told him that what they taught me to do was to yell at the top of my lungs "Airborne!" as soon as I jumped.

Matthew agreed to give it another go. Mustering up all his courage, he climbed up the board muttering, "Airborne, Airborne, Airborne" under his breath. He walked to the edge of the board and gave a tremendous scream that closely resembled, "Airborne!" He did it and he was so excited that the next four times he forgot all about his fear. His focus on his new word and saying it just right distracted him from his fear and allowed him to take action to accomplish his objective.

This may have been akin to a little parlor trick, but dwelling on what we are afraid of magnifies our fear and the outcome that we do not want to see. What if they say no? What if they laugh at me? What if I get hurt? Sometimes a little distraction allows for better clarity in the situation. It allows you to ask better questions or come to different conclusions. Certainly they might say no, but I have heard no before and that has never hurt me. Laughing at me is a possibility, but chances are they have the same question. Getting hurt is always a possibility, but remote as I am prepared and ready for this.

Ignorance and fear keep people trapped and held captive in their own minds. Fear is an unproductive emotion unless it provides the stimulus for action.

Acknowledge Your Fears

In the Army Airborne running cadence that opened this chapter, you will find a small key to the psychology used by the army. The entire time I was in Airborne School, we would run every day to some of the most morbid songs imaginable. One cadence in particular was called "Blood on the Risers" and was sung to the tune of the traditional church favorite, "The Battle Hymn of the Republic": "...Gory, gory, what a hell of a way to die. Gory, gory, what a hell of a way to die..."

We all knew there were chances of getting hurt or possibly killed, so why didn't the army teach us happy songs to take our minds off of what could happen? Why didn't they distract us with positive upbeat cadences instead of ones centering on the worst possible scenario? I understand the bravado of the military and recognize part of this as a long-distinguished tradition. Beyond this, the cadence had the effect of making us face our fears head-on and assess the worst possible scenario. Once fear is faced and action is taken, then mastery over fear is achieved.

Fear Means Well, But...

It is important to listen to fear yet not be controlled or overwhelmed by it. Fear is an ally and should be considered as a counselor, part of your team. You should allow your counselor to be heard, but you must keep it in check. Like a small child without boundaries, fear on its own will attempt to seize the role of controller rather than counselor. Remember, fear works for you, not the other way around. When fear speaks to you, listen and then weigh what fear is telling you versus what you are trying to accomplish. Many times you will find that your fear simply wants to be heard. Like the boy who cried wolf, fear gives off signals many times when there is nothing to be afraid of.

Most people allow fear to overcome, overwhelm and shut them down. Fear can be physical or mental. There are many different kinds of fears including physical harm, failure, success, poverty, embarrassment, etc.

Napoleon Hill wrote about how fear can be a cancer in your life if you allow it to take control:

This fear paralyzes the faculty of reason, destroys the faculty of imagination, kills off self-reliance, undermines enthusiasm, discourages initiative, leads to uncertainty of purpose, encourages procrastination, wipes out enthusiasm and makes self-control an impossibility. It takes the charm from one's personality, destroys the possibility of accurate thinking and diverts concentration of effort. It masters persistence, turns will power into nothingness, destroys ambition, beclouds the memory and invites failure in every conceivable form. It kills love and assassinates the finer emotions of the heart, discourages friendship and invites disaster in a hundred forms. It leads to sleeplessness, misery and unhappiness—all this despite the obvious truth that we live in a world of overabundance of everything the heart could desire, with nothing standing between us and our desires, excepting lack of a definite purpose.

Reframe/Rethink Your Fear

I have some friends who talk to me at times about how stuck in a rut they feel in their jobs, but would be terrified to start their own business. My reframe on this has always been about spreading my risk. Now that I have my own business I have several customers, yet when I worked for someone else I only had one. My dependence on several spreads my risk. If any one of my customers fires me, I still have others. In my job, I was 100 percent dependent on that one customer. I would be terrified if I only had one customer. Different thoughts and angles of approach to a situation produce different emotional outcomes leading to either fear or confidence. In my own business, I believe success or failure is largely within my control. Working for someone else, I felt that my success or failure had far more variables outside my direct control. This is just an example of differences in perception and how the same situation can produce a different reaction.

Face Your Fears

Fear must be a subordinate and kept in its proper place. You have tools at your disposal to combat fear when it tries to overwhelm you and unlawfully control you. Understanding the full situation, practicing courage to develop the skill, obtaining knowledge, making forward progress—these are action steps in facing and overcoming fear. When fear tries to take control of your life, you must face it as you would face an adversary on the battlefield. Associate, observe and spend time with confident people. Confidence breeds confidence. Your courage will grow through confidence in your preparation.

Fear can be both learned and unlearned. Sizing up the situation and facing your fears head-on provide tremendous growth opportunity. Careful planning and preparation are essential. Planning and practice lead to preparedness, which in turn builds self-confidence and a determined will. A resolute spirit moving forward with confident action allows you to grow and imbeds these traits in the foundation of your character. Unless you move beyond your comfort zone, you will not grow. Dorothea Brande believed, "All that is necessary to break the spell of inertia and frustration is this: Act as if it were impossible to fail. That is the talisman, the formula, the command of right-about-face which turns us from failure towards success."

Conquering Fear; Breaking Barriers

On October 14, 1947, Army Air Force Captain Charles "Chuck" Yeager did something no human had done before. Strapped into the experimental Bell XS-1, Chuck Yeager traveled faster than any man ever flew before him. Flying faster than the speed of sound at Mach 1, Yeager did what few people thought possible and what many died trying previously: He broke the sound barrier. Within a few years pilots routinely did what Yeager once did heroically. Now Mach 2 and beyond is ordinary for military jets. Ordinary now, but had Captain—later, he retired as a general—Yeager not pushed beyond what was possible, we would not have had the advances we take for granted today.

This decorated World War II ace and war hero must have felt some panic as his instruments pushed beyond the red line and the rocket he was prisoner in began to buffet and shake violently. But he pushed through his fear.

Each time you face and conquer your fears, you break barriers. Not all of your victories will be as historic as Chuck Yeager's, but this in no way diminishes the cycle of success you develop for yourself. Imagine the most courageous person you know or can think of, someone you feel is very successful and fearless. This person used a cycle similar to the analogy mentioned previously about weightlifting. Facing fear produces growth and strength.

Look back ten years or imagine yourself back in high school trying to deal with some of the issues you routinely face now. It is incredible how we can grow and adapt after we take our proper position and dominion over fear.

Dominating Fear Action Plan—JUMP!

In my first experience preparing as an Airborne soldier, I was lined up to be second out the door. After the guy in front of me jumped, I stood in the doorway and waited for the go command followed by the swat to my backside as a nonverbal reminder. It was merely a second or two standing there and quite honestly at that second, I was not afraid. When the command came I did what I had practiced and prepared for hundreds of times over. My body knew exactly what it was supposed to do. The first jump was absolutely exhilarating.

Upon executing a proper parachute landing fall, I realized I had conquered my fear. The second jump still produced the fear emotion with all of the telltale signs, but I was able to use it as my counselor rather than my controller. This time I had the experience of the previous jump as another tool in my bag. Each time I jumped, I experienced fear. Without fear as a counselor, or what others might term "healthy fear," you lose your advantage in the situation as complacency or laziness sets in. Lack of respect for the situation you are in could lead to serious injury or death.

Fear in control as part of your advisory board is an excellent tool to keep you safe from harm. I still have fear in certain situations but have learned to recognize it for what it is and use it to my advantage. Fear should be an evaluation point, not a shutdown mechanism. We all have fears as a natural inborn survival mechanism. Fear as an evaluation tool is healthy. We can learn to face it, embrace it, distract it, redirect it and use it as a tool. Developing success patterns of positively dealing with your fear gives you the control. This allows you to dominate your fear and make it a servant—not the other way around.

Act with Boldness and Purpose

Contrary to what some may think, boldness is not bravado. Boldness is acting with courage. Applied action confidently toward your objective encourages and emboldens those around you. Certainly test pilots and astronauts have fear and yet they are respected for their boldness. You would be hard-pressed to find a timid test pilot gingerly going about his or her job. Recognize that everyone is afraid, but the strong learn to take action in spite of the fear. The weak shy away and are shut down by fear. Apprehension breeds doubt and hesitation. This not only eats away at your resolve like acid on metal, but it also weakens your determination and dilutes your efforts.

Bold and Audacious

People with an optimistic belief in themselves are people who take action because they believe they possess a great deal of control over their own lives. Pessimists feel as though the world controls them and their fate. People with optimistic attitudes have a strong desire for success because they know that desire will create action, which will create results to be built upon. These initial actions may be nowhere close to the end result, but the act of starting allows for the foundation of future success.

A great example of this is the goal President John F. Kennedy set for our nation in the early 1960s. Before a joint session of Congress on May 25, 1961, President Kennedy galvanized the resolve of the nation with one simple clear-cut and definable goal: "...First, I believe that this nation should commit itself to achieving the goal, before this decade is out, of landing a man on the moon and returning him safely to the earth."

The initial astronauts began the Mercury Program, where individual men would sit atop dangerous rockets and break the bounds of earth. Failures gave birth to success and the knowledge was acquired many times at a very steep cost. Everything learned in the Mercury Program was passed through to the next phase of the Gemini Program.

The Gemini phase consisted of two astronauts. It pushed the limits of knowledge and the boundaries of understanding in space travel. Eventually the incremental success of Gemini gave birth to the Apollo Program.

Apollo took everything before and combine it into the most audacious endeavor ever undertaken. Apollo carried three men, allowing two of them to separate away into a lunar module that would eventually put man on the moon as the successful conclusion to President Kennedy's initial vision.

The process all from Mercury to Gemini to Apollo was about baby steps. Each launch carried with it an opportunity to push just a little bit further. Each mission provided an opportunity to learn, understand and grow. Each mission was another log on the stack.

There were setbacks and even some failures. The most notable failure occurred on the very first attempt of the new Apollo program. *Apollo 1*, commanded by Gus Grissom, a veteran of the first two stages of the program, caught fire on the launch pad and killed the three-person crew. Even through missteps, failures and learning opportunities, the overriding goal of the program was eventually achieved. President Kennedy's goal for our nation was met on July 20, 1969, when *Apollo 11* commander Neil Armstrong stepped off the now famous lunar module *Eagle*'s ladder and placed the first human footprint onto the surface of the Moon.

Certainly the NASA space program was an accumulation of knowledge and victories added together and reinvested back into the program. If you graphed out the program, it would absolutely follow the pattern of the J-shaped curve. Believe in yourself and the destination you strive for. Take the path with thoughtful decisions and deliberate actions. Be bold. Take the next step. As adjustments are needed, make them. As mistakes are made, learn from them, try again and continue moving forward.

"You gain strength, courage and confidence by every experience in which you really stop to look fear in the face. You are able to say to yourself, "I've lived through this horror. I can take the next thing that comes along." You must do the thing you think you cannot do."

–Eleanor Roosevelt

CHAPTER 9

Learn to Convert Discouragement, Disappointment and Setbacks into Fuel for Your Success!

. . . .

"It is the Law that any difficulties that can come to you at any time, no matter what they are, must be exactly what you need most at the moment, to enable you to take the next step forward by overcoming them. The only real misfortune, the only real tragedy, comes when we suffer without learning the lesson."

—Emmet Fox

. . . .

Can you imagine a technique, so powerful that you could recycle every failure, disappointment, setback and discouraging situation into a stepping stone for your success? Remember back in Chapter 2 we discussed the STACK Strategy for success? Let's review and then apply the most relevant principle: accepting results simply as feedback.

117

STACK Strategy:
Five Steps to an Outcome

S – Set your destination and course

T – Take immediate action

A – Accept results simply as feedback

C – Correct your course based on feedback

K – Keep on Stacking the Logs!

The Power of Perspective (Reframing)

Reframing a situation is taking a look at the situation from a different point of view or looking for outcomes other than those originally intended. Many times we get trapped into linear thinking and fix our minds on a certain outcome. Although it is tremendously difficult to see at the time, often disappointments occur for our own good or to our benefit. Could you imagine having married the first person you thought you were in love with? When our intended outcome does not come our way, we are naturally disappointed. Reframing allows us the chance to reassess what opportunities might come from the outcome we received rather than the one intended.

For instance, assume you are up for a job promotion in your company and instead it goes to someone else. The natural inclination might be bitterness, hurt, anger and resentment. Using the power of perspective to reframe the situation, you might look at the message you received (accepting information only as feedback) to better prepare yourself for the next opportunity. You might find a better opportunity shortly down the road for which you would have been unavailable had you received the promotion. You have the opportunity to demonstrate your commitment to the organization which will serve you long-term. There is any number of benefits you might see when you look for them.

It is a given in this life that the chips will not always fall in your favor. You will not always get what you want. The reframe on this is the great number of opportunities you will have to practice and demonstrate your skill in this area. Your ability to take what other people see as bad or difficult situations and turn them around with a positive attitude will quickly separate you from your peer group. This ability is very much an Incremental Advantage skill. As you apply this to all areas of your life, you will find situations start working out to your favor significantly more often. Others may call it luck, but you know the power of perspective allows you to stack the chance of winning significantly in your favor since you literally know the cards before they are dealt. Others will be disappointed more often than they win. You know that through the power of perspective and reframing, you have the opportunity to win nearly every time. Certainly not every win will be what you wish for, but even a learning experience is a win if you apply it to your important goals.

"When defeat comes, accept it as a signal that your plans are not sound; rebuild those plans, and set sail once more toward your coveted goal."
—Napoleon Hill

Abraham Lincoln's Journey

History is filled with many rags-to-riches stories. There are countless examples of men and women who rose through adversity stronger and better for their trials and tribulations. The history of disappointment and setbacks experienced by Abraham Lincoln are documented. Before he was 23 years old, Lincoln lost an infant brother, sister, and his mother, nearly drowned and almost died when a horse kicked him. After his 23rd birthday, the disappointment, setback and failure parade continued to march on.

    1832—Lost job
    1832—Defeated for state legislature
    1833—Failed in business
    1835—Sweetheart died
    1836—Had nervous breakdown
    1840—Filed for bankruptcy
    1838—Defeated for Speaker

1843—Defeated for nomination for Congress
1848—Lost renomination to Congress
1849—Rejected for land officer
1850—Son dies
1851—Father dies
1854—Defeated for U.S. Senate
1856—Defeated for nomination for vice president
1858—Again defeated for U.S. Senate
1860—Elected 16th president of the United States

In spite of all this failure and defeat, most historians agree that Abraham Lincoln was one of the best presidents this country has ever had. The failures of Mr. Lincoln are so well known because they are in such stark contrast to the success he proved to be. Many believe, myself included, that Abraham Lincoln could have never been the man he proved to be without going through the setbacks, frustrations, tremendous losses and deep disappointments he suffered.

The negative events in Lincoln's life helped him define the character qualities that proved so vital as President of a country split in two and in desperate need of a leader with character; a leader who had experienced the very essence of sorrow and adversity. His life certainly parallels the J-shaped curve and his most successful years were after a long period of what appeared to be fruitless failure. Through the eyes of history, we can clearly see the man made great through his triumph over failure, situation, setback, adversity and other obstacles placed in his way. Lincoln himself remarked, "I do the very best I know how—the very best I can; and I mean to keep on doing so."

Practical Optimism—Action Is the Key

You may be sensing a theme that action is an integral part of the success process. Discouragement, disappointment and setbacks are natural to everyone. The difference in how you respond ultimately determines your result and outcome. Most people are stopped cold. If you can use discouragement, disappointment and setbacks as feedback to learn and improve, you will apply the process of failing forward. As you become adept at shaking off and moving through these frustrating obstacles, you will build strength and significant advantage in attaining what you set out to achieve. It is not so much what happens to us in life that matters, but rather how we respond to what happens.

There is usually a good side to every situation if you are inclined and know where to look. A practical optimist sees opportunity in chaos whereas a pessimist sees chaos in opportunity. To find the success or benefit in any situation, learn to become a practical optimist. To learn to convert discouragement, disappointment and setbacks into fuel for your success, change your thinking. When you view every problem as an opportunity, it will change your life. This is not Pollyanna thinking. Everything you do and every action you take in response to a situation or event will depend on how you assess the situation.

As a practical tip, when you are confronted with a serious problem, dwell on solutions and opportunities rather than the problem itself. Nearly everyone who comes to me for advice on serious problem has blinded himself or herself to the view of opportunities and solutions by holding the problems or worries too close. This is like taking a piece of paper with your problem written on it and holding it so close to your face that nothing else is visible.

Look at the box below as an example of what I mean. Stare at it for a minute. Observe what you can in the illustration. What do you see?

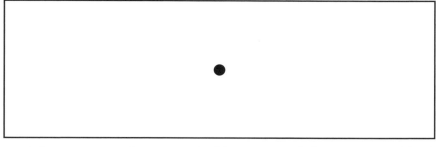

Like most people you probably answered that you see a black dot. This is certainly true. Now take a moment to reexamine the illustration and answer the following question. Within the square, what area represents the overwhelming majority of space? The answer of course is the background area with the black dot being less than a fraction of 1 percent of the entire illustration. The reason you answered the black dot is that we are built and trained to notice the contrast. If this were your life and the prominent area of the page represented good things in your life and the black dot represented problems and challenges and obstacles in your life, you would certainly have a most excellent life with far less than 1 percent problems versus all of the good.

Because of the contrast, the negative stands out and the black dot becomes the focus of the illustration rather than the overwhelming remainder of the box. This is what most people do with problems in their life. We get complacent and forget about the good, the blessings and advantages that we are provided with and too quickly find the black dots in our lives that represent the negative. Sometimes we can take this approach to a far extreme, focusing so much energy on the black dot that we can hardly see anything else. While this is a simple exercise, it demonstrates how quickly we look for, identify and dwell on problems rather than on the positive aspects of our lives. Train yourself to be optimistic and opportunity driven. Look for opportunities everywhere and in every situation. Read the following paragraph and then construct some options for yourself.

Jane is outgoing and talented with a fantastic attitude and a solid set of skills. She is comfortable in her current administrative position though it lacks room for growth. She has been with the company for seven years and has always gotten excellent reviews and maintains a good relationship with her supervisors as well as coworkers. Jane capitalizes on opportunities to learn. She takes on additional responsibilities outside her normal job duties.

In her spare time, Jane enjoys writing and challenging herself to learn about things she is interested in. She is involved in her community and active in her family's lives. Recently Jane and her supervisor began to discuss opportunities for her to develop within the company; possibly in a completely different area. Now, due to a situation outside of her control, Jane and a good number of her coworkers may lose their jobs as part of a company-wide restructure. There is a period of several months where the situation remains in limbo while the company's management filters down the new plan.

If you were in Jane's position, what opportunities would you see? Certainly the norm would be feelings of despair and of being a victim of the company, economy or circumstances. Most people would feel bitter and betrayed about promises not kept. In a vacuum and personally removed, it is slightly easier to look at the situation and assess options for Jane that may later prove that a bad situation provided a blessing in disguise. Suppose Jane took the opportunity to go back to school and pursue a different career or upgraded the job with a different company. Suppose she sought a different position within her company in a different area like sales, marketing or operations that ultimately leads her to a higher income and more satisfying career. Maybe Jane decides to transform her skills and hobbies into her own business to better dovetail her ambitions with her family situation. There are countless chances for Jane's situation to ultimately improve due to this adversity or setback if Jane remains positive and open to the opportunities provided.

It is certainly easier to look at a situation like this and to find these opportunities when it is someone else. There will be many disappointments and setbacks in your life that are in reality opportunities-in-waiting and blessings in disguise. Imagine if you were currently married to the first person you thought you were in love with or who truly broke your heart. Imagine if you were still at your very first job. Over time it is much easier to look back on situations that at the time seemed like bitter losses or disappointments but now seem to have worked out for the best. A key skill set in developing practical optimism is looking at situations affecting you in the present and applying the same long-term wisdom and vision. While others are wallowing in disappointment, you have the opportunity to assess your situation and the opportunities presented.

An airplane flying from New York to San Francisco may be off course for a significant time during the journey due to weather, rerouting, traffic patterns and other obstacles to a straight flight. If you narrowly define success as being on course, the flight will be failing more often than succeeding. Pilots understand how this process works and make adjustments and course corrections to get back on track. Pilots don't get frustrated, angry or hurt when they get off course; they take corrective action.

There is a myth that says we must "think positive" all the time. To succeed and to fulfill our dreams, we have to keep focused on our goal and continue making progress toward it. Practical optimists accept feedback on a situation and then seek to take whatever kernel of opportunity is presented to take action within the opportunity. Learning to do this as second nature and as a positive success cycle is the key skill set of the practical optimist.

Our lives are a combination of both good and bad, positive and negative. When we learn to zero in and focus on whatever good may be present in a bad situation, we feel better and more empowered and are more inclined to take action. When we don't, we are more inclined toward a negative pattern and a negative cycle. This neither helps the situation nor our feelings regarding it. Either way we choose to think, life goes on. If someone in a vehicle forces you off the road on the way to your destination, the choice is yours whether you want to have justified anger, resentment, self-pity or any number of reactions. You are certainly justified to have any of these emotions, but as long as you stay on the side of the road, you are no closer to your objective. The other choice is to get past your situation and learn from your experience. Regardless, get back on the road to your objective.

No Growth Without Resistance

As we learned earlier in Chapter 7, there can be no real growth without resistance. Every challenge, obstacle or problem you face will present you with a learning opportunity. As we meet new challenges, we learn and grow to meet them and become better equipped to deal with future challenges. Fourth-grade math may have seemed difficult at the time, but it was a cakewalk compared to calculus. The challenge of fourth-grade math seems to push the boundaries at that level, yet the capacity becomes so much greater as the challenge is met.

Everyone encounters problems in life. It is your choice to be unhappy and upset about the cards you are dealt or to play out the hand as best you can. Just reframe your mind-set so that every problem and challenge you face gives you both an opportunity to show your character and allows you to become stronger by learning and growing through the problem.

The Lesson of a Mistake That Made a Million Dollars

A young wholesale company had a difficult customer. Many times the customer was demanding and overbearing, but each time the company took the abuse and did its best for him. One day the company made an honest mistake and sent a wholesale invoice to the client of the customer rather than to the customer directly. When the customer found out, he furiously called the company screaming and accused the young company of treachery. The customer's client was now upset, learning they were being overcharged and underserved. A period of confusion and turmoil followed with accusations leaving many people unhappy.

After the dust settled, the customer refused to work with their client. The young company, by default, took care of the client even though they bore no real responsibility. The small client of the original customer now became a small client of the young company. The young company stopped doing business with the original customer and lost all of that revenue. In an interesting twist, the small new client developed into a large client in a short period of time. A major mistake became a success catalyst and a negative was ultimately transformed into a relationship worth well over a million dollars in total relationship value to the young company. What began as disaster was converted into an opportunity worth far more than the original relationship.

Successful people have problems just like everyone else. The difference is in their ability to solve problems. Energy spent in worry brings you no closer to a better outcome. In fact, it has the opposite effect as it drains the batteries of your resourcefulness and stifles optimism. Ultimately, fear and worry shut down action toward a different outcome creating the thing feared. Job said in the Bible, "That which I have feared has come upon me."

Phoenix Principle—Reinventing Yourself

The phoenix is a mythical creature whose lore of rebirth in the ashes of death is present in nearly every single culture. From the ancient Greeks and Egyptians to the American Indian, the myth of the phoenix symbolizes immortality, resurrection and new birth. Every society has a slightly different version of the myth, however, the template myth tells of a bird of matchless splendor, unique and unparalleled in the entire world, living beyond 500 years.

According to the Greek version, when the bird felt its death was near (approximately every 500 years), it would build a nest of aromatic wood and set itself on fire to be completely consumed by the flames. After three days, a new phoenix would arise from the ashes and begin life anew until the cycle was repeated. The Phoenix Principle is not about dying, but rather about getting a fresh start and rebirth into a new life. No matter what your circumstances or your past today is a new day and tomorrow is a fresh beginning. You do not need a publicist or a team of spin doctors to reinvent yourself as we have seen examples of from Hollywood to Washington, D.C.

The basis of the Phoenix Principle is that all of your yesterdays are lessons and today provides new choices. The phoenix is merely symbolic of renewal and the opportunity to shed your past. Too many people hold onto the failures and setback of the past like a set of trophies they refuse to give up. Whatever has happened in your past must be left there.

If you have achieved victories, they can be reminders of your success and inspiration to continue on your path. They can provide confidence that you have succeeded in the past so you can succeed in the future. But don't let your past victories keep you from growing. Your disappointments, heartaches, setbacks and even failures can actually be more useful to you than your victories. With reflection and positive perspective, these can provide not only powerful lessons, but also deep reservoirs of motivation and drive. Success can at times cause complacency and failure to push yourself beyond comfort zones. Finding and developing opportunities out of failure provides a double win in the form of new success and the confidence acquired in the transformation.

While Frankie was still in treatment in Memphis, some very good friends with two small children came to visit. One of the nights together we sat in our room and watched *Chitty Chitty Bang Bang*, the classic Dick Van Dyke movie about a quirky inventor who never quits despite his many failures. With persistence and the help of his support structure (along with a flying car), he eventually prevails over adversity, finding success and true love. In the end, in fairy tale fashion, he and his family fly away in the car of the film's title.

This movie is simple yet truly inspiring. I have watched it numerous times in the past as a child and many times with my own children. There is a scene where the father of Dick Van Dyke's character says, "From the ashes of the failure, grows the roses of success." The meaning hit me like a lightning bolt. *Our failures seed our success.* We cannot play it safe and still grow. It is not necessary to take extreme risks to succeed, but you must venture out of your comfort zone. Someone once told me that, "You can't get to second base without taking your foot off first."

Good and Bad Are Related

Good and bad create a contrast to differentiate between. Every situation carries with it elements of both good and bad. You might think winning the lottery is good, whereas the woman who loses her son to drug abuse stemming from the newfound wealth does not. You might look at a car accident as a bad situation, whereas the man who had a close enough brush with mortality to forever change his life for the better might see it as a blessing. In some situations there is only a razor-thin line of separation in the analysis of what is good versus what is bad. Sometimes, the positive result of a bad situation does not show up until long after the event happens. Without the contrast of bad times, how can you savor the good? Without experiencing pain, how can you know joy? Without the distinction of struggling financially and doing without, how can you understand wealth? Without the depth of loneliness, how can you know the peak of companionship and love?

Successful people don't experience fewer disappointments or less pain than others. Instead they view their failures, setbacks and disappointments through a more positive lens directed and focused forward toward their intended objective. Knowing this, train yourself to always seek the positive and avoid as much as possible wasting time lamenting on the negative. This is not to say you should never have genuine emotions like grief, disappointment, anger or sorrow. Recognize these emotions and allow them their proper place. If you try to hide or suppress these emotions, you will do yourself no favors and eventually damage your psyche. Normal emotions are just that—normal. Just remember that you are the master of your emotions and you can train yourself how to respond to rather than react because of a situation.

Our thoughts and emotions are the staging area for our destiny. Everything that happens to us is a byproduct of our thoughts. Our choices and actions have brought us to where we are today. Our decisions, affected by our thoughts and outlook, direct our actions. Events and things that happen to us are but a very small percentage in life. Far greater is the impact of our reaction and response to every situation that comes our way. Things that happen to us and for us in our lives are ultimately the product of what and how we think. More importantly, our actions and responses that arise from our thoughts greatly affect our situation. We can learn, through practice and focus to harness and control our thoughts and direct our actions. In doing so, we can exert a far greater degree of control than someone who allows their life to randomly flow from one event to the next.

. . . .

"To establish true self-esteem we must concentrate on our successes and forget about the failures and the negatives in our lives."
—Denis Waitley

. . . .

CHAPTER 10

Overcoming the #1 Reason People Fail

"All successful people are people of purpose. They hold fast to an idea, a project, a plan, and will not let it go; they cherish it, brood upon it, tend and develop it; and when assailed by difficulties, they refuse to be beguiled into surrender; indeed, the intensity of the purpose increases with the growing magnitude of the obstacles encountered."
—James Allen

Why People Fail

If you had to guess, what would you think is the number-one cause of death in the world today? You might guess cancer, heart attack, accidents or any number of maladies, but you would probably be wrong unless you guessed the heart ceasing to beat as the number-one cause. This is a bit of a trick question in that the truism of the heart stopping as the cause of death does not accurately reflect the true cause. When death occurs as a result of the heart ceasing to beat, it belies the fact that there are always underlying causes creating the condition of a heart failing to beat.

I recently watched a program about the life and death of Elvis Presley. Elvis died due to the horrible overuse and combination of prescription drugs in his system. This underlying drug situation, combined with his weight and other stress factors, caused what the coroner would later report on that fateful August day as death due to a discontinued heartbeat. The questions and inquisition later into why the coroner documented the great singer's death in this way created tremendous conflict. Another medical examiner characterized the nature of the situation with an analogy that when a person is run over by a truck, it would be true to say that he or she died because the heart stopped beating, but it would be a gross mischaracterization of the real cause of death.

What is the number-one separator from people and their dreams and desires? What is the one thing that if you could overcome it would give you a tremendous boost in your success rate in all that you attempt? Is it lacking a skill? Is it failing to plan? Is it lacking motivation? The answer is no. Although all are quite important, they pale in comparison to the real number-one dream killer. I will break the suspense for you. In the words of Thomas A. Edison, one of the greatest inventors and thinking minds of the 20th century: "Many of life's failures are people who did not realize how close they were to success when they gave up."

There are actually three categories of failure that plague us:

1. The failure to know *specifically* what we want.
2. The failure to know how to get it.
3. The failure to take and maintain sufficient action until the outcome is achieved.

The main reason people fail is certainly a combination of all three, with quitting as the main reason since it is part of the previous two. When you fail to know fully what you want, how easy is it to simply quit? There is no sustained action when there is no clear outcome. Many people quit without realizing they even started. Failing to know how to get where you want to go falls under the same category. Action may be taken for a short while, but if you don't know how to get where you want to go, failure to take sustained and determined effort creates the death of your dreams out of neglect.

Most People Fail Because They Quit Too Soon

Quitting too soon, giving up short of the prize, throwing in the towel is near epidemic in our comfortable society. Most generally, we lack the perseverance and fortitude to stick with something through the pain of the learning curve to the fruit of the labor. There is always a learning curve. We have discussed at length the concept of the J-shaped curve with results on the left axis and effort over time on the bottom. Most people quit before they yield what they have sown.

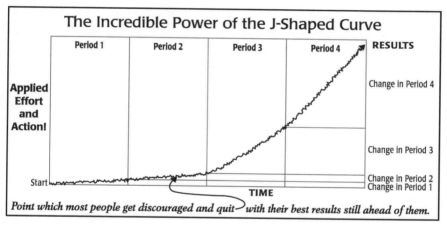

The Incredible Power of the J-Shaped Curve

Point which most people get discouraged and quit → *with their best results still ahead of them.*

We learned early on in this book that success comes as a result of efforts applied, harvested, reinvested and multiplied over time. As the above graph shows, the early results are less than stellar and it is not until nearly halfway through before the efforts start to show a decent result. If the process is followed through to conclusion, the results change in period 4 is greater than the previous three combined period results. Unfortunately, most people will never see their massive payoff because they will have quit and moved onto something else.

Look back to our doubling penny example from Chapter 1. If you got bored with your accumulation efforts after 15 days, you would end up with not half of the final bounty, but rather only a measly .00305 percent. As a matter of fact, you would not reach the halfway mark of your future treasure until the 29th day. Most people get discouraged or bored and change their focus, depriving themselves of the results they initially sought. It is as if they have a magnifying glass out on a hot sunny day with a pile of scattered dry leaves trying to start a fire. Constantly moving the magnifying glass to a more opportune leaf will cause a loss of focus of the beam. Without the heat of the focused sunlight, the fire will not start.

If you plant a seed that takes a year to germinate but get frustrated at the nine-month mark and replant it in what you believe is more fertile soil, it will defer the desired result even longer. In some cases this starts a cycle of frustration and defeat to where there will never be any growth achieved or measured. A seed will not grow overnight and neither will your ambitions be realized in that amount of time.

Goal setting is the foundation of a lifetime of reward, achievement and personal excellence. Few people actually achieve what they truly want in life because they fail to recognize and commit to paper clearly what they desire, and pursue it until achieved. To counteract the forces that cause us to quit before we achieve our desired outcome—failure to know what we want, how to get it, how to persist until it is achieved—there is no better antidote than clearly defined written goals.

Goal setting and goal achieving are tactical processes one follows step by step until the desired outcome is attained. Below is a combination of what I have learned from others and adapted for effect in my own life.

Tactical Goal-Setting Process

1. Decide with clarity exactly what you want in each area of life.
2. Write it down very clearly in positive, present tense, measurable specifics.
3. Create and set a deadline for achieving. If it is a large goal, create milestones or subgoals with their corresponding deadlines.

4. Create a plan of action.

   a. List what you must do, tasks, projects, research, materials to gather, etc. Make this list a live working document and add to it as you go.

   b. Organize into priorities.

5. Take action!

   a. Do something to get started and get momentum working in your favor.

   b. Resolve to do something meaningful every day to move you in the direction of your objective. This is your applied Incremental Advantage in your endeavor. Daily action toward your objective will deliver you to your destination.

This tactical plan will work in conjunction with the STACK Strategy discussed in Chapter 2. The tactical component here is really in developing your plan of action. Most people do not have clear-cut, specific goals. Even fewer write those goals down along with a definite plan of action to accomplish. If you take these measures, you will dramatically separate yourself from the crowd, those being carried through life by the momentum of controlling outside forces. I challenge you to live your life deliberately as the architect of your own future.

Acres of Diamonds

Perhaps you are familiar with Dr. Russell Herman Conwell and his inspiring speech repeated hundreds of times across the country to raise money for the institution now known as Temple University. Russell Conwell was born in 1843 and lived until 1925. He left Yale for a commission in the Union Army to then study and become a lawyer for about 15 years until he became a Christian minister. Dr. Conwell was approached one day by a young man who shared his strong desire for a college education and his disappointment in not being able to afford it. Dr. Conwell made a monumental decision to build a university for unfortunate but deserving students. He had a major challenge, however, in that to achieve his objective, he would need to raise at least a few million dollars to begin construction. Dr. Conwell demonstrated in his actions that for anyone with real purpose in life, nothing can stand in the way of a committed goal.

Many years before this decision, Dr. Conwell was very intrigued by a true story with a direct application and an ageless moral. The story he heard was about a prosperous Persian farmer named Ali Hafed, who lived in Africa. Through a visiting Buddhist priest and his elegant tales of wealth and opulence regarding the diamond fields in the country, Ali became intrigued about his prospects of finding diamonds. Diamonds had already been discovered in abundance on the African continent earlier and these tales stoked the fire of riches within this farmer. Ali Hafed got so excited about the idea of millions of dollars worth of diamonds that he sold his farm to head out to his diamond dream. Ali wandered all over the African continent constantly searching for diamonds and extraordinary wealth, finding neither. Eventually, far from home, old and weary, his former wealth squandered, this now disillusioned pauper gave up completely. He threw himself into a river and drowned.

While Ali Hafed roamed the continent in search of diamonds, the new owner of Ali's farm picked up an unusual-looking rock about the size of an egg. He displayed it on his mantle as a curiosity he called a *mooi klip*, or a pretty pebble. A while later, a visitor came by and told the new owner of the farm the funny-looking rock on his mantle was about the biggest diamond that had ever been found. The new owner of the farm began to laugh as he related that the entire farm was covered with them. True enough, the farm was covered with "acres of diamonds." Indeed, the original diamond was 21˘ carats, or about an eighth of an ounce. The farm would later be developed into the famous Kimberley Diamond Mine, the richest the world has ever known.

The amazing irony of the whole story is that Ali Hafed, the original farmer, was literally standing on "acres of diamonds" the whole time until he sold his farm because he did not recognize diamonds in their natural and unrefined state.

The Kimberley Mine would later come into the possession of Cecil Rhodes who formed the Rhodes De Beers Consolidated Mines, controlling 90 percent of the global diamond production. This mine later brought the discovery of a massive 85-carat diamond, now know as "the Star of South Africa." As the next 40 years progressed the mine was expanded to more than a mile wide and 1,300 feet deep. From this original farm, untold wealth and riches have poured forth.

Dr. Conwell saw a great lesson to be learned from the story of Ali Hafed. He believed that whether or not we realize it, we are each squarely in the middle of our own "acre of diamonds." Before we go charging off in search of richer opportunities and greener pastures, we should develop the ground beneath our feet.

Dr. Conwell told this story many times and attracted enormous audiences. He was soon America's foremost platform orator delivering the speech more than 6,000 times across the country. Over time, he raised nearly $6 million for the founding of Temple University in Philadelphia. Dr. Conwell wanted to encourage people to stick with something until success comes.

Most people fail because they quit too soon. They don't cross what I call the "threshold barrier to success."

Threshold Barrier to Success

It is a simple rule of physics that water will turn to ice at 32° F and boil at 212° F. There is a threshold where 1° is all that separates the phase change. Thirty-three degrees will not do it, nor will two hundred and eleven degrees.

In order to create lift, an airplane wing has to reach a speed through the air for a takeoff. All airplanes are unique with different takeoff speeds. A Lear Jet requires 147 knots of airspeed over the wing to achieve a takeoff. The interesting thing is that a jet can scream down the runway and you may think it is going to take off, but if it does not achieve the airspeed over the wing, it will not fly.

What is your threshold barrier to success in your life? Are you close, but not quite there and need that tiny bit of energy to push you over the top? A key aspect of success is simply know-ing what you want. It sounds so simple, yet vague or unseen targets cannot be hit. Sometimes you are much closer than you think to have your investments in time and effort rewarded. Perseverance pays great dividends!

Manmade Barriers

Up until the mid 1950s, there was an impenetrable barrier in the speed of running. Literally no one thought that a human could ever run a mile faster than four minutes. Even scientists and doctors theorized that the human body was incapable of sustaining the oxygen and energy reserves needed to accom-plish such a thing. Many tried and no one even came close. It was decided in this unity of thought that no man could ever run a four-minute mile—until Roger Bannister proved everyone wrong.

On May 6, 1954, Roger Bannister, a 25-year-old English medical student ran the first sub-four-minute mile in recorded history. He completed the entire distance in an amazing 3 min-utes and 59.4 seconds. Later, when he was asked to explain his thoughts on his historic feat, he answered, "It's the ability to take more out of yourself than you've got." Bannister was also quoted as saying, *"Après moi le deluge."* Translated and slightly paraphrased, what Bannister meant was that once the seem-ingly unbreakable barrier was broken, many would follow.

Indeed, Bannister was correct in that thought as in the two years following his historic run more than fifty other runners ran sub-four-minute miles. Probably a more familiar quote from Bannister is, "The man who can drive himself further once the effort gets painful is the man who will win." The reason people fail is they end up quitting on themselves. Real and imaginary limitations keep us from our dreams until we realize that noth-ing is impossible when we put our mind and all of our focus to something and pursue it till the goal is achieved.

Don't Vacation on "Someday Isle"

Have you ever said, "Someday, I'll be happy when…I lose 20 pounds…live in a bigger house…get a new boyfriend/girlfriend…make more money…get a different job…"?

You get the picture. Someday Isle is not a dream vacation spot. It is the imaginary destination to where you will never arrive. It is the carrot on the stick perpetually in front of you. So close you can see it; yet you never seem to reach it.

This isn't saying you shouldn't have goals and dreams. Certainly all of the above may be worthwhile endeavors. The issue is that you need to be content and happy where you are and in the *progress* you are making toward your destination. Delayed happiness is not the same as delayed gratification. We need to be content in who we are yet constantly improving and making progress toward who we want to become.

If you delay happiness and contentment, you will never be there. Content in our imperfection yet striving for improvement and taking steps toward our destination is a key Incremental Advantage attribute. We usually have things backward, hoping that when our surroundings or environment change, we will change. But the truth is, when we change, we can change our environment and circumstances.

Most people are like a thermometer, merely reflecting the temperature or the attitudes around them. Good stimuli produce a good day. Negative stimuli or events produce the corresponding negative effect. The challenge is to affect your attitude and direction each day in relation to your desired destination or output rather than outside factors.

Remember the legendary Earl Nightingale's analogy of a person sitting in front of a cold stove waiting for it to produce heat before the man will add any fuel? We can all see how ludicrous this situation is, yet how many times do we fail to recognize that our experiences are a reflection of our attitude and actions. When we spend time dwelling on what we do not have, we are focusing on the wrong thing. To get the heat from the fire you must have fuel first. To get the results and rewards we desire, we first need to increase our service or value to others. People who won't do more than they are paid for, rarely advance. Studies of successful men and women throughout time will show a clear trend that even when in the lowliest of jobs, these future high income earners and successful business people sought to do more than they were paid for. In some cases the early reward was not money, but experience and opportunity in the guise of work that no one else wanted to do.

Avoid Someday Isle or the equally damaging "I'll be happy when…" syndrome. Focus on what you do have and the progress you are making. Trend analysis helps here as a quick test to see if you are on the right track. Focus on where you are and what you have. When you focus on what you don't have or allow yourself to be happy and content only at some time or event in the future…you never will be. "I'll be happy when…" is a sure fire road to disappointment and discouragement.

Beliefs of a Winner

Roger Bannister had a belief that did not constrain him to barriers restricting every other runner before him. He maintained a belief consistent with a reality he wanted to create. His firmly held belief created a new reality. Studies and observations of successful people over time have shown amazing consistency in beliefs held by these men and women. In his excellent book, *Think Like A Winner!*, Dr. Walter Doyle Staples lists 10 main beliefs held in common with all men and women of peak performance. His list outlines the very essence of an amazing and empowering belief structure, which in turn provides a strong framework from which decisions can be made and action can be born. Winners have an empowering, supportive and challenge-oriented belief structure that allows them to continue on and learn from setbacks and adversities. Winners still struggle and are faced with adversity, but their belief system "corrects course" based on feedback whereas others are shut down.

We all have a belief structure. Which beliefs are working for you and which are working against you either consciously or subconsciously? Which need a little work? Your belief structure keeps you going when you want to give up. To avoid failing by not knowing the outcome or quitting too soon, apply the STACK Strategy. Failure for most does not always happen in black or white, but rather in the grays. Failure happens in the twilight, somewhere between the light and the darkness as the life is slowly let out of your dreams and ambitions. The breakdown can happen at any one part of this five-part strategy. If you are not achieving the result you want to achieve, you are stalled in one of these steps. All of the components of the STACK Strategy are important, but without the tenacity to continue on or to keep Stacking the Logs as the final step suggests, you will fall short of your desired objective.

To Change Your Result, Change Your Approach

If you do not like your result, change your approach. Either way, continue to Stack The Logs! and keep on making forward progress. The key is moving forward. You do not have to continue to hit problems straight on or headfirst. Sometimes, to finally break through a barrier or to create success in an endeavor you have been struggling with, you need to change your approach as you maintain your forward progress.

Are you familiar with the Dr. Seuss children's classic book, *Green Eggs and Ham?* The persistent protagonist name is Sam. He is trying to convince his counterpart to just try the green eggs and ham. Success does not come after the first attempt. In fact in the book, Sam changes his approach 18 times, with his objective remaining steadfast. He is never contrary or pushy. Rather he uses question techniques and pursues alternative scenarios to entice the attempt of his questionable culinary delight. We can learn a valuable lesson in this example of creative persistence to continue on until our objective is met.

· ·

"No matter how great the talent or effort, some things just take time: you can't produce a baby in one month by getting nine women pregnant."
—Warren Buffett

· ·

Part IV

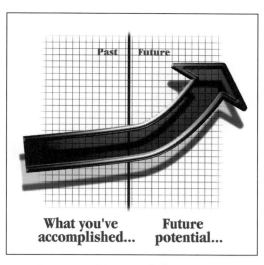

Past | Future

What you've accomplished... | Future potential...

CREATE A POSITIVE SUPPORT STRUCTURE

CHAPTER 11

Your Absolute Best Advocate…YOU!

. . . .

"All that a man achieves and all that he fails to achieve is the direct result of his own thoughts."

–James Allen, author of *As a Man Thinketh*

. . . .

The Master Incremental Advantage Skill…Practical Optimism

Thoughts are alive. The application of those thoughts in a positive, results-oriented manner creates optimism. Optimism is a vital component to a happy and successful life. It seems a simple concept and yet it is so misunderstood. Most people relate optimism to the analogy of the half full/half empty glass of water. While this certainly is part, it goes far beyond. The other facet of optimism that is misunderstood is the two very distinct types of optimism. There is the wishful-thinking, everything-is-going-to-work-out, rose-colored-glasses, Pollyanna optimism. This type of optimism is passive and sometimes proves harmful rather than helpful. This manner of optimism gives up control to circumstances and is merely an internal positive "spin" to fool yourself out of worry.

The other type of optimism is a more proactive and strong-minded optimism that allows you to inject control into your situation. This practical optimism is the skill set similar to mental judo. Judo as a martial art is the redirection of force an opponent uses against you to give you leverage against your opponent. Practical optimism as a skill set allows you to be proactive and exert control to redirect and rechannel whatever situation you are in, to provide you with personal leverage in your situation.

. . . .

"A pessimist is one who makes difficulties of his opportunities and an optimist is one who makes opportunities of his difficulties."
–Harry Truman

. . . .

Have you ever known anyone to actually admit to being a pessimist? Most pessimists like to refer to themselves as realists. I am not knocking realism as it is certainly critical to assess reality in your current situation. Our very thoughts about every situation and our attitude create opportunities for us to grow, learn and succeed. The way you think, whether positive or negative, creates emotions that reflect your beliefs. The words you speak and the actions you take tell your whole story. College football coach and motivational speaker Lou Holtz aptly observed, "Ability is what you are capable of doing. Motivation determines what you will do. Attitude determines how well you do it."

Within each thought is a choice to grow healthy plants of practical optimism. Conversely, every thought regarding each situation might plant seeds growing bitter roots of negativity, anger, resentment or apathy. Over time these thoughts produce a cumulative result as well. Surely you can think of two people as examples of each end of the spectrum. Think of a person who no matter what happens always remains optimistic and hopeful, making the best out of every situation. This person has all of the normal emotions including anger, fear, sadness, grief and yet even in those situations has the ability to keep negative emotions at bay. This person is fun to be around, especially in tough situations.

Now think of a person at the other end of the spectrum. He or she enters and you can feel the mood of the room change. This person walks without purpose, with shoulders slumped. He or she lacks hope and complains about situations rather than taking meaningful action to change them. If forced to read a book like this one or go to a seminar, this type of person will be immediately drawn to any inconsistency or flaw to discount the growth opportunity.

Now the tough question. If you created a scale of 0 to 10 with the practical optimist as a 10 and the other as a 0, where would you rate yourself? The good news, regardless of how you scored yourself, is that you can adapt and learn to increase your skill set of practical optimism. This is absolutely a master skill that will provide tangible benefits and certainly a personal Incremental Advantage. Go back to the two people you thought of from the previous example. If you were an employer, which would you rather fill your company with? Who do you think will earn more money over their career? Who will have a more satisfying relationship with their spouse, family and others?

The Art of Practical Optimism

Optimism creates confidence and confidence breeds success. Success is always preceded by a desire for it. Negative thoughts are precursors to negative emotions, which are precursors to negative actions and feelings of depression or despair. There is a big difference between practical optimism and self-talk that is unrealistic and self-delusional. Sayings that are mere platitudes of comfort to mask the anxiety when you feel your world is crumbling are ultimately not effective. Saying you feel terrific when you feel like crap or chanting a mantra that your worst days are behind you and your future is nothing but roses is not really what practical optimism is about. Practical optimism is certainly an Incremental Advantage success characteristic. It can impact your life and provide a harvest of benefits in every aspect.

Practical optimism is understanding and appreciating your situation and then searching for the blessings, benefits or opportunities contained therein. More importantly, practical optimism allows you to take action to take the best from whatever a situation provides. There is the positive expectation that even bad things or situations can carry seeds of positive things within. Successful people use their imaginations to rehearse success, taking the very best of the opportunities presented to create an Incremental Advantage. Successful people still have trials and tribulations; they just learn how to assess the best response to each situation.

As an example, in our situation with Frankie's illness, we found some tremendous blessings. We had new experiences, made excellent new friends, grew together as a family and I even found new time to work on this book project. I certainly would not want to repeat this event nor would I ever wish it on anyone, but we made the decision early on that we would actively look for and be thankful for whatever blessings came our way in this adversity. A key characteristic of practical optimists is that they understand and accept what they cannot change. Beyond this fact, they find and develop active strategies to mine the opportunities presented. It is easier to become optimistic when you begin to take action. Any action is sufficient to begin to improve your outlook and your feelings of optimism. As action happens, solutions begin to appear.

We are born who we are. We possess a unique set of attributes and a unique set of limitations. Our choices, made up in the small increments, allow us to define ourselves and create our own destiny. Destiny is a power word and might scare people. Replace destiny with destination. Create your own destination. Your destiny is nothing more than your self-charted course to the future you desire. A relatively small percentage is actually born into the "lucky sperm club," with affluence and opportunities their birthright. If this is not you, take heart. We are all given opportunities. Stories abound about people succeeding after tragedy or overcoming great poverty to achieve wealth. Our destiny is not found in the gifts we are given or the tools we are provided with. Rather, *our destiny lies in the cultivation and use of what we are provided with.* We are all equally empowered to reach our highest potential. We need to define and create our own destiny as a self-charted course. Our successful future is the one envisioned and acted upon. The biggest secret as well as the biggest obstacle to your success is you. The formula is there for everyone to know; however, there is a big difference in knowing what to do, and doing it.

Strategies to Develop Practical Optimism

When a tricky situation comes your way, take on the identity of a problem solver. Think how someone you greatly respect in this area might handle your same problem or challenge. Look for multiple options in every situation. Search for applications and creative solutions outside normal thinking. Anticipate problems in advance and accept reality. Create strategies and contingency plans to break though difficulties that will appear in your path.

In grief and in hard-hitting situations, allow true feelings to be released (even if they are negative). Now, I am not in any way advocating becoming negative. But emotions are important in our lives and even the negative ones serve a purpose. When my father died, I grieved. When my son was first diagnosed with leukemia, I was scared and filled with sorrow and dread. All of these emotions at the time were healthy. Over time the emotions changed and adapted to allow me to take a more practical and proactive approach to my situation.

Identify yourself with your strengths not your weaknesses. Create beliefs to support what you want rather than what you don't want. Follow your thoughts. Create a new self-fulfilling prophesy for yourself. Our identity is who we think we are. We have the power to control our thoughts.

Belief Influences Actions

According to many experts, you will produce more than 50,000 random or directed thoughts in a single day. That works out to around a thought a second. What amazing brain power! Every innovation, every work of art, every bit of science all began as a seed within 1 of those 50,000 random daily thoughts. Our thoughts are the single most dominant energy force determining our lives today. Your thoughts are the precursor to everything else; the genesis of any creation and all your endeavors.

Belief definitely influences actions. As a Christian, I believe God owns everything and I am merely a steward of what he entrusts to me. I tithe and give at least 10 percent of my first fruits back to God. My belief influences my actions. You may have a different underlying belief that would cause you to take a different action I would. Different beliefs lead to different actions. Consciously or subconsciously, we act how we act and achieve the results we achieve largely due to the underlying beliefs we hold and then act upon.

Our belief system is our underlying set of rules and operating frame of reference for how we see, judge, create and live our reality. Our belief structure resides within our subconscious mind. Although we may be able to articulate some beliefs, others are there whether or not we recognize them. Your beliefs are your filter on your conscious reality. If you subconsciously believe you are impoverished, a sudden windfall of money will not last since your belief thermostat is set at poverty. If you are fat, it is because your subconscious thermometer and belief system is set at fat. All the diet gimmicks in the world will not permanently change your weight until you can change your belief system. Beliefs control attitudes, which control emotions, which control actions. When you subconsciously believe something, you are hard-wired to have a result consistent with that belief.

In my own life I have literally lost a thousand pounds on yo-yo dieting using many different methods. It was not until I could change my belief and my subconscious programming that my results changed. This was also the same for me with regard to my income. When I saw myself making $20,000 a year, I did. Slowly this nudged up, but I still maintained limitations on what I thought my earning power was. There were years that I made a lot of money, but lost a lot of money at the same time to net out what my image of myself was. My income did not dramatically rise until I corrected my belief and reset my financial thermostat.

Act As If

To become the person you want to be, you need to first change who you are. To change who you are, you first change how you think, which affects how you act. One interesting twist is the fact that you can create a positive "self-fulfilling prophesy" by changing the way you act. When you can begin to visualize and see yourself as you want to be, you will find yourself moving closer to your goal.

Harvard psychologist William James observed, "If you want a quality, act as if you already had it." William Shakespeare said, "Assume a virtue, if you have it not." Dale Carnegie remarked, "Act as if you were already happy, and that will tend to make you happy." Dennis Waitley maintained, "If you believe you can, you probably can. If you believe you won't, you most assuredly won't. Belief is the ignition switch that gets you off the launching pad."

Self-Limiting Beliefs

The famous German philosopher Goethe made a profound observation in dealing with others: "Treat a man as he is and he will remain as he is. Treat a man as he can and should be, and he will become as he can and should be." These words are true in how we relate to others. This observation also applies directly to how we relate to ourselves. Self-limiting beliefs are a major downfall for most people. The cycle starts when we are small and continues through adulthood until we end up doubting our abilities and afraid that failure lurks behind every corner.

Assume you were told that a university was doing a study on luck and you had a chance of winning $1,000 based on the outcome of a coin toss. Just one toss, your call in the air; heads or tails. Ask yourself this simple question: What does your small inner voice tell you immediately after your choice is made and the coin is in the air? You know you have a 50 percent chance of winning $1,000. Do you have confidence that your 50 percent chance will fall in your favor, or do you secretly believe that like most things in your life, this one will fall opposite of what you are hoping for? If you are a golfer, what does the last voice you hear say to you before you try to drive the green across a small pond? If you are running late for an appointment, what does your inner voice tell you about traffic lights?

Art of Talking to Yourself and Others

Keep a log of your inner thoughts both positive and negative…you may be surprised with the patterns that emerge. Many people find they think they are positive when they are not. If you don't want to take the time to go through a log, try this simple exercise. Place a rubber band around your wrist and every time you catch yourself thinking a negative thought or negative emotions such as fear, doubt or worry, or finding yourself running mental movies of bad situations, snap the rubber band. Caution: You may find yourself with some serious welts. This experiment can go a long way in at least recognizing the overbearing nature of negative thought patterns.

If you do keep a log for a while, take a look at the negative attitudes and try to ascertain their origination. Are they your thoughts and beliefs or do you continue to garden seeds that were planted by someone else? Sometimes a careless comment by a parent or teacher leads us to create a belief structure that is inaccurate.

Why are some people gloomy and negative? You can easily spot them a mile away, can't you? Do you like to be around those people, or would you rather be around someone positive and affirming? If you (currently) happen to be a negative or gloomy person, you have the choice to reprogram and reset your beliefs to be more reflective of the person you wish to be rather than the person you thought you were.

Listening to Your Inner Voice (Self-Talk)

We have brain capacity far greater than any of the computers in use today and yet most of us never learn to use or practice even the most basic self-computer programming. Over time, with practice and persistence, we can change the dynamic of our inner voice. We talk to ourselves every day. Unfortunately for most people, their inner voice is an enemy rather than an ally. We get used to berating and doubting ourselves. It is evident within our self-talk.

You are not stuck with the inner voice you now have. There is a factory recall and you are eligible for a new and upgraded model. As a matter of fact, you qualify for the top-of-the-line inner voice with features and benefits designed for the best and highest quality self-talk possible. All you have to do is learn how to program the thing. Most of us already have what we are looking for; we just somehow find a way to sabotage ourselves. We only need to learn how to reset our thinking away from the defective factory settings to avoid allowing our inner voice to take us off track.

Programming Positive Expectancy— The Power of Affirmations

Affirmations are not mystical or New Age. They are optimistic statements about yourself written as though your desired positive outcome has already been attained. It is a mental programming technique to convince your subconscious to carry out the programming you implant. There are numerous examples of the opposite and many that you most likely can readily point to in your life. Statements disguised as self-effacing humor can have the effect of cementing into your subconscious the very opposite of what you wish. Allowing your inner voice to have free rein undercuts your confidence and eats away at your belief for positive outcomes. Lowered expectations ultimately decrease opportunities for success as confidence is diminished.

The only way to change your situation is to change your thoughts because they are the precursor to action and action is the engine of success. If you are convinced your life is lacking and you are a failure, you will remain in that situation until you convince yourself your life is filled with abundance and you are a success.

Affirmations and self-talk are only effective if you can use thoughts or words with emotion. Have you ever been driving down the highway listening to music with a really strong beat then look down only to find yourself going significantly over the speed limit? You may not get out of a ticket with this explanation, but your emotions through the music affected your body and your actions on a subconscious level. Affirmations spoken to music are extremely effective as they cut through the clutter to implant a success consciousness with emotion.

Would you have as your best friend someone who was negative, constantly criticized you, always pointed out your flaws (even to strangers), second-guessed you, gave credit for your accomplishments to luck and always whispered in your ear predictions of your failures in all that you do? Of course not. Why then do we do this to ourselves? Why do we belittle and berate ourselves, point out our flaws, make excuses for our talents and successes? Worst of all—why do we allow negative self-talk to steal our ambition and derail our dreams?

Positive expectancy is not about overlooking the evidence pointing to negative events or outcomes. It is not viewing the world with rose-colored glasses or being blissfully ignorant. Positive expectancy is about training yourself to be optimistic about your results because you have planned, are prepared and have the right frame of mind for success. This is not to say that you will not have failures and setbacks. As we learned earlier, those are all part of the process of learning. Positive expectancy is about believing in yourself and your dreams, even when no one else does. Positive expectancy is about seeing what you want to happen rather than what you don't want to happen. The law of attraction basically states that whatever we focus on, we draw to ourselves. When we are focused on our desired outcome, we create the conditions we seek and work to bring that to reality. Fear, doubt and worry fill our minds with what we don't want and subconsciously sabotage our actions to bring about exactly that.

The Thermostat and Thermometer

The thermostat is an often misunderstood modern convenience. A thermostat "sets" the target temperature as designated by the programmer (you). If the thermostat is set for 74 degrees and the temperature in the room is 80 degrees, the thermostat will allow the air-conditioning to turn on and run until the temperature in the room is the desired 74 degrees. If the room is too cold, the heat will come on until the desired temperature is achieved.

A common misconception of thermostats is you can speed up the process by over-correcting. If the room is 80 degrees and you would normally set the thermostat to 74, overcorrecting and setting it to 70 will not get the temperature to 74 any faster. Many times people dramatically overcorrect and never actually get to the desired temperature setting.

This phenomenon of "chasing the thermostat" happens in our lives as well as we pendulum-shift far to one side. Then, frustrated before we see our desired outcome, we shift far to the other side. If you lack patience with a thermostat, you will never be at the correct temperature. It is the same with your life: If you lack patience to follow through on the path to your desired outcome, you will never get there.

A thermostat is a device used to set and control the temperature in a room. A thermometer is designed only to provide a reflection of what the actual temperature is. A thermostat is active and in essence drives the change, whereas a thermometer is passive and can only observe the change. Many people would like to change their surroundings or their environment, but instead are merely thermometers acting only as a reflection of the environment.

There is an interesting phenomenon I have noticed with some people who begin to achieve outside their comfort zone or their reality of themselves, they find a way to return to their original setting. If a person makes $25,000 a year and has a self-image of a $25,000-a-year performer, it takes a massive thermostat change to allow him or her to be comfortable outside of around 20 percent—say, $5,000—in either direction. They start to achieve and then the thermostat of fear, doubt and worry creeps in and pushes the person back to their set point of income comfort. It might happen the same way if the income drops. The discomfort causes a change until they are back to being the person they believe themselves to be.

I have seen this with people who have amazing talent and ability. As they began to see real success, they would somehow sabotage themselves to avoid the success that would challenge their internal thermostat set-point perception of who they are. You might know people or have fallen into this pattern yourself. Look at the fate of rock stars and TV or movie celebrities who have either died or taken action that seems so contrary to the success they exude in public. Drugs, drunkenness, arrests, suicide and murder are commonplace in a crowd you would assume has it all. They have convinced the world, but not themselves. If your set point is low and you lack value in yourself, outward success, fame or riches will push you to take action contrary to what you should.

Take a minute right now and do the following exercise. Imagine in your own mind what you annual salary is. Now imagine quadrupling it. Four times more than you are currently making? Do you feel a little uncomfortable? Is there a small still voice saying you could never do that? Do you feel a little fear, doubt and worry? Do excuses pop up as to why it could not happen? I used income merely as an example. Other examples might be your weight, your job or your habits. This resistance to change is very natural, but we can reprogram ourselves to not only accept this reality, but create it.

If you internally believe that you are a lazy underachiever, unworthy of success, your subconscious will not buy into your goals. You might find some initial progress, but after a few weeks you will get distracted and your internal thermostat, still set on lazy underachiever unworthy of success, will bring you back to that reality.

Self-Discipline—
Your Personal Support Structure

I used to own a business in the personal and professional development industry and would often have the opportunity for public speaking. One theme that seemed to resonate with audiences revolved around making an ally of self-discipline and its relationship with success. In these speeches I would say, "The price must be paid. You have a choice to pay the price of success up front in one lump sum through planned discipline, focus, determined and sustained action." I then boldly held up a $100 bill representing self-discipline and the full price to be paid for success. "Or, you have the choice to pay the price of failure…on the lifetime installment plan." Then ripping the $100 bill, I would say in mock resignation, "I didn't really want to send my kids to school." *Rip!* "The house we live in now is okay, I guess." *Rip!* "I didn't really want to be fit anyway and have to buy all new cloths." *Rip!* Each lowering of standards, each dismissing of dreams brings a *Rip!* of the $100 bill. "The choice is up to you. Either way the price is paid; the choice is yours."

You would not believe the physical cringing at the ripping of the currency. The effect worked and the point was driven home that self-discipline is not easy. Hard process; easy results. Lacking self-discipline is easy; the results are not. Self-discipline to spend less than you earn, saving at least 10 percent of your income and avoid going into debt, at first is not easy. You do without and your results are initially painful. Over time, this price paid up front reverses as you achieve an Incremental Advantage in your finances. Cash in the bank allows you to save money when you pay cash. You are completely unburdened by debts and can make work choices based on what you want to do rather than what you have to make to sustain your cash burn.

Over time the self-discipline of this habit or any other is an Incremental Advantage invested at a tremendous rate, yielding a return far superior to results of those who lack self-discipline.

(Note: Being ever frugal, I was always careful to rip the bill for effect yet preserve the value of the currency so I could tape it and exchange it at the bank.)

Taking Control and Developing Self-Leverage

It would be nice to delegate our life results to someone else, but this will not happen. No one will do it for you nor could anyone if they wanted. Your parents cannot. Your spouse cannot. Your boss, friend, minister, therapist, children…cannot. You are the center of your own world and as such, you are the only one who has the leverage to take control and to affect your outcomes.

There is no one who can be a better advocate for you…than you. As you learn to reset your thermostat and to affect your environment, as you learn positive programming, as you learn to harness self-discipline…in all of these you create an Incremental Advantage and self-leverage.

"We must all suffer one of two things: the pain of discipline or the regret of disappointment."
—Jim Rohn

CHAPTER 12

Develop and Enhance Your Inner Circle

. . . .

An ant and an elephant were walking together when they came to a large rope bridge with wooden planks spanning more than 40 feet across a great crevasse. As they began to make their way across with the ground more than 200 feet below, the bridge began to heave up and down. Once safely to the other side after all of the perilous movement, the ant turned to the elephant and said, "Man did we shake that thing or what!"

—Unknown

. . . .

Human Relations

Life is a group sport, yet we are the only ones who can apply personal leverage to our lives. That said, we can achieve success and enjoy our lives more fully with other people. Relationships from our most intimate family to mere acquaintances are extremely significant in life's journey. We affect and are affected by others. We have a greater opportunity to achieve what we want when we have a basic understanding of how vital other relationships are to our lives, and how we can improve our lives by improving the quality of our relationships.

Crabs in a Bucket

Crabs in a bucket together will usually find a way to coexist. There is usually not a problem until a crab attempts to climb out of the crab-in-the-bucket community. What prevents this exodus? The other crabs will pull the first and any subsequent jail breaker back down into the bucket.

Unfortunately, sometimes our base human nature wants company in the misery. If crabs were smart and understood the synergy of their dynamic, they could easily all escape. Instead of helping one get out to then assisting the others, they engage in cheap crab-community bickering and politics aimed at keeping the crab status quo. I may be carrying this a little far, but hopefully you get the picture. If you are continually venting, blowing off steam, talking about things you can't control, involving yourself in problem-highlighting rather than solution-finding conversations, you are negative. Stop it! You affect others. Learn to cultivate and develop upwardly spiraling relationships.

It is great to be in a conversation with someone who listens and focuses on solutions. Try to avoid negative people and relationships. If you are in a relationship like that, transition by shifting focus to solutions rather than problems. We cannot necessarily choose our relatives and sometimes we are in situations we feel we have no control over. Align with positive people. When you are with someone who is not, try to steer the conversation to productive ground. If they want to stick with the negative you will frustrate them and they may just leave you alone to find someone else to commiserate with. I think it is beyond coincidence that the root word of commiserate is misery. Commiserate is literally *co-misery*. When I was growing up, my father had a plaque in his office with a quote from Admiral Hyman Rickover that read as follows: *Great Minds Discuss Ideas…Average Minds Discuss Events…Small Minds Discuss People.* Try to associate with positive people discussing ideas and avoid those who seek company in their misery. You have a choice: If you find yourself surrounded by negative people pulling others down, it may be time to find a different bucket!

Law of Entropy

This is a fancy physics term basically meaning that for everything living, from the smallest organisms to the largest, there must be energy added or the organism will die. Entropy is death or the process of dying through loss of energy. You have personal entropy if you do not allow for renewal and recharging in your life. This is also true in a more abstract way with both your dreams, and also with your vital relationships. For both to remain healthy, energy must be added. If you have a relationship with someone, yet never put any effort into it, the relationship will eventually atrophy and die. Perhaps you can look back 10 years and think of several people you would have considered close, but have not talked to in many years. When you have a dream but never put energy into it, your dream will die. Personal entropy occurs when you do not take care of yourself and allow for renewal. You begin to rob yourself of the energy needed to sustain your dreams.

How do you counteract the effects of personal entropy? Attach yourself and align with optimistic and positive people. To keep yourself revitalized, your dreams moving forward and your relationships healthy, find and put effort into growth relationships with others who are on the same journey as you. There is a basic truth that people either leave you higher or lower after you are done with your interaction. Think about the last three people with whom you interacted. Did they lift you up? Or did they bring you down? Here is a tough question: If the same question were presented to those same three people, what would their response be in regard to you?

There are many methods and opportunities to stimulate and reverse the natural trend of personal entropy. Change your intellectual and mental habits. Change your input to change your stimulus to grow. Continue education and continue learning and growing. Learn new skills. Study a foreign language; read books outside your normal interests. Change habits and routines. Try a new restaurant or type of cuisine. Watch different TV shows, go to bed considerably later or earlier than you normally would and do the same rising. Interrupt your routine!

Step out of your comfort zone. Get out of your rut. I once heard "rut" defined as, "a grave with the ends kicked out." Don't allow your routines—ruts—to develop and stagnate your progress. One of the greatest disadvantages of our current society is the comfort level and complacency that has developed. This complacency calcifies ambitions and does not push us to new levels. Feed your spiritual needs. Spend time with a young child and try to match their curiosity and enthusiasm. Listen to their questions and sense of humor and try to keep pace with them. Meet new people. Laugh; humor is a vital success tool. If you apply just some of these techniques, you will soon find that any burnout or loss of energy will start to change into a new sense of purpose. Sometimes all it takes is a fresh perspective.

Create an External Infrastructure

I realize this sounds a little like an oxymoron (e.g., jumbo shrimp or military intelligence), but it is important to develop your external infrastructure. Look at the illustration like a dartboard or bull's-eye with you at the center. The next ring out would be your family, and then close friends, then friends all the way to mere acquaintances. As you create and develop the external infrastructure you build a mutual support system allowing for and creating mutual benefits. Every interaction with another person is a transaction. Each transaction creates an effect for both parties. Over time each singular transaction in the form of conversation, physical contact, correspondence, proximity, etc., creates an input. This input over time creates the Incremental Cumulative Effect for this relationship. The relationships you have as well as the ones you used to have but currently do not maintain, are where they are because of these individual transactions.

It is necessary to put care and effort into all our relationships. Taken for granted and untended, the garden of your relationships will begin to grow weeds, choking the life out of your blossoms. Many of us have lost touch with people as our lives have changed. We adapt to jobs, spouses, and external situations that affect the fabric of our relationships. You cannot maintain an inner circle relationship with everyone you meet. It is imperative to select and maintain the relationships important to you.

Your external infrastructure has layers. The further from the center, the lower the gravitational pull to maintain that relationship. The relationships vital to you need care and tending for them to flourish. Your support structure begins with you. In order to change the world, you must start by changing yourself. To truly be successful, you will not journey alone. Learning to effectively combine strengths with others for mutual benefit is the bedrock of your success foundation. It would be difficult to imagine anyone truly accomplishing anything of great significance and importance without the help and assistance of other people. Whether it is your family, church, peer group or any number of other support mechanisms, it is tremendously important to have a support structure.

Aesop, the author of hundreds of the now famous *Aesop's Fables*, was a Greek slave living more than half a century before the birth of Christ. His truths and insights into human nature and behavior are as completely relevant and applicable today as they were almost three thousand years ago. Many of Aesop's fables, like the one paraphrased below, worked around the theme of unity and human relations.

Aesop's Fable of the Father and His Sons

A father had a family of sons who were continuously quarreling and fighting among themselves. When he failed to mend their disputes by his pleadings and exhortations, he determined to give them a practical illustration of the wrongness and perils within their lack of union. For his illustration he one day told them to bring him a bundle of sticks. After they had done so, he presented the stick bundle into the hands of each of them in succession, ordering each to attempt to break it in pieces. They each tried with all their might, yet not one was able to break the group of sticks. He then opened the bundle, took the sticks individually, and one at a time placed them into the hands of his sons. This time the sons were able to easily break the sticks. Then, in the solemn wisdom of a wise father, he addressed them in these words: "My sons, if you are of one mind, and unite to fully assist each other, you will be as this [group of wood], uninjured by all the attempts of your enemies; but if you are divided among yourselves, you will be broken as easily as these sticks."

Life is abundance. We achieve in relations what we seek and dwell on. It is necessary to put care and effort into all our relationships. Taken for granted and untended, the garden of your relationships will begin to grow weeds, choking out the life of your blossoms.

"The only way to have friends is to be one."
–Ralph Waldo Emerson

There is an easy way to get a friend—be one. Your attitude plants the seeds creating the harvest of personal relationships. Within your relationships there is sowing and there is reaping. As in nature, for there to be a bountiful reaping at harvest, it must be preceded by the equivalent of greater sowing during the planting season. Give to give rather than give to get. When you give to others you receive a benefit and you build a relationship. When you give to get, your relationship will remain shallow. As you give to others of your time and your attention you begin to make deposits into the emotional bank account and solidify your relationship.

Internal Communication

Communication happens first internally as self-dialogue. Sometimes it is a focused and purposeful dialogue. Other times it is a meandering, tangent-filled excursion of mental gibberish. How you communicate with yourself is important. It sets the tone and direction for how you communicate with others. There is logical commonsense wisdom in the question, "If you don't respect yourself, how can you respect anyone else?" The same goes true for communication at the most basic level. "If you cannot correctly communicate with yourself, how can you fully communicate with anyone else? If you have negative or fear, doubt and worry self-talk, how will your communication reflect differently, outwardly to others?

The corollary of this is the understanding that the most direct route to improving your communication with others is by improving your communication with yourself. This takes some effort as you have thousands of internal dialogues yet most likely do not pay attention to them. To correct the habit pattern, you need to first recognize it. As discussed in Chapter 11, you most likely are not aware of the dominant negative, angry, fearful, resentful thoughts rattling around in your head. Again, try the rubber band method if you did not do so before. Every time you find yourself beyond the quick flash of a negative thought and into a sustained negative thought pattern, pull back the rubber band on your wrist and give it a snap. It is painful on two levels. Your wrist will definitely have welts and you may find yourself aghast at the level of negativity you have. Even if (especially if) you see yourself as a positive person, this may come as quite a shock.

There is a natural law called the law of correspondence at work within every relationship. It basically means the outside world is like a mirror reflecting back to you whatever is going on in your inner world. Everything that happens outside you corresponds to something happening inside you. The law of correspondence is in your relationships. Your relationships mirror back to you exactly the kind of a person you are. When you are content, happy and optimistic, your relationships also have the same attributes. When your thinking is negative, fearful, depressed or angry, it is reflected in your relationships as well.

Talking positive, calm, confident goal-directed thoughts internally to yourself sends a strong verbal and nonverbal message externally to all you communicate with. Changing your internal dialogue will change actions you undertake. Changing your internal dialogue will change how you communicate to others. As you change and learn to more fully respect yourself, you may be surprised to see others follow suit.

Lessons of the Flock

I'm not much of a naturalist, but in doing my research I found some interesting facts regarding geese. If you have ever watched a flock of Canadian geese flying in their triangular pattern, you will witness fuel efficiency in action. Each individual bird takes advantage of the rising air from the bird in front of it. This is a remarkable increase in efficiency nearly three times that of a single bird. The effect is similar to drafting in bicycle racing.

Ultimately, the reduced wind resistance coupled with the energy boost from the rising air reduces the individual bird's workload. As the lead bird tires, it changes position and moves to the back of the formation with another bird taking the front position. Flying in this V formation, the geese appear to move effortlessly through the air, even with a headwind. It has been calculated that geese flying in this V formation will burn up 72 percent less energy flying the same distance compared to a lone goose. Each member of the flock shares the responsibility for the success of the journey. Geese in the rear of the formation honk to provide encouragement for those in front as well as to assist them in maintaining the proper pace. When a goose is wounded or becomes ill, at least two geese fall out of formation and stay with the impaired goose until it gets better or dies. Depending on whether the goose gets better or dies, the remaining geese will catch up or join another flock.

There are some real lessons to be learned and applied in the example of geese. When you are traveling a common direction and share a sense of community, you can get where you are going more easily if you travel on the thrust of one another. When we stay in formation along with those headed where we want to go, we allow for efficiency and lift unavailable to us individually. As with geese, it is to our advantage to take turns doing the hard tasks and sharing in leadership roles. We must encourage and motivate each other. When one of the group is in trouble, treat his or her concerns as important as your own. Nurture and care for those in your flock who need it. This delivers a far more powerful message than any words could.

Creating an Inner Circle

When I was younger and starting out on my entrepreneurial apprenticeship, I had one problem; I had no master or mentor and had to learn my craft the hard way. Sometimes it is very difficult to ask others for help. Eventually, I chose some mentors. I opened the door to allow my father to share his wisdom after being closed to it for a long time. I created and developed friendships with others who were doing what I wanted to do. I even found mentoring opportunities in people I had not yet met and in some cases with people who were no longer living. No, I was not involved in any séances or New Age mysticism, but I did find a way to benefit from the lives of other people (even the deceased). I read biographies and autobiographies of people I was intrigued by or people who accomplished what I wanted to accomplish.

The biography of Ben Franklin gave me tremendous insight into this great man. When faced with a problem of human relations, I would reflect on what he might do in my situation. I was only able to go through this mental exercise because of my knowledge of the man and how he responded to certain situations. From founding fathers to war heroes to great men and women of business to sports figures, there are lessons to be learned and applied to your life. Sometimes it takes a little creativity to step out of your own skin and ask yourself how someone else might respond to your same situation.

Sometimes, because of pride or fear, we force ourselves to be prisoners in a situation unnecessarily. Chances are whatever you are going through, whatever hardship, trial, difficulty or challenge, someone has gone through the exact same or very similar situation. It is important to open ourselves up enough and be willing to ask for help. There is no shame and no embarrassment necessary when you need help from others. Cultivate and develop friendships. Create opportunities to trust others and learn to grow together. Learn to find the ultimate leverage in a few important friendships in the spirit of harmony.

Power of the Mastermind Alliance

The concept of the "mastermind" is the same as synergy found in nature applied to specific and definite purpose. A mastermind alliance is simply the coordinated effort of knowledge and resources of two or more people working in harmony to achieve a specific purpose. Two batteries hooked together will have more voltage than the two individual batteries' power. In effect a third battery is created. Have you ever heard the expression, "Two heads are better than one"? Like grouping chords of steel together to increase the strength over the combined sum alone, a group of people with like-minded goals working together can achieve more than each could individually. The human mind has electrical energy that can be both monitored as well as measured. Like a bank of batteries, two or more brains working in cooperation and in harmony create a bank of mind power that is in essence a new mind.

This effect was popularized by Napoleon Hill, who first referred to the phenomenon and bedrock success principle from all he studied as the concept of the "mastermind alliance." He observed giants of industry and intellect of his day and noted, although each man was great in his own right, each also had strong relationships with other great men to collaborate and work together in the spirit of harmony. The founding fathers in creating the Declaration of Independence and the Constitution operated in a mastermind collaborative framework. Whether consciously or not, nearly all successful people have a mastermind or collaborative alliance at the heart of their success.

Napoleon Hill did not discover or invent the phenomenon of the mastermind, but he is most closely associated with it from his observance of more than 500 successful business executives of the early 20th century. Mr. Hill suggests a mastermind is the "coordination of knowledge and effort, in the spirit of harmony, between two or more people, for the attainment of a definite purpose." This applies to all areas of life. Successful families embody the principles at work in a mastermind alliance.

Many people over time have used it and nearly every successful person today will probably admit to having a mastermind alliance. King Arthur was part of the legendary Knights of the Round Table. Benjamin Franklin created a group of thinkers and doers he called "Junto." Franklin and his mastermind group solved community problems. One tangent of their creation was the library system of the United States. Another was the genesis of the present day volunteer fire department. Jesus of Nazareth had His disciples, who after his death became the epicenter of Christianity spreading the gospel to every part of the world.

You don't have to agree to have a working mastermind alliance. Different perspectives and even heated arguments are part of the process as long as there is still harmony and a definiteness of purpose. Our political system is a great example. Congress even with all its acrimony and spirited debate pushes forward the agenda of America. Occasionally self-interest gets in the way. However, in aggregate and over time as demonstrated through the last 200-plus years, the system works. America, even with problems is one of the best places to live in the entire world. There is a key distinction between agreement and alignment at the core of a spirit of harmony. Alignment allows for groups to have the same focus and same spirit of definite purpose without having complete agreement.

It is important to believe that people want to contribute and are committed to support you because you are committed to their success. I have a friend and partner in business named Chris. He and I could not be more different in some ways. He can look at numbers or math problems and know the answer before I have time to turn my calculator on. His analytical prowess fascinates me and I am thoroughly convinced he is a genius. In many of the key areas where Chris is strong, I am challenged. He and I disagree completely on politics and nearly completely on religion. Chris is single; I am married. He has a dog and I have children. We look at problems and opportunities differently and we frequently get into spirited debates regarding situations arising at work. I tend to look toward opportunities and gaining benefits whereas Chris focuses on protecting what we have built and avoiding losses. Outside of commonality in sports teams, it appears we have little in common.

The funny thing is that Chris and I have a great relationship and an excellent supportive friendship. I know our company would not be where it is today without it. Although different, we have common goals and a true mastermind alliance. We trust in each other and rely on each other's using each of his strengths to our corporate advantage. We focus primarily on our common objectives rather than our differences. We know we are different, yet respect and place high value on each other's opinion. Neither of us has dramatically changed any of our beliefs (or is willing to admit it), however, we are both more inclined toward independent thought rather than blindly following party line or jumping on the bandwagon without forethought. We trust and respect each other's strengths and how that plays into the overall synergy and effectiveness of our team.

Another partner and friend, Tom, and I are very much alike. We share many of the same experiences and are in many ways as similar as Chris and I are different. Whereas Chris and I have learned to focus on our opposite skill sets, Tom and I have learned how to play off of our common strengths to our corporate advantage. I value my friendship and my partnership with both Tom and Chris tremendously. During the six months I took a complete sabbatical from our business, I not only had their complete support to be with my son in Memphis, but they ran the entire operation without me.

Did the business suffer because I wasn't there? Was the relationship strained when I came back? Absolutely not! Actually, quite to the contrary. My inner circle, radiating out from Tom and Chris to several other key players on our team, stepped up and took complete stewardship of our business to where it flourished in my absence. When I was able to return, I joked with people that I was only allowed to return to work for a 30-day probation period. The truth is that our relationship was even stronger upon my return. A shared vision and sense of purpose create synergy. It makes the journey easier for all.

Reverse Egocentrism

No person is as important to you as you. Egocentrism literally means "centered around me." We all tend to view every situation with a "What's in it for me?" lens. It is our base human nature. But we are not prisoners of our base human nature and there is one key that literally unlocks the secret of beyond belief human relations. Everyone feels the way you do. The golden rule did not become the golden rule by accident. Treat others as you would like to be treated. Listen the way you'd like others to listen to you. Help others like you want to be helped. Step outside yourself to break the egocentric trend.

Like Napoleon Hill's *Think and Grow Rich*, Dale Carnegie's *How to Win Friends and Influence People* goes far beyond descriptions like timeless, classic and must-read. Both of these books, though written in the first half of the last century, are principle based and researched diligently from nature and the successes of many great people. You their influence in all of the great thinkers of today.

Stephen Covey in his excellent book, *The 7 Habits of Highly Effective People*, says we need to, "Seek first to understand, and then be understood." To build friendships, we must be a friend first. To advance your agenda, find out how it helps advance their agenda. There is an old adage in sales that, "nobody will care how much you know until they know how much you care." Fundamentals of human relations boil down to the basics of placing the needs of others in front of your own. Dale Carnegie chose this Henry Ford quote to be one of the finest insights into human relationships: "If there is any one secret of success, it lies in the ability to get the other person's point of view and see things from that person's angle as well as your own." Unfortunately, the more complicated and scheduled our lives become, the easier it is to get wrapped up in ourselves and further away from the needs and concerns of others.

I heard a marriage counselor offer these choices in dealing with a spouse during a disagreement: "You can choose to be right, or you choose to can be happy!" This is equally true in all human relations. In disagreements with others, do you want to be right or do you want to be happy? Do you ever catch your-self proving you are right or correcting others when there is nothing important at stake? It is a natural tendency most of us are guilty of while at the same time not doing it consciously. Benjamin Franklin said the same thing in a slightly different way: "If you argue and rankle and contradict, you may achieve a vic-tory sometimes; but it will be an empty victory because you will never get your opponent's good will."

No one wants to be proven wrong. No one wants to be em-barrassed or have their sins confessed or uncovered to others. The object in human relations should be to advance the agenda that best serves everyone. Learning the most effective way to get the most from every human interaction will allow for a greater probability of cumulative success in every encounter.

Develop the habit to sincerely treat each person you en-counter as the most important person in the world and you will be surprised at how your relationships will improve. You natu-rally develop an affinity for people who treat you this way. It is easy to feel this and yet very difficult to practice. The gravity of our own planet is sometimes too great to overcome and we have a difficult time breaking free of ourselves. The interesting para-dox is that when we learn to break the bonds of our own gravitational pull to put forth the needs of others, our needs get met far more often. When you are generous with others, they will be generous with you.

The Amazing Power of a Smile

The old adage of never getting a second chance to make a first impression is very true. People will get an impression of you initially and then later will look for evidence and clues to sup-port their beliefs. Every interaction with others is an opportunity to build a connection and set the stage for what will follow in the remainder of your interaction. One of the most amazing, yet completely underrated, techniques for connecting with people is to smile before you speak and during your conversation.

Practice smiling, I guarantee it will make a difference. A smile at the beginning or end of an encounter sends a positive message to your brain. This physiology affects not only you, but also the person you are interacting with. Have you ever been in a room with people and someone yawns and then everyone starts to yawn? When you smile, you trigger a chemical reaction in your own body causing you to feel slightly euphoric. This also happens to the person you are smiling at with the result being a better connection between you. A genuine smile with good eye contact is the building block to a solid connection and rapport.

In Frankie's time in the hospital we encountered many doctors from new residents to senior attending physicians. Everyone we dealt with communicated a message to us. Some were open and friendly and relaxed us with their body language and demeanor. A few talked to us with their arms crossed or without making eye contact. My wife and I felt distinctly different about those encounters even when the message was good.

Pay attention to your body language and the message you send to people. If someone asked you a yes or no question that you wanted to answer in the affirmative but said yes while you were shaking your head no, what message would be received? There truly is power in a smile. Smiling will produce a tremendous Incremental Advantage in your relationships. A smile tells the other person, "You are important. Your presence here is having an effect on me. I like you." Harvard psychologist and renowned expert, largely credited as the father of psychology in America, William James noted, "The deepest principle in human nature is the craving to be appreciated." If we can enter into every interaction with the intent to make others feel genuinely important, every interaction has a greater probability of working out for our mutual benefit. In keeping with the concept of ICE, the Incremental Cumulative Effect of these encounters builds lasting mutually beneficial relationships.

Life Is Vibration

When present in your life, hate, jealousy, anger, frustration, irritation, disappointment and fear vibrate through your thoughts and emotions. Love, enthusiasm, passion, zeal, excitement, confidence, thankfulness and gratitude also create vibration but at a much higher rate. Napoleon Hill observed, "Thoughts that are mixed with any of the feelings of emotions constitute a 'magnetic' force, which attracts other similar or related thoughts."

Vibration is essential to all life. Your thoughts are accompanied by vibration. If you don't believe this, observe people and see if you can guess their mental state by clues other than what they say. When you are relating well to someone it might be said that you have a good vibe. Vibrations of happiness, positive expectation and success are far different from the vibe of hatred, anger, fear and other destructive emotions.

Modern physics tells us that the matter in the universe is not static or passive, but rather is in a continuous movement in the form of vibration. The rhythms of these movements are determined at the subatomic level. Everything within the scope of the entire universe has vibration and movement. In this world of vibrations, resonance is what links two or more compatible people with similar vibrations.

Law of Resonance

The law of resonance has a tremendous impact on human relations and with how we as individuals relate to our world around us. Resonance has its roots in physics. In acoustics, resonance happens when an elastic body starts to vibrate due to a sound (vibration) produced close to that body. In electromagnetism, two frequencies of identical characteristics would be said to be on the same wavelength. When the two identical frequencies overlay or come together, the ensuing wave is amplified, reaching new levels called points of resonance. Simplified, resonance is like vibration or being on the same wavelength. These phrases are used to describe people of like minds or ideals. The opposite of resonance is dissonance, when the frequencies or vibrations are in opposition.

Assume that you and I are in a room together having a discussion. Between us there are two independent sources of waves, or vibrations, representing our emotions. In this example, there are two main possibilities in our relations. If our emotions and ideas produce waves and vibrations with like frequencies, they would resonate or amplify each other (resonance). If the waves have equal frequencies and are opposite each other, they work against each other creating dissonance or discord.

If you have two guitars tuned exactly the same, place them together and pluck one string, you will produce a sound through the vibration. If you look at the other guitar, you will observe an interesting phenomenon. The corresponding string on the other guitar, which was untouched, will also vibrate, producing a sound similar to that of the first guitar. This is the phenomenon of resonance. The two guitars together create a *resonant system*. If you take a tuning fork for the note of C and strike the fork in the same room as a properly tuned piano, the same amazing thing happens. The same chords of the piano will vibrate or resonate. Like attracts like and positive people tend to attract other positive people and situations. Negative people tend to attract the negative.

Interpersonal Resonance

An outburst of anger between two people is a materialization of the phenomenon of resonance. The angry person creates waves or vibrations of anger, which is transmitted into the person's surroundings creating the same emotion in the receiver. When two people agree on a subject, they are attracted to each other as they resonate. When a group of people are in step, the power of the thoughts and feelings becomes greatly amplified.

If you have ever been to a pep rally or a political or religious event, you have probably experienced this. Terms like synchronicity, coordinated, harmonized, corresponding, matched and analogous all describe this phenomenon. Harmony might well be characterized as positive resonance. Listening to harmony on the radio is soothing and comforting. Discord, like the music used in the movies for suspense or horror, produces an entirely different effect on the body. Discord in this environment is negative resonance. A group or company in harmony is positive whereas the same in discord would be in conflict or disagreement.

This occurrence of resonance can be very well applied to our inner world of thoughts, feelings and emotions as well as how we associate with other people and our surroundings. Our thoughts, emotions, ideas, feelings attract, stir up and intensify each other through resonance. What we think and how we feel dictate our emotions and actions. We are radio towers broadcasting our frequencies to others. With this knowledge, we must be careful what we project.

Your Inner Circle—Getting by Giving

Harmony with others is a key component of developing and enhancing your inner circle. Many people mistakenly believe that success and wealth are achieved at the expense of other people, but this could not be further from the truth. Applying the law of resonance in our lives allows us to bring about an attraction with other like-minded people. The best and most satisfying victories come through serving other people. Serving may be a misunderstood term. Serving others is to meet their needs. As you learn to provide value to others, you will find more value come back to you.

In 1988, I had the privilege of attending a powerful seminar and then briefly meeting Zig Ziglar, a man whose name is synonymous with success and motivation. Zig offered a jewel of wisdom as a centerpiece of success. In the midst of insight and humorous motivational quips, he said something so profound that it would completely change my perception of striving for success. When implemented and applied as an Incremental Advantage in the concept of the ICE, this one practice over time will yield benefits beyond belief. Zig Ziglar's insightful wisdom to unlock the secret of success in human relations: "You can get anything in life you want, if you'll only help enough other people get what they want."

Part V

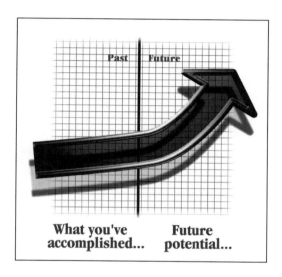

What you've accomplished... **Future potential...**

STAY POSITIVE, STAY FOCUSED

CHAPTER 13

Program Yourself to Create the Attitude of a Champion

. . . .

"What a man thinks of himself that is what determines, or rather indicates his fate."

"I have learned this at least by my experiment: that if one advances confidently in the direction of his dreams, and endeavors to live the life which he has imagined, he will meet with a success unexpected in common hours."
—Henry David Thoreau

. . . .

Much has been written about attitudes and their relationship and correlation to success. In many ways, I believe these truths have gotten lost amidst the clutter of the overwhelming flood of success communication. This repackaging of old ideas, shortcuts and New Age gimmicks becomes a sort of patterned wallpaper subtly hiding the great truths in the design. Have you ever gone to a store filled with signs and communication yet come away without remembering any? In this same way, the fundamental notion that we can set our course by controlling our attitudes is largely missed in all of the clutter.

Although we are born with this amazing supercomputer, the most complex and incredible instrument known in the universe, it does not come with an owner's manual. Success principles are not secrets; they are hiding in plain view. Famed journalist Edward R. Murrow remarked, "The obscure we eventually see. The completely obvious, it seems, takes longer." They are not reserved for the rich or famous, but to everyone who will apply them. We are inborn by our creator with tools to guide us and protect us, and to open the world of abundance to us; if only we will let it. Just as you understand that the law of gravity will place you on your bottom if you violate it, principles of success are laws of nature. Every idea you produce consciously produces subconscious activity to fulfill what was first created in your mind. A farmer choosing what to plant in a field is like the conscious mind. The field itself is the subconscious mind. Whatever the farmer plants, the field grows. The field does not possess a will of its own; it must grow what was planted. It would be ridiculous to think of the farmer planting corn and having beans grow. In the same way your subconscious mind will carry out the actions your conscious mind directs. If the farmer neglects the field and plants nothing, there will still be growth. The growth will be wild and weedy based on whatever was accidentally planted. Over time the field will be out of control with weeds. In the same way our minds if not consciously directed will fill with mental weeds.

Imagine two people equal in most ways. One listens to audiocassettes in the car and reads books to educate and nourish her life. Friendships are uplifting and encouraging. The other listens to the radio and has a steady diet of tabloid and exploitive TV. Friendship is biting, sarcastic and stabbing others in the back.

You probably know people like this and probably relate more to one end of the spectrum. The first life produces fruit whereas the second example is choked with weeds. John Milton, author of *Paradise Lost*, said, "The mind in itself, in its own place, can make a hell out of heaven and a heaven out of hell." In essence, your life will reflect the dominant thoughts you hold in your mind.

"Men ought to know that from the brain and from the brain only, arise our pleasures, joys, laughter and sorrows....Through it, we think, see, hear and distinguish the ugly from the beautiful, the bad from the good, the pleasant from the unpleasant...To consciousness, the brain is messenger."
—Hippocrates

The Power of Your Subconscious Mind

Many people unwittingly program themselves to fail by not understanding the nature and workings of the human mind. Your subconscious is your success mechanism or servomechanism, or it can be programmed to be your failure mechanism. When your subconscious mind processes and accepts an idea it goes about immediately working toward those ends. Whatever you focus on will come about because of this programming. There are several key natural laws that are the underpinnings of explaining why the human brain and the subconscious operate the way they do. For all the amazing things we know and understand about the working and the capacity of our brains, we have yet to scratch the surface. There are several key natural laws that are important to discuss and revisit. These laws are natural laws of the universe with a basis in science and physics. It is not necessary to fully understand them to apply them any more than you need to understand the law of gravity to fall off a ladder.

Natural Laws as Applied to Your Supercomputer

There are natural laws governing our universe applying to everything, everywhere, all the time within our universe. These laws allow the universe to function in an orderly fashion. Through study and application we can lead more successful and productive lives. Successful people have an intuitive understanding of these natural laws as they apply them consistently in their lives.

These laws and their inner workings may or may not be consciously understood by the individual. Either way, it is the application that is at the center.

Law of Attraction

Like attracts like. Whatever you focus on will be drawn to you. Subconsciously, you magnetize the conditions you seek. Most of the time, you attract what you seek by default rather than by choice. Many times we react to our day by shifting focus to problems needing to be solved or issues that crop up. In taking this action, we actually create more problems and more opportunity to attract what we don't want. You are a human magnet attracting the image of what you think about. If you focus on lack and scarcity, you subconsciously attract more lack and scarcity. The opposite is also true. Proverbs 23:7 says, "As a man thinks in his heart, so is he." Everything regarding the law of attraction is about what we choose to focus on and where we keep our dominant thoughts and desires.

Law of Expectancy

The famous author John Steinbeck wrote, "It is the nature of man to rise to greatness if greatness is expected of him." The law of expectancy says in essence that what we prepare for we receive. Sometimes this works against us if we are not careful despite our best intentions. Fear and worry about getting sick sometimes brings it about as it was expected. The subconscious cannot tell the difference between what is real and what is vividly imagined with emotional intensity. People worrying about poverty and lack of money subconsciously program their subconscious to magnetize the conditions they seek. As expected, money issues and struggles seem to creep up.

You are probably aware of the phenomenon known as a "self-fulfilling prophecy." This is the misapplied or unintentional violation of the law of expectancy. Sometimes people with good intentions open themselves up by sending out the invitation to bring about what is not wanted, but is nonetheless expected.

Many superstitions come about from negative expectancy. A black cat, a broken mirror, walking under a ladder or any number of initial events happen to someone. The person harbors fears coming from the events and implants a negative expectation. Insignificant occurrences innocently happen and are attributed to the event further cementing the expectation. Things don't go the person's way and that is attributed to the initial event further rooting the negative expectation into the subconscious. The negative cycle continues, further taking hold and producing a deeper belief and more negative results.

Expectations lead to outcomes. If I like you and my expectation is you will like me in return, you are more inclined to like me. Certainly in our world there are those whose conditions and opportunities are so lacking and void of choices that they are true victims. Yet contrast this with those of us living in North America where even in the direst of situations there is opportunity. What a misfortune so many people in the civilized world are impoverished in a land of plenty. They starve at the buffet table. What are your expectations?

Law of Correspondence

The law of correspondence might also be called the law of the mirror. Whatever we feel or believe within is reflected to our outside conditions. Your outer world is a mirror reflecting back to you whatever is happening in your inner world. Everything happening inside corresponds to something happening on the outside. In relationships, our outward relationships will mirror back, or reflect, the kind of person you are on the inside. Whatever emotions are deep-seated will find corresponding outward attributes reflected in our relationships with others.

Your Subconscious— A Laser-Guided Servomechanism

In early 1990, prior to the Gulf War, I had the remarkable leadership experience to attend my Armor Officer Basic Course at Fort Knox, Kentucky. I was then a young first lieutenant training for six intensive months in all facets of military leadership. This training was available to me after earning my commission with two years in Army ROTC while at college. In addition to comprehensive leadership, basic and advanced military skills and small unit tactics, I was given a unique opportunity. I was trained and provided the chance to learn on what would later that same year prove to be the star of Desert Storm, the incredible M1A1 Abrams Battle Tank.

The M1A1 Abrams was a marvel of modern technology. One of the experiences that stuck with me more than anything was learning about and observing the stabilized gun mount and the ballistic fire control computer with laser tracking. Once the laser was sighted, the long turret remained completely fixed on the target regardless of the movement of the tank. Even though the tank would move up and down and sideways and be bumped in every body-jarring way imaginable, the long turret remained 100 percent immovably focused and locked on target.

Here is a physical example of what I mean: Extend your arm with your pointer finger extended and fix the point directly on a target. Your arm should stay rigid and straight pointing directly to your intended target. Now swivel your body to the left and right or duck down and rise up without taking your pointer finger off your target. That is exactly what it was like with the turret of the M1A1 locked on and pointing to its target. Many unfortunate Iraqi tanks would soon learn the lesson the hard way; once sighted and locked on, the outcome will be "steel on target!"

Another easier example is one I learned from my four-year-old daughter Rachel. One day she was looking at herself in the mirror and turning her head left to right and up and down. She exclaimed, "Look, Daddy, my eyes don't move when my head does!"

Rachel discovered the same principle used in the M1A1 and in fighter jets to create a "lock on the target." Next time you look at a mirror try this for yourself. Turn your head different angles and notice how your eyes don't move as they are locked on target. This is also an example of how your subconscious locks on to a target of whatever is firmly held in the mind.

Winners concentrate and put laser focus on activities that, as Brian Tracy observes, are goal achieving rather than tension relieving. A purpose or compelling goal is like an engine that powers your life. Clearly defined and written goals are the most effective tool for directing both our conscious and subconscious brain in what to focus on. Achievement in life comes from the incremental actions applied over time. We can either move about blindly waiting to see where we end up or we can plot a course with the shortest path possible. Your mind is a supercomputer, but it needs input.

Servomechanism

A servomechanism is an engineering term for an automatic operating device to regulate a system or machine's variables. It can control large power output and all variables contained within through a small power input device for maintaining the correct and specified operating conditions in the mechanism. Have I confused you? In essence, a servomechanism is merely a type of feedback control system. In simplest terms, it is a device's autopilot. Servomechanisms are used for the control systems engines, guided missiles, aircrafts, bombs, manufacturing machinery, industrial equipment, battle tanks and nearly every piece of complex equipment to direct, control, coordinate all of the sophisticated and numerous subsystems at work within the system.

As the law of attraction relates, what you spend a lot of time thinking about, either positive or negative, becomes attracted to you. Your subconscious computer does what it is instructed. When you fear something and keep it constantly in your mind you begin to manifest it into your life. What you think about and dwell on with emotional intensity will be created by your mind. It really is the essence of the term self-fulfilling prophesy. Inadvertently or by conscious choice, our brains—as instructed and programmed by us—create the conditions to bring about what we seek. Be careful what you think about.

Your servomechanism will allow you a direct path to your objective. Picture a river in all of its meandering. If you ever get the opportunity, study the great Mississippi River from its point of origin to the mouth at the Gulf of Mexico. In many cases the meandering river winds back on itself. To me this could be a representation of life—long, lazy and winding. For some people, this is all they aspire to do. If the great river were more direct from start to finish, it might cut the true length of the river in half. When you are not directed, your life is long and meandering without purpose and sometimes without direction. When you can direct your path, you may still find yourself off target at times. Small, clear course changes redirect your activity. Your focus brings you to a more express path to your goal. Employing your subconscious as a servomechanism allows your brain to set your target and then use the reticular activating system to pull it all together.

Reticular Activating System

The reticular activating is another extremely complex part of your servomechanism. The term "reticular" means network. At the most base level, the reticular activating system is the part of the brain that turns consciousness on and off. It allows you to sleep, shut down, refresh and reawaken in the morning. As your servomechanism controls all of the various systems in a coordinated effort, your reticular activating system is the filter and the order giver to direct the servomechanism. In a tank crew, there are four soldiers with four distinct jobs and responsibilities. There is the driver, the loader, the gunner and the tank commander.

In an M1A1 Abrams battle tank, the gunner would be the servomechanism, ensuring everything works together to keep the turret pointed directly on target at all times. The reticular activating system would be the tank commander who takes in information, makes the decisions and issues commands to the gunner. Everyone in the tank takes their direction from the tank commander. The ammunition to be loaded, the movement of the tank, the decision of target acquisition and ultimately firing are all done at the command of the tank commander. The gunner acquires the target but does not fire until the command is given.

The reticular activating system activates, or turns on, areas of the brain in the cerebrum for thinking as well as emotion. There are several thousands of neurons interspersed throughout a large portion of the brain. Your brain is assaulted by thousands of messages each second. Everything you see, hear, smell, feel and touch is a message entering your brain. The reticular activating system filters through all the messages received. After filtering and categorizing, it decides which ones will get access to the conscious part of the brain. In other words, the reticular activating system will pass on anything remotely related to the important issue if directed from the conscious brain.

Applying this practically means that, if you want to achieve a goal or need to solve a particular problem, it needs to be firmly implanted into your subconscious mind. As you think about your issue, talk about it, write about it, affirm it, imagine it completed and ask positive outcome questions related to it, your reticular activating system goes to work. It acts like a giant search engine looking for results and information for you. The more you take action to consciously employ your reticular activating system, the wider and deeper and more active the search becomes. This is one of the reasons written goals, visualization, affirmations and questions work. This is also why it is very important to frequently review your goals.

You and I have a conscious mind that takes in sensory information and allows us to make conscious decisions regarding this information. We also have a subconscious component of our brain constantly taking in information then filtering, processing and sorting. When we are clear and direct about our focus, the subconscious is able to take an active part in assisting us to complete our journey.

Have you ever gone car shopping and decided on a certain make and model of vehicle? Later, you probably had the experience of seeing many more of those vehicles than you did previously. Actually, the more likely scenario is that there were the same number before as after. This time your subconscious mind was tuned into what you had a specific desire for. This happens all of the time without your even realizing it. When your mind can focus on a clear target, your subconscious will assist you by allowing you to notice things otherwise unnoticed or assist you to take action where before there was inactivity. The energy of our lives needs to be focused on outcomes of our design or we squander our potential. Like a high performance race car stuck in second gear, you and I were not designed to merely go through life reacting to the situations we are placed in.

Our life is not meant to be some cosmic sitcom where we have to get ourselves out of contrived messes; we are the writer and director. We have more control than we sometimes allow ourselves and we have far more tools at our disposal to make what we want to happen come about. It is all about programming and you are the programmer!

Programming Your Supercomputer

Many years back, Eastern European scientists performed an experiment in which a criminal slated to be executed was placed on a table with a small incision made in an area he could not see. A small amount of water streamed over the incision and trickled into a bucket. The prisoner had the sensation of bleeding to death as the flow of the water mimicked his blood and the bucket collecting the water created thoughts of massive blood loss. During the procedure, the scientists talked among themselves about the progress of the patient's "bleeding out." Within a short time, the man with no real blood loss died on the table, suffering all the symptoms of bleeding to death. His life was ended because his subconscious mind created a reality based on wrong information.

Here is an experiment not nearly as violent, but just as potent. Right now I want you to notice that you have an itch on your head. Don't scratch. It is really bugging you now, but don't scratch the annoying persistent itch on your head. I know you now have an irresistible urge to scratch, but don't. You may not do it right this instant, but I can assure you that at some time within the next hour your subconscious will cause you to scratch your head. You are probably doing it right now and oh, by the way, you have just been hypnotized.

The basis of hypnosis is autosuggestion. It is a way of activating a process that works for you below the conscious level. Hypnosis is much less glamorous than TV portrays. In truth, it happens all the time. With a little effort and some practice, you can easily harness the massive power of your conscious and subconscious brain to work for you rather than against you. There are many techniques and methods in the marketplace designed to assist you in programming or reprogramming your subconscious mind. Subliminal tapes, self-hypnosis, NLP, flashing lights, biofeedback, autosuggestion, visualization, sound generators, mind control and many other techniques are available. Some techniques are more effective than others, and some have never been proven to be effective beyond the still potent placebo effect. The interesting fact is, you currently use three of the most powerful mind programming techniques and are probably not even aware you are doing it. The three techniques you currently engage in are *visualization*, *affirmations* and *questions to yourself*.

Unfortunately most people are negative and conditioned to have self-limiting beliefs and attitudes and will never learn to rise above their circumstances. Most people affirm what they don't like about themselves, visualize negative events and outcomes in their lives and ask themselves the wrong questions. With all that has been learned and proved in the recent past, what a tremendous shame people will chose not to learn to harness the power of their minds. As a consequence, they will largely give up control over their lives.

The mind is a tremendous computer, far more advanced than any computer on earth today. Don't ask for success and then act as if you are preparing to fail. This immediately short-circuits your opportunities and you subconsciously set your course for failure. You cannot completely control your subconscious as it processes everything it observes. You can, however, create plans and desires and work to consciously direct your subconscious mind. The purpose of this is to assist you in harnessing the most powerful tool in the known universe, reprogramming your sub-conscious to work for you as your success autopilot. The subconscious mind is thought to be over a hundred times more powerful than the conscious mind, yet the programming of the subconscious is left up to random images and what the TV advertisers want you to believe.

The subconscious mind is a supercomputer that will allow programming. This programming can be good or bad, positive or negative. It is what you chose. This programming can be done consciously, but I must warn you that it is also happening sub-consciously all the time. Think of what you put into your mind in the last 24 hours. What was good and what was bad? Did you nurture your programming with positive and affirming messages or did you allow negative programming in. We are bombarded with gossip, trash TV, negative news, negative people, problem-oriented conversations and negative self-talk. If you think and dwell on the negative, you will seek and you will reap negative results. If you think and dwell on the positive you will find positive results.

This is the law of attraction and the law of correspondence at work. It is the law of sowing and reaping. Farmers don't plant corn and then expect beans to grow. Most people understand this but fail to take it all the way to conclusion. They try to think positive and then when a negative result or situation happens they think the process is a failure. If you think and dwell on the positive, you may still very well have negative conditions or cir-cumstances come your way. If you use the tools of optimism, you will see seeds of benefit and opportunity even in the nega-tive and learn to reap the positive.

"The greatest discovery of my generation is that human be-ings can alter their lives by altering their attitudes of mind."
—William James

Four Highest Leverage Incremental Advantage Mental Programming Techniques

There are many ways to attempt to reprogram our supercomputer; however, in all my research and in my personal life experience, I have found these four to be by far the most effective and the easiest, most cost effective way to create an immediate change in the focus, direction and control of our conscious and subconscious mind. It makes no sense in life to put forth tremendous effort consciously only to take away advantage and sabotage what you have worked for. Without conscious programming, reinforcement and a strong filtration system, your subconscious mind will fill with negativity, self-doubt and any number of emotions counterproductive to the person you consciously want to be.

You certainly have the opportunity to abdicate this responsibility and go on your merry way in this life allowing fate and circumstances to dictate your life's outcomes. Or, you can take control of your life by learning how to direct your thoughts and your underlying belief structure to make your life work intentionally rather than by luck of the draw. These four techniques are based in science and natural laws. They have been proven effective by thousands of people over time. They have been practiced and used in many cases long before they were understood. The four Incremental Advantage mental programming techniques are:

1. Clearly defined and written goals
2. Visualization
3. Affirmations
4. Positive questions

Whatever you can indelibly impress on your subconscious mind through written goals, visualization, affirming self-talk and asking the right questions will manifest itself into your present reality. Reality imagined equals reality achieved. If your present reality is not what you desire, it probably will not change until you can reprogram your thoughts and reset your thermostat. The reality is: a mind not directed is a mind off course.

Clearly defined written goals, visualized, practiced and experienced in the theater of the mind, supported with affirmations to cement the image and the reality create a clear instruction for the subconscious to act upon. Positive questions allow us to reflect on our situation and get feedback to our subconscious for positive course correction input throughout the journey. It is all very straightforward. Employing these techniques as daily success habits and implanting success consciousness, in essence allows you to put your brain on autopilot. Your laser-guided servomechanism takes over and steers you to your intended target. At the core of all of our thinking is our belief structure. Our belief system is our thermostat and will affect all of the conditions in our life to maintain whatever setting is put in. All four of these techniques go immediately to work at the belief level as this is the thermostat setting. Their goal is to allow you the control to permanently reset your thermostat or belief structure, from which everything else will come.

Mental Programming Technique 1— Clearly Defined and Written Goals

Without clearly defined and written goals, you have no target to shoot for. The most sophisticated and technologically advanced tank or fighter jet (which, by the way, are less sophisticated and advanced than your brain) cannot be successful with its weapons system if there is no target. This seems so basic, yet why do so many people start their day without really knowing what their overriding objective is? Right now, do you know what your goal is and why you are taking the action you are taking? Of course, many people have broad stroke goals of "taking care of my family," "building for my future," "trying to be happy" and many other similar yet unfocused and unspecific targets.

With a firm target in mind first, you can then begin to take directed action toward that target. When you have a clearly defined goal, you can enlist the help of nature through the law of attraction, resonance, correspondence, expectation, etc. Imagine asking a friend for directions. Being your friend, they enthusiastically reply, "Certainly, I would be glad to help, where are you going?" Without a clearly defined written goal, your answer is, "I don't know, but I think I will know when I get there." This, of course, is ridiculous, except it happens in probably better than 95 percent of the population every single day.

Having your goal in mind is the first critical step. The next part is writing it down. Why is this so important? First, writing it down helps to provide clarity. Your mind sees the goal and the physical act of writing creates a subtle kinesthetic response. When you write your goals down and continue the processes, it provides spaced repetition to further activate your sometimes dormant reticular activating system with regard to your objective.

Having a target to focus on makes a tremendous difference. Here is an experiment: Stand up and put your arm straight in front of you with your index finger pointing out. Now keep your feet planted, rotate your body absolutely as far as you can and take mental note at what you are pointing to. Repeat this experiment but now consciously set new a target slightly further than your previous target. Isn't it amazing that you thought you went as far as you could the first time but you easily exceeded your mark when you had a clear-cut objective?

Another experiment would be to simply hold your breath as long as you can. Note your result. Now set a goal to exceed your result by 10 percent. With the new specific target in your mind, you can easily surpass your first result. These are certainly very simple illustrations to prove you can achieve more when you have a target in mind. After you read through these examples and the element of surprise is gone, try them on someone else to see the natural improvement in simply having a new target.

Mental Programming
Technique 2—Visualization

*"Losers visualize the penalties of failure. Winners visualize
the rewards of success."*
—Dr. Rob Gilbert

Running through giving a speech or flying an airplane or
skiing down a mountain can all be safely practiced without the
risk of embarrassment or physical injury. Your mind is a safe
place to practice success before your have to try to perform
success. Could you imagine getting a 1,000-piece jigsaw puzzle
dumped out in front of you without the aid of the picture on
the box? It may not be impossible, but the effort would be far
more difficult than if you had the outcome in mind as you put
together the pieces. Most people suffer from the same common
malady. They don't know what they want so they can't visualize
it. The technique of visualization and mental rehearsal is more
widely practiced than is publicized. Olympic athletes have been
using it as an Incremental Advantage slight edge tool for decades. The top 1 percent of salespeople and earners in America
relate it as a key skill to their success.

In our imagination, what we think about with intensity we
are drawn to and can become. What we have thought or been
taught to think in the past has made us what we are and gotten
us to where we are (Incremental Cumulative Effect). If we want
to be somebody different than who we are today or achieve a
different result than what we have today, we must learn to change
our thinking. Doing this redirects our future Incremental Cumulative Effect. Visualization is imagining what can be.
Visualization is the theater of your mind; it is a mental rehearsal.
When you daydream, you visualize without purpose or direction. Your subconscious is on a random journey indirectly moving
from one tangent thought to another. Visualization is your imagination at work.

How do you visualize? Try to picture a blue triangle inside a red square. Can you do it? If you can, you just visualized or created a mental image in your brain. It is very simple although it takes discipline and continued practice. Visualization is imagining, imaging, creating mental pictures or movies; it is about actively seeing in your mind what you want to happen. If I asked you to write a number down on paper, before you actually write the number, you most likely will hold the number in your mind. If I asked you to draw a picture of a symbol, you would first imagine it before you could draw it. If you want to achieve a goal, you need to learn to first see it clearly in your mind before you know how to obtain it.

We are not necessarily responsible for every thought jumping around in our brain. Instead, we are responsible for the thoughts we place, hold and reinforce there. Instead of allowing advertisers and mainstream society to plant seeds in your brain, why not take control and plant your own "dream crop" of positive visions. Create and focus on the positive outcomes you desire and over time the law of attraction will work in your favor. Avoid negative thoughts. Don't think or dwell about what you don't want or you will be like the Biblical Job from the Old Testament who said, "What I have feared has now come upon me." It is your imagination; you should always win and reign as the victor! The mind is like rich farmland capable of growing abundant crops. If left untended the field will certainly weed over. That said, there is certainly no reason to plant the weeds!

Visualization is not a gimmick or a New Age technique. It is simply thinking about and using your imagination to work out the situation in your mind before you do it. If you visualize yourself going to the store, you can run a mental movie or picture and vividly see yourself doing this in the future as you have done in the past. Daydreaming is a stream of conscious form of visualization going from one random thought to another. Worry, however, is the misuse of imagination. It is negative visualization—or visualization gone bad.

Research has proven that the subconscious mind cannot tell the difference between a real event and one that is vividly imagined. One famous study used two groups of basketball players to determine if visualization as a tool could boost performance. Both groups had a baseline determined, then one practiced over a set period of time while the second did not touch a basketball, but mentally practiced shooting and making free throws. Not only did the group that used visualization improve over their baseline, they improved more than the group that practiced. This is no secret and nothing new. In the past 50 years, Olympic athletes and collegiate and professional athletes have been using and developing new strategies to better harness the proven power of positive visualization.

Mental Programming Technique 3—Affirmations

We need to find a way to control our thoughts to keep them as allies rather than adversaries. In her book, *The Secret Door to Success*, the late Florence Scovel Shinn talks about having a watchman at the gate of our thoughts. Her assertion is that we have the power to choose our thoughts. She uses an analogy of a single sheepdog herding frightened sheep into a pen through gentle determination: "We cannot always control our thoughts, but we can control our words, and repetition impresses the subconscious, and we are then master of the situation." Although her book was written in the early 1900s, she hits upon a tool that is one of the best and yet underutilized tool for controlling and programming your thoughts: the power of affirmations.

Affirmations as a mental programming technique is an extremely powerful tool, yet one that is scoffed at by many. Affirmations are tremendously misunderstood and very much underutilized. What you may not realize is that you use them all the time although usually not to your benefit. Affirmations are simply statements of intent. You can develop into all that you desire to be based on what you chose to affirm about yourself. You subconscious will create over time with the concept of ICE based on what is programmed and affirmed into it. Mohammad Ali is one of the most widely known and recognized sports figures. Ali is famous for repeating an affirmation he used with great effectiveness to convince not only himself, but also his opponents and the rest of the world: "I am the greatest!" Mohammad Ali's affirmation created his legacy.

Like goals, affirmations work best when they are worded in the present tense as "I am" or "I achieve" type statements. The mind cannot hold a negative. To affirm at the core is to hold true. Affirmations are nothing more than affirming the truth as you wish it to be to instruct your subconscious mind to take action in that direction. It is really very simple. Affirmations help you believe in your dreams and what you wish to be. Belief is essential to convincing your subconscious to act the direction you want to go. Your dream must be vivid and real, compelling to your servomechanism. Affirmations are like exercise: You will not see results immediately. You create a habit that over time helps you build strength in yourself and in your beliefs. This ultimately affects your actions, which affect your results. An affirmation in some cases might be a lie at present, but you are in a sense trying to convince your subconscious that it can be true to make it a reality in the future.

> "To affirm anything is to state that it is so, and to maintain this as being true in the face of all evidence to the contrary. Repeating an affirmation is leading the mind to that state of consciousness where it accepts that which it wishes to believe."
>
> **—Ernest Holmes**

Sometimes we inadvertently affirm and reinforce old established beliefs: "I am so stupid." "I'm going to lose this account." "I always flub this shot." "There is no way I can make this deadline." "I gain weight just smelling chocolate." "I need a drink." "I am a horrible golfer." "I can't speak in public." "I could never write a book." "I am such a pig." "I am such a klutz." "I never win." "I'm not smart enough to do that." "I could never do something like that." "I am such an idiot sometimes." "I would lose my head if it were not attached."

Have you ever said things like this to yourself? Or worse, to others about yourself? Of course you have, we all have. This kind of talk while sometimes self-effacing and done for positive effect, can actually have negative consequences. If taken to the extreme and developed into a habit or pattern of self-talk, the message and programming can be damaging. The issue that separates the successful from the unsuccessful is an underlying attitude and belief about oneself. How do you respond to setbacks and adversity? Do you take it in stride, or do you take the glum and negative approach of "this always happens to me, I never catch a break," etc.?

The other choice is to create, affirm and reinforce our desired positive beliefs. This happens all day long and takes hold a little at a time. "This is easy." "I only eat when I am hungry." "I feel great when I exercise." "I know I can drop the pounds when I put my mind to it." "What an awesome day!" "I don't run and hide from problems, I attack." "I feel great!" "My life is really working." "I see a lot of opportunities in this situation."

I have one friend who repeats to herself a daily affirmation of, "I feel healthy, I feel happy, I feel terrific!" Every time I see this person, I can tell it is working. Another friend of mine when asked how she is replies glumly, "I'm here." Which person is progressing faster in her life? Which one has more abundant opportunities "luckily" come her way?

One person constantly affirms, "I am so broke!" Another person consciously thinks daily, "Money flows to me like the water of a raging river!" Both are saying affirmations and communicating with their subconscious. Who do you think will have more luck with Sara (serendipity) regarding money?

In a very real way, negative affirmations are the language of failure and lack whereas positive affirmations are the language of success and improvement. Every time we think and say things like this we're affirming it to ourselves. Each time we bring the reality of what we say a little closer and we believe a little bit more. Long time habits are difficult to break because we inadvertently support them through our thoughts and words. It is like saying yes with your mouth, but nodding your head no. It is incongruent and takes away from your efforts. You are affirming your beliefs every day through the thoughts you are thinking and the words you say.

When you learn to change and direct your internal communication your life will reflect the change (law of correspondence). Creating affirmations can change your beliefs and change the course of your life. In order to be effective, your positive declarations should embody most or all of the following characteristics:

1. Personal (usually a statement beginning with "I")
2. Positive (the mind cannot hold a picture of a negative)
3. Present tense (the time is now)
4. Short (easy to remember and apply)
5. Specific (a specific target allows for a specific course of action and the most direct route)
6. Emotionally intense (necessary to break through the clutter of the thousands of thoughts and images you are bombarded with on a daily basis)

The objective is to embed a positive goal into the subconscious to allow it to do the yeoman's work. The only real obstacle is convincing your subconscious that you are serious and committed and that you truly have a burning desire for what you want. Long-term change will only happen when there is congruency between who you think you are, how you act and behave and the choices you make.

Affirmations Are a Catalyst for Success

Positive affirmations mixed with emotional intensity produce amazing results. Music is an amazing mood catalyst. To really get the most out of affirmations and create an incredible Incremental Advantage in their effectiveness in your life, I suggest recording your affirmations to inspiring music. A good friend of mine challenged me to do just this 10 years ago. I purchased an inexpensive karaoke machine, put an upbeat instrumental tape in and recorded all of the affirmations I could create to change behaviors and support my goals.

I literally wore my first tape out listening to it, but it created significant leverage and results for me. I know the vast majority reading this will not make the commitment to this habit. It is a shame, but for those of you who do, I promise results in every area of your life. I constantly look for, borrow, adapt and write down affirmations. I cannot claim originality for all of them as they have been collected and changed over the years. Below is a sampling of some personal affirmations. Say them aloud with emotion and notice the immediate physical effect they have on you. Sure, it feels uncomfortable, but remember about uncomfortable methods to achieve comfortable results.

- I acknowledge *no limits* on my abilities and my ultimate success.
- I turn challenges into opportunities. I am creative and adaptable to any situation and make the best of whatever comes my way.
- I seek out new opportunities to learn and to grow.
- I look for opportunities to serve and increase my value to other people.
- I see people not how they are, but rather, as they can become. I work to help them unlock their hidden potential. I am a developer of people.
- I enter into every activity with success in mind and give no mental recognition to the possibility of defeat.
- I expect challenges and obstacles and am prepared mentally to grow from each challenge before me. Every challenge I overcome makes me stronger.
- I am flexible and adaptable in every situation. I look for creative alternatives and seek out new ways of accomplishing my goals.
- Organized activity and maintained enthusiasm are the wellsprings of my power.
- I have all the money I need to accomplish my greatest destiny.

- I am physically fit and vibrant filled with energy and positive enthusiasm.
- I am worthy and achieve all I set out to accomplish because I have a passion for my life and am dedicated to the attainment of my goals and objectives.
- I love myself and I love others. I am the person I choose to be and others love and respect me for who I am.
- I have singleness of purpose in my life and am dedicated to the achievement of my dreams and goals.
- I love my family and work every day to show and demonstrate my love.
- I value my relationships with others and seek out only positive and affirming relationships.
- I magnetize the conditions that I seek. Like calls to like. Water seeks its own level. I am positive and draw other positive people into my life.
- Organized activity and maintained enthusiasm are the wellsprings of my power.
- I am prepared for great achievement. I have worked hard and allow victories to come my way.
- I love to learn. Leaders are readers! Reading stimulates my creativity and my hunger for knowledge.

Mental Programming Technique 4— Positive Questions

Most people ask themselves the wrong question, which produces a negative subconscious effect. You can learn to program your supercomputer brain by learning to ask yourself the right questions. The key is to ask yourself solution-based, positive and empowering questions rather than negative, disempowered, problematic questions. In the past, you may have asked questions like the following: "Why am I so fat?" "Why is my life such a failure?" "Why do bad things always happen to me?" "Why am I so stupid?" These questions and others like them take a terrible toll on you. They start with a negative assumption, stated as fact with the question supporting the wrong conclusion.

If you ask yourself, "Why is my life in the crapper?" any answer you provide supports a negative assumption. This is worse than any attorney taking a person down the path to prove the lawyer's point. Next time you find yourself doing this, interrupt yourself with the quip, "Objection, your honor; leading the witness!"

Improving your condition comes through asking yourself better questions. This allows creative inspiration to work through your subconscious to bring about or magnetize the conditions you seek. You not only have the ability, but also all the resources necessary to learn anything you need to learn to fulfill any ambition or achieve any goal you desire. The goal for your questions to yourself in any situation should be outcome- or solution-based. The assumption is that there is an issue that needs to be fixed. Rather than what was presented above, look at an approach leading to an action conclusion. "What do I need to change about my habits to get to my fitness goal?" "What do I want to do with my life that gives me meaning and satisfaction?" "What do I need to do differently to change this string of results?" "What can I learn and apply from this?" "What is affecting my mood that makes me feel my life is not going in the right direction?"

Tony Robbins asserts, "Questions provide the key to unlocking our unlimited potential." Probably the single best question you can begin to ask yourself in any situation is, "What outcome do I want from this event/situation?" You may certainly wish to adapt this slightly, but when you go into a situation, whether it is a business meeting or negotiation or class, knowing your desired outcome is vital. As I began to work on this habit in earnest for myself, I was simply amazed at how many actions I took and how many activities I worked on without asking this clearly up front.

I need to research a better mortgage for my house. What is my ideal outcome? Is it lower payments, less interest over time, more house for my money, flexibility? Without knowing the right question, the answers don't help much. What outcome do

I desire for my relationship with my spouse and children? Do I know and plan or just let it happen?

We have the power through understanding and training of our subconscious minds to plant the seeds and affirm health, security, happiness, abundance. We also have the opportunity to allow society's programming to plant the seeds of lack, insecurity, fear, doubt and negativity. I am not speaking about deep hypnosis or anything out of the ordinary. It takes practice to keep your mind free from worry and insecurity. It takes dedication to constantly feed your mind new information and positive stimuli that will provide positive associations. It takes vigilance to associate with positive people and positive influences. Make sure your questions ask for what you want, not what you don't want.

The Power of Belief

James Allen, the author of *As a Man Thinketh*, observed, "Belief is the basis of all action, and, this being so, the belief that dominates the hearts or mind is shown in the life." There is a hierarchy we hold in our mind of our beliefs about ourselves. This belief structure controls our identity, which controls our self-directed prophesy through our actions resulting from the previous. Again, our belief structure is our thermostat. We are who we define ourselves to be. If I see myself as an overweight person with no control, my actions and habits reflect this programming to bring about that result. If, instead, I see myself as a fit person in control, my eating habits and exercise activity over time bring about that reality.

We should be involved in a conscious process to determine how we want to define ourselves. Unfortunately, many times the subconscious mind holds programming created by events or circumstances in our life that we have handed control over to. If you were fat as a kid and are still struggling with your weight, you are fighting programming from your childhood. If you have an event in your life where you were embarrassed, chances are programming has carried forward into your feelings and your success in that area of your life today.

We need to create a filtration system for events. Reprogram your old out-of-date operating system. Create new targets in the form of clearly written goals. Affirmations, visualization and better quality questions are the easiest ways to begin to alter your belief system. This is why visualization (vivid and detailed), positive self-talk and supporting and affirming questions are critical to the success of reprogramming our subconscious and changing our mental thermostat.

A scrawny 12-year-old named Milt dreamed of being a world-class athlete. "My junior high coach told me that if I was willing, I could be a good athlete. But that wasn't good enough for me. I told everyone I was going to be the greatest athlete in the world. That became my dream. My family shook their heads in disbelief. Others laughed at me. I didn't care. I knew what the prize was going to be and I was out to get it." World-class athlete? Greatest in the world? Hardly! Scrawny and weak, Milt would be the last person anyone would believe could even make it to the Olympics let alone win the gold medal. No one believed he could do it save one: Milt Campbell.

Milt not only developed himself into a world-class athlete, he competed and won the silver medal in the 1952 Olympic decathlon. In 1956, Milt Campbell won the gold medal in the decathlon. Milt not only realized his Olympic dream, but he earned All-American honors in swimming, a national championship in hurdles, became a professional football player and later was inducted into an amazing 10 different halls of fame. Milt Campbell started out a very unlikely athletic hero, but he followed his dream and employed all of the techniques to program his mind to create what he wanted to be. His efforts and dedication allowed him to transform himself from ordinary to extraordinary.

I had the rare privilege and pleasure several years back to introduce Milt Campbell's stirring presentation: "Good. Better. Best! Never let it rest, until your good is better and your better is best!" This was Milt's main affirmation he used to transform himself into a gold medal Olympian. His transformation happened in his mind first. After Milt conditioned and reprogrammed his mind he created a system of belief surrounded in massive sustained action and carried through with relentless practice and determination. As his mind created the programming, his body followed.

Daily Programming

Programming your supercomputer is your job and yours alone. Like the previous example of Olympic champion Milt Campbell, you can program yourself for the attitude of a champion. Write down your goals. Define them. Affirm and visualize them with emotional intensity. Positively question them and your desired outcome. You are the owner of an amazing asset. It did not come with an owner's manual, but these techniques and methods when applied will allow you a significant advantage and leverage for your dreams.

Use the concepts and use them together to achieve a force multiplier effect. The success you have with one technique can be leveraged and reinvested into success in other areas. Your current beliefs, attitudes, actions and results did not happen overnight. They were solidified over time. To break free of these entrenched beliefs, you must approach them as a battle. Throw everything you can at them. Allow the principles to work together in synergy to change your future results to what you ardently desire, who you choose to be and where you choose to go.

"Self image sets the boundaries of individual accomplishment."
—Maxwell Maltz

CHAPTER 14

Destroy the Cancer of Success—Negativity and Unfocused Activity

· ·

"Sow a thought and you reap an act; Sow an act and you reap a habit; Sow a habit and you reap a character; Sow a character and you reap a destiny."
—Samuel Smiles

· ·

What I Learned About Cancer...

This chapter was titled before my son was diagnosed with leukemia, a cancer of the blood and bone marrow. I wrestled with keeping or changing the title that hit a little too close to home. After careful consideration, I decided to let it remain as an apt metaphor describing the combination affliction that is equally destructive to people's lives.

There are many types of cancer, but quite simply, cancer is a mutation of a cell that rapidly multiplies. These are mutated and bad cells unable to perform the function of healthy cells. These bad cells end up crowding out, pushing aside and destroying good cells. Without treatment, cancer cells grow and spread. If not eradicated, cancer will eventually cause death.

Cancer is not usually the direct cause of death, but rather the instigator. Depending on the type, cancer can kill healthy organs or will shut down systems vital to life. In my father's case, the cancer stopped his immune system from working. He eventually died of a simple cold with which his body's natural immune system could no longer fight.

Cancers of Success

It may appear melodramatic to classify negativity and unfocused activity as cancers to success. But these two negative traits, above all others, if not eradicated, will be like a cancer in your life, destroying good things, good relationships and good opportunities. Can you name five successful people you know of or know personally who are negative in their attitude and wander through life without purpose? Can you name a couple? You might possibly be able to name one as the exception to prove the rule, but chances are you will not be able to think of anyone who has attained (not inherited) any measure of success while possessing a negative disposition and aimlessness in their activity. Why is it so prevalent today for people to be self-sabotaged?

Attitude—The "Kingpin"

In the logging camps of the great northwest, thousands of logs are sent down river in the spring. When the logs get too bunched up some get turned crossways causing a jam. To get things moving again, the loggers look for the main log that is causing the problem to straighten it out and get all the logs floating downriver again. The problem-causing log is referred to as the "kingpin." Do you have a kingpin negative emotion or attitude that is jamming up your life?

When you find a way to release negative attitudes and straighten out your kingpin log of negative emotion, your other positive logs can once again move downstream to their destination. For many people, there is an event or series of events keeping them bound to the past.

The Earned Baggage Theory

It is important to treat your mistakes as necessary lessons to be learned, to understand that each lesson brings with it an opportunity for a certain amount of wisdom to be applied to the next situation. Many people can never achieve the success they dream of because they will not or cannot leave their past behind. They refuse to tear down the monuments they've built to their old troubles and hurts. Most people have a difficult time accepting personal responsibility because of anger with others.

I had a very good friend when I was younger who could not get on with her life because of resentment of people and events in her life. Her parents were tragically killed in an accident. Her husband divorced her leaving her with two small children to raise alone. She had challenges in her job and in her relationships with others. She was a great person who at that time could simply not let go of the injustice done by others and by fate. She unintentionally stilted her future by holding onto the past too tightly. She had simply been through too much to let it go. One of the sayings of Buddha is a good descriptive. "Holding on to anger is like grasping a hot coal with the intent of throwing it at someone else; you are the one who gets burned." Please do not misunderstand. Her personal responsibility was not necessarily in the events outside her control. Her personal responsibility was in letting go of the past and things outside her control to grasp firmly on the future. Her responsibility was to look for opportunities to improve from where she was at that point and go forward.

It is said that monkey traps in Africa work based on the premise similar to the earned baggage theory. Monkey traps basically allow a monkey to slide its hand into a container holding a large piece of fruit. The monkey sticks its hand in and grabs the fruit, which then makes the monkey's hand too large to fit through the opening. To obtain freedom, all the monkey would have to do is let go and remove its hand. Instead, the monkey will hold onto the fruit and will not release it even to avoid capture. This is very similar to those who have invested a great deal into their situation (even a bad one) and refuse to let go. In essence, what is being said is, "It is mine, I earned it and I am not about to let it go. Do you realize how much I have been through?"

The negativity we hold from our past binds us to that past. In order to move beyond the baggage we carry, we must find a way to forgive others and more importantly to forgive ourselves.

The Practice of Forgiveness

Have you ever noticed a large rock in the middle of a stream of moving water? The rock stays firm while thousands of gallons of water flow past it. The water's direction is changed by the placement of the rock and not the reverse. Forgiveness is like being like the rock allowing the current to move past. When someone wrongs or hurts you, the natural inclination is to harbor negative feelings. Hatred, bitterness, rage, hurt, revenge—all are cancer to your system. If allowed to grow they will mutate and multiply, negatively affecting everything else. When these emotions take hold and become an increasing presence in your life they close off opportunities and harm healthy relationships.

All relationships involve more than one person, as does any breakdown of a relationship. If someone has hurt you, take the first step—don't wait for the other person. If you've offended someone, take responsibility. Forgive yourself first and allow yourself the ability to grow and right any wrongs or correct any slights. Ask for forgiveness and seek reconciliation. Even if your attempt is rebuffed or your relationship never goes back to what it was, you will feel better and you will eradicate one cancer in your life.

Words Have Meaning

To eliminate negativity and unfocused activity in your life, the first and easiest place to begin with is your vocabulary and the words you use in communication to yourself and others. It may seem like a trivial matter or mere semantics, but studies prove that words trigger an emotional response. Choose your words carefully in light of the response you seek.

A similar word to "response" might be "react," which has a different, somewhat negative connotation. If you take medication for an illness and respond to it, the meaning is positive toward resolution of your ailment. But if you react to the medicine, the inference is now that something unintended or bad has happened. It's a slight difference, but although react and respond are very similar in their definitions, respond has an advantage in the implied meaning. Another example are the words "problem" and "challenge."

A problem implies something serious with negative implications. I prefer the word "challenge." I enjoy challenges whereas I do not enjoy problems. Sometimes in place of "problem" I euphemistically employ the word "opportunity." To me this is more in line with my belief that problems carry the seed of alternate benefit (opportunity) when you train yourself to look for it. Crisis and situation, adversity and obstacle, situation and issue, failure and learning experience—all are just a few examples of word choices to direct your meaning. There are many more examples and in most cases your background or experience will dictate your meaning and your feeling of positive or negative.

Positive and empowering words can create a positive attitude and thought process. As this is developed as a skill set, it allows for a chain reaction of positive thoughts to bring about actions leading to events that ultimately create positive outcomes. A positive attitude reflected in word choices creates a spark for applied optimism. Applied optimism becomes leverage and a catalyst for creating extraordinary results in your life.

The Power of Positive Expectancy

Positive expectancy is certainly linked with optimism. Here is a very real example of the power of positive expectancy. As I was writing this information regarding positive expectancy, our family had another situation in need of resolution. Because the house we were building wasn't going to be ready until three months after we moved out of our old house, we needed short-term housing. My wife and I were still in Memphis with Frankie and could not look for a three-month residence, so we gave it up to prayer and decided to tap into the law of expectancy. Within one week a casual conversation between friends 400 miles away from where we were turned up an opportunity with the timing and circumstances that could not have been better scripted.

In the late 1900s, there was a surge in popularity of positive mental attitude (PMA) programs, books and methods. Motivational teachers like Zig Ziglar, W. Clement Stone and Norman Vincent Peale inspired a generation to the benefits of what a positive mental attitude could accomplish. "Your attitude will control your altitude" and other mantras of motivation were widely used until a new incarnation of the self-help genre emerged and pushed PMA to the back shelves of history. The empowerment movement and the technique driven motivational programs along with new generations of gurus and teachers relegated some of the foundational truths to near obscurity. There is absolute merit to the evolution of the personal development industry, but many of the underlying principles have been overshadowed by sexier and more glamorous approaches. It is important to realize that methods come and go. Foundational principles and laws of nature and the universe, however, are constant.

Martin Seligman, a professor of psychology at the University of Pennsylvania and the author of *Learned Optimism*, explains that optimism is not about always being cheerful and happy or not acknowledging adversity, setbacks, problems, fear, loss, sorrow, etc. No one will go through life having only positive experiences. Rather, optimism is a habitual way of explaining setbacks and disappointments to yourself as a response to learn and correct for the future. If you blow a sales call, you can reflect negatively or you can take the optimistic approach.

The negative approach, although funny, might resemble the self-talk of Tommy Callahan as played by the late Chris Farley in *Tommy Boy*. He smacks his forehead with the open palm of his hand as if to stamp on the label or beat into his brain his three-word belief of himself, "Stupid! Stupid! Stupid!" Perhaps a better approach after stumbling would be a more balanced and optimistic approach. "Boy, that was not what I had in mind, but I know I can do better than that. Next time when dealing with Mr. Johnson, I will have my numbers down and my research complete. This hurts, but I know I can learn from this. I will get better!"

Optimists, who by the way it has been proven have better immune systems and are generally healthier, are not afraid to strive for improvement or to try to squeeze the good out of a less than desirable situation. When a pessimist gets bumped from a flight and has to stay the night in another city, he or she will look for all the bad, seething about the injustice. Pessimists will seek to ruin the day of other unsuspecting victims as they complain and relive the incident countless times.

The optimist is disappointed and upset, but then quickly assesses the situation to look for opportunities. Tune into the self-talk of the optimistic personality in the same situation: "This stinks, I really wanted to get home. Oh well, here I am. Maybe there is a free flight out of this if I treat the gate agent with more respect and courtesy than the negative person in front of me. Maybe I can take some time to catch up on some reading, after all they are putting me up at a hotel, and I could sure use a chance to get caught up on a little sleep after this trip. Oh well, let's make the best of it."

It is human nature to remember the bad over the good. If nine great things and one bad thing happen to you in a day, your natural tendency will be to think disproportionately about the bad thing. Try to concentrate on what is positive rather than what is negative as you will be drawn to what you think about. When you are frustrated, recognize where you want to direct your energies as it is a choice. The energy of negativity produces bitter fruit that is acid in your stomach. The energy of positive optimism may not always bear good fruit, but the chance is better that over time your harvest will be far superior (and edible).

Trend Extension Assessment

"The greatest thing in this world is not so much where we stand, as in what direction we are going."
—Oliver Wendell Holmes

It is unrealistic to expect any lasting monumental change to happen immediately. What we need to strive for is consistent and incremental improvement and managing the trend. Ask yourself this question: How is my trend in this area of my life? Trend is either down, neutral or up. "No change" is not neutral; it is down. It takes power and effort to remain neutral. The great artist Vincent Van Gogh observed, "Great things are not done by impulse, but by a series of small things brought together." Knowing you are on the right track assists you to eliminate negativity and unfocused activity.

Sometimes it becomes difficult to know for certain that you are getting close to achieving your goal. Sometimes we may still be weeks, months, even years away from certain goals. You may have changed your diet and exercise habits only to look in the mirror or step on the scale and feel as far away as when you began your journey. It is easy to get frustrated. What is important is to perform a quick trend analysis on your situation. Look at your trend and find motivation in the seeds planted for future harvest.

When I was learning to fly, I learned visual recognition techniques. Quite simply this would be to look at the visual cues around me and then compare what I saw to the map to determine my position. Once position was determined, an updated course could be plotted to the destination. It is important to do this in relation to your goals. Sometimes answering a simple question is all you need to keep you on track. "If I continue on my current trend, am I on pace to achieve my goal by my deadline?" "If I continue to get the results I am getting, will I move closer or further from my goal?"

Immediate results will most generally not be impressive nor will they be able to motivate you if you can't visualize a longer-term trend. If you are 50 pounds overweight, start to take action, then jump on the scale the very next day, you will be crushed to find that your results are less than spectacular. Even a week or a month may not show results that will continue to motivate you. You must use the trend test to evaluate your progress.

This is no different than driving in a car for a 600-mile journey with small children. Our own inner voice of, "Are we there yet?" frustrates our efforts in just the same way the small child's incessant questioning will not improve the time to destination. Of course, as adults when we are in this situation, we can figure 600 miles at an average speed of 60 miles an hour would be about a 10-hour journey. Factor in breaks and you are looking at about another hour. If you have traveled for three hours, you still have about six or seven to go. Most importantly, you know that although you are only about a third of the way to your destination, you are absolutely on the right trend. If you continue on the road in the right direction continuing the progress you have already made, you know that you will certainly reach your destination.

Why do people get frustrated and quit before they have reached their goal destination? It is important to realize that to achieve success in what we are trying to achieve, we must continue taking incremental action and seek incremental improvement. Just as a bicycle will stop rolling and fall over sideways if you stop pedaling, your movement to your goal will be pushed over if you stop taking action.

Our destiny is always a work in progress with the outcome not yet written. The script is ours to write. It is very much like the character Ebenezer Scrooge in Charles Dickens's classic *A Christmas Carol*. Scrooge was given a rare gift of insight of who he would become if he continued down his current path. The frightening reality of that destiny caused him to alter his thoughts and behaviors and change his destiny. What is your current destiny if your path remains unchanged?

Take a moment to reflect upon the course of your own life. If you take your life today and extrapolate all of the key areas out 10 years, will you end up at your desired outcome? Where do you see your trend with respect to your finances, family, career, social, health, spiritual, educational, and mental aspects of life? If you are less than excited about your trend or are downright scared, you must make changes now.

Sometimes we need to stop and ask ourselves about the trend we are in and contemplate the consequences.

Poison in Your System

When you have negative attitudes like hate and resentment they literally cause poisons in your system that can bring about a negative physical effect. Poison and acid in your prevailing thoughts produces poison and acid in your blood and organs and will eat away at your insides. Many people with physical maladies cause their own ailments by keeping their prevailing thoughts negative.

We learned about the four most powerful mental programming techniques in Chapter 13 (written goals, affirmations, visualization and self-questions). Some people without consciously doing so misuse the last three. When this happens, you undercut all opportunity and bring negativity into your life. This has the effect of creating a cancer in your life as negative emotions breed negative results, furthering the cycle as the results compound the attitudes.

This is not an exaggeration. Perhaps you know someone or have even been there yourself on a smaller scale. A bad attitude leads to a bad day, which brings negative results and on it goes. The only good news is that the string can be broken if you are conscious of it. This actually happens quite frequently.

The biggest source of poison, unfortunately, is other people.

Avoid Negative People

You only have this one life to live and only so much time available. If you want to be happy and make your life meaningful and full of joy, you need to eradicate situations of negativity. It may sound harsh, but you don't have time to waste with negative people. Unchecked and unchallenged, they will drain your energy and pull you down. When they find a willing audience, they stick around and try to convert others into their negative worlds. Certainly they may have real and justified concerns, however, too often they get involved in trivial matters as they blame and look for excuses outside themselves.

When you hand over custody of your happiness to someone else instead of assuming responsibility to solve your own problems, you succumb to negativity. You can still be compassionate, polite and encouraging to negative people, but you cannot let them take you to their level. It is fruitless to get into a gripe session without looking for a productive end. Clearly, everyone has problems, but not everyone allows their problems dominion over their lives. *You can offer a temporary safe house to your friends without allowing them to become a permanent resident.* You are not a martyr, nor are you obligated to sacrifice your life to the problems of another. Communicate with people in a meaningful way that shows you appreciate how they feel and suggest they look for solutions. Apply what you know to help redirect their mental energy.

This may sound cruel, but I assert just the opposite. When I am feeling negative or bitter about a situation, the friends I appreciate the most are the ones who will not allow me the temporary pleasure of self-pity or the comfort of negativity. Their standards lift me up and remind me of what I know. The friends or acquaintances who will wallow in self-pity with you do you no favors. Align yourself with positive people. Give negative people notice that you are working to change your attitude and let them know you would appreciate their help in keeping you in check.

If it does not work, minimize your time with negative people and their influence on you. Be wary of dream stealers. They seem positive at first but then slowly let the air out of your dreams. They use the pretense of "for your own good," but they manage to plant seeds of doubt into your garden of ambition. Be wary of whom you ask advice. Look to plant positive and optimistic people in your life. Life is simply too brief to be saddled with the negative baggage of others let alone your own adversities and challenges.

Destroying the Cancers of Success

In the disease of cancer, there are three basic ways to deal with it and eradicate it from your body if it has not progressed too far. There is chemotherapy, which uses drugs and chemicals, both poisons and toxins, to kill the cancer cells. Even though this is done in a controlled and measured environment, the toxins directed at the bad cells also affect the good cells. Radiation therapy is another alternative where high amounts of directed radiation are used to focus on the cancerous area to kill those specific cells. As with chemotherapy, radiation has a downside and also the potential to damage healthy cells as well as cancer cells. The third alternative is surgery whereby all the cancer cells and affected tissue is removed completely. In very general terms, the earlier the cancer is found, the better the chance it can be contained and removed before it spreads.

What cancers do you have in your life? For some it is apathy. For others, it might be the Internet, computer games or the TV stealing their ability to think and brainwashing them into the status quo reality Hollywood portrays. For some it is proximity to negative and sour people who decay and rot inside themselves then seek company for the journey of self-destruction. For others it is self-doubt, fear or lack of possibilities. Negativity and unfocused activity will destroy a person's opportunities and forever hold you in a prison of limitations.

Daydreams are unplanned and unfocused visualizations. They are not real goals since the first real obstacle or resistance shocks us back to the prison of what we create as our reality. We allow negative self-talk to discourage us and slowly slip away from what we initially aspired to. You may have set out to write a book and then before you get a single word on paper, you find excuses and self-created limitations to push you from your intended target. "I barely passed freshman English. How in the world could I ever write a book?"

Sometimes, as when sailing, the wind is at your back and life is good. Sometimes there are impediments to your goals, but you can sail into the wind. The prevailing winds over the Atlantic Ocean are from west to east. How were the great sailing ships before the advent of the engine able to sail west? Ancient mariners learned you can set your sails in such a way that wind can blow into one sail and be directed to another. Sailing against the wind is certainly not the desired course, but when you need to travel west and the wind is blowing east, it is important to have strategies to overcome the obstacle.

Program Yourself for Success

Look for the good in every situation. This does not mean to turn into a modern-day Pollyanna or to delude yourself into thinking positive while the *Titanic* is sinking beneath you. The lesson is to assess each situation for the opportunities and the benefits that are surely there. This is often difficult due to the emotion clouding the situation. Losing a job is an event that happens to millions of people each year. You could look at this predicament and see only the negative or you could see the opportunity presented.

The Chinese symbol of yin and yang represents the coexistence and the benefit played by problems and opportunities. Former President Richard M. Nixon explained the same type of dichotomy in the Chinese symbol representing the word crisis: "The Chinese use two brush strokes to write the word 'crisis.' One brush stroke stands for danger; the other for opportunity. In a crisis, be aware of the danger—but recognize the opportunity."

Learn to recognize opportunity and remain alert for the situations able to give birth to success. To do this it is important to get and maintain a positive attitude. When you practice this attitude it allows you to see the possibilities when opportunity comes—because it usually shows up disguised as adversity and no one else recognizes it.

"The pessimist sees difficulty in every opportunity. The optimist sees the opportunity in every difficulty."
—Winston Churchill

CHAPTER 15

Develop the Power of Challenge Alchemy— Consistently Convert "Lemons to Lemonade"

"Every adversity, every failure, and every heartache, carries with it the seed of an equivalent or greater benefit."
—Napoleon Hill

Several years ago, an exceptional 19-year-old Spanish athlete was goalkeeper for the world-famous Real Madrid soccer team. A promising sports career was derailed when a tragic car accident left this young sports phenomenon near death and paralyzed. For more than three excruciating and painful years he underwent the difficult recuperation and rehabilitation process. Most people in this situation would have been devastated and lost all hope, with a bright future torn away and no time to plan or contemplate a different alternative. This young man, however, accepted a gift from a physician's assistant in the hospital given with the intent to raise the young man's spirits. The former soccer star, still at the beginning of a long journey to even walk

219

again, began to play the guitar and even to write songs. As the song of his life began a new verse, the young man did recover. He studied law before his new passion for music began to open opportunities.

The young man later reflected on his journey: "I think having that experience changed the direction and the philosophy of my life, going through all that made me who I am today. I was a sporting, flirty young guy before that. All that pain gave me a sensitivity to everything around me. I became a poet without writing, a singer without singing." Perhaps you have heard of this singer who eventually recovered the use of his legs and whose passion and art grew out of the ashes of adversity. Perhaps you might recognize the voice of a man now known around the world, a man whose music and passion inspired millions and earned this crooner fame and fortune beyond comprehension. Perhaps you have heard of a man named Julio Iglesias.

The success story of Julio Iglesias is not unique. There are thousands of tales of adversity giving rise to a life and opportunity far better than what was originally intended. McDonald's and the "golden arches" would not exist today if Ray Kroc had succeeded in his first several ventures. Instead they ended in bankruptcy prior to the opportunity of meeting the McDonald brothers and purchasing a little hamburger stand that later became the preeminent fast-food franchise in modern history. Had Walt Disney not failed in his initial dreams to the point of bankruptcy, the enchantment of the Magic Kingdom and the hundreds of Disney-related businesses would not exist today. It can be a hard pill to swallow, but allow yourself to be open to what life is teaching you and apply it later when the opportunity presents itself.

Our lesson from all of this is that we must learn to condition ourselves to look for and create within us opportunity awareness even in the midst of tragedy. I hate what my son Frankie had to endure during his initial bout with leukemia, but he helped remind me of these principles. Even though he was separated from his family, being stuck with needles and dealing with pain and discomfort, he began to share blessings with me. From new people we had the opportunity to meet to the hundreds of cards, letters and gifts from friends and loved ones, our family began to experience blessings in the midst of a bad and uncertain time. I would not have had the time, opportunity or life lessons to write this book if it were not for the opportunities presented during Frankie's illness.

Look at how many first and second generation Americans there are today who escaped poverty and oppression to get to America. They came here with literally nothing but the clothes they were wearing. How is it that these people with no money, no possessions, no advantages and in most cases no ability to even speak the language are able to become successful in America? Creating optimism in the face of adversity does not mean you must pretend everything will be okay and lull yourself into a false belief. Realism is okay. It is important to face reality and what happens. We sometimes cannot control what happens to us, but we can control our thoughts and response to our situations.

Challenge Alchemy

Alchemy was the medieval science of trying to turn lead into gold. Lead and gold are very close in atomic makeup on the periodic chart. It was thought (mistakenly) that you could somehow take a low value metal like lead and convert it into the precious commodity of gold. While the scientific evidence disproved the possibility for this metallurgic conversion, there is a more symbolic and valuable type of alchemy available to us. Challenge alchemy is converting problems and challenges into something more valuable. In essence, challenge alchemy is the science/art of converting lemons into lemonade.

The phrase has become overused and trite, but there is still value in it. At different times in our lives, we will be provided with the proverbial lemons. How we respond determines our overall outcome. In the opening quote for this chapter, Napoleon Hill observed through the study of success in hundreds of people that every negative situation brings with it a seed of greater or equivalent benefit. This has been said other ways in commonsense wisdom. My mother always used to tell me that when God closes a door, He opens a window. "In every dark cloud there is always a silver lining." The famous philosopher Frederick Nietzsche said, "That which doesn't kill us makes us stronger."

I have a good friend who recently had the opportunity to apply this philosophy. He and his wife were expecting their first child and living with his wife's parents at the time. Their true desire was to own their own home. The challenge they both had was the fact they had both been divorced and had other children and financial baggage from the past preventing them from being in an ideal situation to get a mortgage.

Knowing their desired outcome, they took action and followed all the right steps to achieve the outcome of their design. They were working with an acquaintance new to the financing business who wanted to specialize in situations similar to my friends. This mortgage broker worked hard on their behalf and got them the financing they needed so that my friend and his wife could make an offer on their dream house. They searched and eventually found exactly what they were looking for in the perfect neighborhood and school system. They negotiated with the seller and came to a very satisfactory conclusion.

Then something unfortunate happened. In spite of the best of intentions, the mortgage broker made some critical errors early on in the process that were not discovered until just prior to closing. Unfortunately, financing fell through at the last minute and they ended up losing the house. To make matters worse, they lost their earnest money and money they'd spent on an appraisal.

As difficult as the situation was, my friend is a student of the philosophy of greater or equivalent benefit and took this very unfortunate situation as an opportunity to apply this principle. He took a few days to deal with his normal emotions of frustration, anger and resentment. Then he took stock of the situation, assessed his options and began to take proactive steps toward his desired outcome. He and his wife realized that although not ideal, they could rent and take the time to pay off old debts, increase their incomes and save money for an even better situation.

They met a builder who just finished some nice apartment buildings. It turned out that the builder wanted to build duplexes and worked out an arrangement with my friend to apply a percentage of his rent over the next year to a down payment on a duplex he would build for my friend and his new family. In addition, the duplex was in the design of their choosing and large enough to meet his family's needs within his budget. As an added bonus, this new situation allowed my friend and his wife to create an income property as well as their dream house. The new situation would allow the rent of the additional unit to nearly cover the entire mortgage. Needless to say, in retrospect, he is happy with the outcome. None of the benefits would have come to him had he not looked for advantages and opportunities in the midst of his adversity.

How would most people have handled that situation? How do you think you would have dealt with it? Can you look back at your life and see other situations to prove this point? Sometimes things naturally work themselves out for the better over time. Having the skill to search out opportunities in adversity and train yourself to maintain a proper perspective in the midst of a perceived crisis will serve you well and dramatically separate you from your peers. This ability to discern and create advantages out of disadvantages or "lemonade from lemons" is a master Incremental Advantage skill in controlling your own destiny.

Judo Principle—Situation Transformation

Judo is the martial art of redirection. The basic premise is to use the force and momentum of your attackers against them. When they throw a punch or lunge at you, they have taken themselves off center and presented you with an advantage. The momentum of their size and strength has shifted and you can redirect it to your advantage. Judo is thousands of years old and has a tradition of allowing smaller opponents to win over much larger and even stronger foes. In a way similar to challenge alchemy, the judo principle of situation transformation takes a situation others may classify as bad or negative and allows you to redirect the energy to your benefit.

This skill set does not come easy at first. We are trained to see problems as situations to be avoided at all costs. This principle is about energy redirection. Escape and fear from adversity should not be the thought, but rather the benefits to be gained through the adversity and overcoming it. Like everything else we discussed previously, the process begins in the mind. It starts with the imagination as the tool employed in redirecting the momentum of a situation. A rich vibrant imagination is the fertile breeding ground for solutions to any problems or challenges you now face.

Discovery is about seeing what everyone else sees but then thinking originally and creatively. It is about relating the normally unrelated. Newton observed an apple fall from a tree and from that began his scholarly thinking regarding the nature of gravity. Benjamin Franklin observed nature and was prolific in his scientific discoveries from lightning and electricity to the earliest understanding of weather patterns and the effect of the Gulf Stream to modern-day refrigeration. Nearly every great discovery or invention came about from an observation relating the normally unrelated. Another way of phrasing this might be nonlinear thinking or thinking outside the box.

Life will from time to time give you lemons; what will you do with them? I have always liked the "lemons to lemonade" theory and have had the "opportunity" to apply it with many "challenges." The first time I read Napoleon Hill's words, the theme instantly resonated with me. He said, "When life gives you lemons, make lemonade and then sell it to all of those who get thirsty from complaining." Everyone will have adversity in their lives. You can be beaten down by it, or you can chose to forge your mettle as you learn, adapt and apply the situation for your future benefit.

Practice Perspective—
Take a Step Back from Your Problems

The other day, I asked my son to get something from the table for me. After several minutes, he called out in frustration, "Dad, I can't find it." As I approached, I could see the item I was looking for just slightly out of his view; his search parameters were too narrow. I walked up behind him and gently pulled him back two steps to where he could easily see it. If you take this book and put it so close to your face so that your nose touches the page, you will not be able to read a single word. Go ahead and give it a try. If you pull the book an inch or so back, you will be able to read about a third of the book. Another few inches and the entire book will come into focus. This is the way it is many times with our problems. They are too close. The saying "Can't see the forest for the trees" is another illustration. When you are too close, you cannot see patterns or alternatives emerge from your solutions.

Become a Turn-Around Specialist

On April 11, 1970, astronaut Jim Lovell, with his crew of Jack Swigert and Fred Haise, commenced a voyage to the moon. Two days later, when *Apollo 13* was more than 200,000 miles from the earth, an oxygen tank exploded and the crew was placed in extraordinary and unparalleled danger. Any number of events or components of the situation could have killed the entire crew.

On top of the critical issues that potentially would leave them stranded in space and separated from earth, they had the more immediate life-threatening crisis of running out of oxygen. The air filters or scrubbers as they were called were designed to remove the harmful and toxic waste product of normal human breathing. The scrubbers for the command module were round, while the scrubbers in the lunar module were square, precluding their use, which would have kept the air safe to breath. Without fixing this critical problem, the remaining issues would not matter since the asphyxiated astronauts would float forever into space entombed in the vessel that had failed them.

Captain Lovell and his crew most likely felt a range of emotions from fear to anger with the situation. They could have blamed the stupid engineers who might have prevented the problem with additional forethought. They could have been upset and aggravated with each other. They could have allowed themselves to be frozen in inactivity due to the panic and terror of the situation. What they actually did was to choose to access the situation and take action with whatever resources they had available. Both in space and hundreds of thousands of miles below on the earth, scientists, astronauts and technicians worked to create a solution to the problems they faced. They prioritized the eventualities and took action in that order. Duct tape and socks provided one of the solutions for the scrubbers, which led to the ability to work on navigation and eventually a safe reentry. Had the astronauts put themselves in a fetal position and waited to be rescued, they would have never survived the first day. Through knowledge and contingency training for similar events, they were equipped to turn their situation around.

This is so simple yet so difficult to grasp completely. The outcome of our lives lies not in what happens to us, but rather how we respond to what happens. It is not by what life brings our way, but rather by our attitude and what we bring back to life.

What Would MacGyver Do?

In times and situations where you are feeling powerless and circumstances are taking control of your life rather than the other way around, it is sometimes helpful to ask yourself this question: What would MacGyver do? *MacGyver*, for the uninitiated, was a show in the late 1980s and early 1990s starring Richard Dean Anderson. Called only by his last name and placed in the most precarious and unenviable situations, MacGyver was the absolute epitome of resourcefulness. Combined with his training and knowledge, he was somehow able to convert ordinary items into extraordinary tools to get him out of any cliff-hanging situation. MacGyver would evoke his magical blend of creativity and applied science and triumph as the poor man's

James Bond. I don't know whether the science was always real or not, but the show taught me a mind-set that has served me whenever I feel trapped and out of options.

Maintain the attitude and mind-set of a creative problem solver. Learn to develop opportunity awareness. Learn to think about possible benefits and opportunities hidden even in adversity or hardship. Learn to visualize any negative situation as an opportunity for metamorphosis to an enhanced situation, like a caterpillar changing into a butterfly. Earl Nightingale believed, "A great attitude does much more that turn on the lights in our worlds; it seems to magically connect us to all sorts of serendipitous opportunities that were somehow absent before the change." Sometimes creativity in your personal situation is relating the normally unrelated or looking at a combination of things that you had not thought of previously. When you get into a pinch requiring a healthy dose of creativity, step out of yourself and your normal patterns to ask yourself, "What would MacGyver do?"

Army Leadership Reaction Course

One of my favorite army officer training experiences was a challenging field classroom like an obstacle course only far more mental than physical called the Leadership Reaction Course. The LRC provided each of us an excellent opportunity to demonstrate and practice leadership, followership, problem solving and the discipline of thinking creatively to utilize resources available to complete the mission. A mission objective would be provided along with the available resources for the group to apply. Many of the solutions were tremendously counter to linear thinking. The goal of the LRC was to teach soldiers and small-group leaders to think unconventionally. Life does not always present us neat situations with clear-cut alternatives. Unfortunately we deal with uncertainty and many times very limited resources for achieving our desired end point. You may never have the opportunity to benefit from a course like the LRC, but you can learn to think critically, linearly as well as nonlinearly, and to ultimately develop the skills to find and expand alternative solutions regardless of the situations.

Concept of Backward Planning

Have you ever seen the triangle puzzle with 15 holes and 14 golf tees? The object is to jump an adjacent tee and then to remove the tee jumped until there is one left remaining in the middle of the puzzle. You would think this is easy, and for those officially in Mensa, it might be. For me, however, I would leave an embarrassing three or four pieces remaining. The way I finally figured how to solve this was to do it backward. Starting with the final piece and the final desired destination, I worked the puzzle backward to find the pattern I would need to use from the beginning. With this knowledge, it is much easier to work the puzzle. Like watching a murder mystery with full knowledge at the beginning of who performed the heinous act, you have a much clearer picture of events, sequence and how all the clues fit together. This is absolutely applicable in your life from the smallest of situations to the largest of obstacles.

Backward planning is a technique I learned in army leadership courses. The concept is very simple yet rarely used. An easy example would be catching a 9:30 A.M. flight in a city 90 minutes away. Start with the departure time and work backward to plan and figure your time intervals. If your flight is a 9:30, you know you need to be at the airport an hour early (8:30), it will take an hour and a half to make the drive and a half an hour for parking and buffer time, so you need to leave your house at 6:30 A.M. You know that you need 45 minutes for your morning routine, so you set your alarm for 5:45 A.M.

The natural progression of this example seems like a real no-brainer and you may already utilize the technique without knowing it. This works with goal achievement as well. Take your focus off of your problem for a minute and instead put it on what your desired outcome would be. Take where you need to end up and work backward step by step and interval by interval until you are where you are currently. Think of what each step and each preceding step needs to be. As you work backward from where you want to be to where you are now, you create a roadmap. By the time you work it backward all the way from where you want to be, you have created a plan of action for yourself to apply going forward.

Developing an Entrepreneurial Mind-Set

You don't have to quit your job or even start your own business to have an entrepreneurial mind-set. The word entrepreneur as defined by a more traditional dictionary is a person who assumes risk to organize and operate a business leveraging that potential risk for potential profits. This definition still applies, although I would add that being an entrepreneur is more about applying creativity and alternate approaches to the process you are involved in currently. You might be a district manager for a large company charged with results from your territory and be able to apply an entrepreneurial mind-set to your situation to positively affect your outcome. You could be a minister of a church, teacher in a school, secretary in an office or the head of a large company and have the opportunity to utilize applied creativity to your situation to achieve the results you seek.

An entrepreneurial mind-set challenges the status quo and allows you to look at situations and resources in a different way. Do not misunderstand; being an entrepreneur is not license to be a loose cannon or maverick creating troubles and headaches for supervisors. Being an entrepreneur is about applied creativity to focus all your resources on solving problems. It is about taking a scrap of opportunity or knowledge and applying it or converting it into something beneficial.

Creating Your Personal Horatio Alger Story

You have probably heard it said before, "That is a true rags-to-riches Horatio Alger story." Who is this Horatio Alger and what is his story? Living from 1832 to 1898 on the U.S. East Coast, Horatio Alger was a writer and a poet by desire and a Unitarian minister and social worker in New York by trade. Alger found inspiration in the poverty-stricken, poor and homeless of New York and wrote hopeful rags-to-riches stories of characters overcoming obstacles to achieve success. His books were extremely popular as they touched a chord in America, whose immigrant-based population strongly related to the theme of hard work persevering. His moving stories captured the emotion and spirit of a nation.

A Horatio Alger–type story is still one of the most popular genres in America today. As in the classic movie, *Rocky*, starring Sylvester Stallone, these inspiring stories tell of nobodies, who after hard work, grit and determination, manage to lift themselves up by their own bootstraps to uncommon and extraordinary success.

The original screenplay of *Rocky* was written by Sylvester Stallone whose life story is itself a classic Horatio Alger tale. Stallone was an out-of-work nobody, a struggling actor divorced and penniless. He was completely without resources and desperate to the point that he eventually had to sell his dog, his most loyal companion, to survive. All the while he held onto his dream to write and sell a screenplay and become a famous actor. His early results were of little value and most ordinary people would have long given up. Like his character of Rocky Balboa, Stallone refused to quit and continued "stacking logs," holding steadfast to what he sincerely believed was his destiny. Ultimately, and against all odds, he realized his dream and became a famous movie actor with wealth, power and prominence in his chosen profession. The result line on his success graph turned dramatically upward in classic J-shaped fashion.

A few years back, I had the great fortune to personally meet the real man behind the inspiring movie *Rudy*. Daniel "Rudy" Rudy Ruetigger spoke at a conference I attended and retold the story of his persistence and courage to follow his dreams to play football for the "Irish" of Notre Dame. Beyond his small stature and meager athletic ability was a heart filled with passion and a determination to "stack the logs" until he could no longer be ignored. Through this tenacity and determination, Rudy ultimately achieved his dreams. Beyond common sense and beyond normal, Rudy was clear in his outcome and persistent in his approach. He eventually fulfilled his dream of playing for the Fighting Irish. Rudy's success did not end with his initial dream. In addition to that he wrote a book, sold the rights to Hollywood, created a movie about his life and is now a sought-after public speaker.

"Within us all there are wells of thought and dynamos of energy which are not suspected until emergencies arise. Then oftentimes we find that it is comparatively simple to double or triple our former capacities and to amaze ourselves by the results achieved."

—Thomas J. Watson, founder of IBM

Part VI

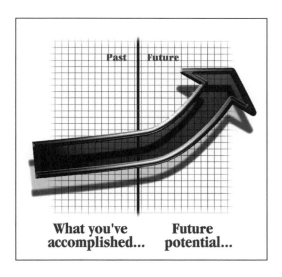

Past | Future

What you've accomplished... Future potential...

MAINTAIN YOUR MORAL CHARACTER

CHAPTER 16

Accept Personal Responsibility— The Great Liberator!

"You are free to choose, but the choices you make today will determine what you will have, be and do in the tomorrow of your life."
—Zig Ziglar

I Should Have Been Rich

When I was a child, I spent my entire summers with my grandparents living in a small town outside of Pittsburgh. My grandfather, whom I was named after, was an awesome man of marvelous skills and talents. He was an engineer by education and a carpenter, architect and craftsman of the finest German tradition by practice and patience. My grandfather designed and built his house by himself. He had a wood shop in his basement and could do miracles with creations from scratch, or repair anything from electronics to fine china. He had great patience in his tasks and I can recall only once in all of our time together when he lost his patience and raised his voice. My grandfather was the go-to guy for all of his and my grandmother's relatives living in the area, always willing to help in any task, undertaking or in any creation. His hands, as directed by his brilliant mind, could build or fix anything. My life was profoundly influenced and guided by mentoring from my Pop-Pop. He was and remains to this day one of my all-time heroes and models for my life.

When I was about 12, I learned something amazing about my grandfather. Pop-Pop invented many things and eventually patented several of his inventions. While a student at Carnegie Mellon, he actually invented the system of windshield washers to deliver fluid to the wipers but never got his designs patented. Instead, someone else took his idea and somewhere out there another man's grandson and other heirs are filthy rich. At the time and my maturity level, I could not believe what I heard. When I asked my grandfather about it, he confirmed what I had heard and showed me his drawings. He laughed and shared with me his philosophy about life and personal responsibility.

Wealth was never the dream or within the scope of importance for my hero. He believed in God. He believed in family. He believed in service to others and he believed in taking and accepting complete responsibility for his life and his situation. As the oldest of five children born at the turn of the century to German immigrant parents, he worked in the coal mines as a child to help support his family. He missed out on nearly everything a young boy of today would take for granted. He took responsibility for his life by taking advantage of all the resources in a life with seemingly no opportunities.

He worked full-time and educated himself later earning a college degree. At 25 he was the youngest supervisor in the plant where he would later be an engineer. He lived through the Great Depression, lost his first house in a flood and survived countless obstacles that would paralyze most ordinary men. He created a good life for his family and a legacy of "logs stacked" beyond comprehension. At his funeral, it was as if a head of state had passed away. All those who knew him understood and knew exactly what he stood for.

Unfortunately for me, somehow I didn't inherit all of my grandfather's talents in mechanical and carpentry skills. I ended up with C's in shop class, and I am allowed to try to fix things around home only as the absolute last resort and with adult supervision. But though I missed out on the physical skills, I did inherit something that has proven far more valuable to me and provides benefits way beyond lost wealth earned through birthright. I picked up his work ethic and many of his life philosophies. The legacy and overriding inheritance I received from my grandfather was the understanding and application of accepting personal responsibility for my life.

I have had many great influences in my life from family and friends mixed with education and experience. My own philosophy regarding success has certainly evolved from those; however, they have all been built upward from the original foundation laid by my father and his father before him. I am not a proponent of New Age mysticism. I believe we have a creator who has given us the ability to think, create, adapt and choose. Our power of choice is our great liberator. We can choose our emotions and our actions and set our own course. Applied over time, we are basically in control of our own destiny. We are where we are and generally where we chose to be, good or bad. We have assets and liabilities and the power to make changes in our life. We may not be able to control all of the circumstances or situations in our lives—loss of life or loved ones or disease or how other people treat us. We can control our attitudes, our response and the actions we choose to take.

It saddens me to see people who let life happen to them and take no action other than to complain and further allow the roots of complacency to set in and grab hold. Life is to be lived and there is a world of abundance ours for the asking. We only have to learn how to ask.

Flying Lessons

When I was 16 years old, I began to take flying lessons. I actually started flying when I was 14, but the rules were that you could not fly solo until you were 16 so I briefly stopped and used that time to earn money for my newest passion. I really enjoyed flying and the biggest thrill of my life at that time happened when one day after practicing takeoffs and landings, my instructor told me to taxi back to the hangar. I was disappointed because I thought I had been doing pretty well. My disappointment turned to shock when my instructor got out and told me to go do three takeoffs and landings…by myself! I had confidence and knew I could do it, but I was alone and could look to no one but myself for this task. I successfully soloed and continued to grow in my confidence as a pilot.

The remainder of my training was a combination of instructor training mixed with solo flight. A funny thing happened toward the very end of my training. When I was by myself doing cross-country flights, night landings or other maneuvers, I felt very confident and sure of myself. When my instructor would fly with me, however, I felt nervous and tense and seemed to constantly make stupid mistakes. I couldn't figure out why this happened until he wisely filled me in. When I was flying in the left seat, I was pilot in command and totally responsible. Like most new pilots, I let the fact that a more experienced pilot was in the aircraft distract me from the fact that I was personally responsible.

Have you ever had to make an important phone call where others were listening? Have you ever had to perform a task with others watching? Did it make you tense and self-conscious and even more flustered? This is what was going on with me at the time. I learned over time that sometimes a safety net can also be restrictive to your freedom. Until you embrace the understanding of your personal responsibility, you will never be totally free.

In life there will always be outside forces acting upon us. There will be times when we have to adapt and take responsibility. The more responsibility you take on, the more your self-confidence and directed energy grow. You feel completely up to the task and competent in any endeavor. My grandfather believed that accepting complete responsibility was the cornerstone to one's foundation of self-esteem, pride and worth as an individual.

"If it is to be, it is up to me!"
—Oft quoted motivational saying

Success does not come from luck or inheriting money or being born with great talent. The only path is to take control and assume responsibility for your own destiny. Instead, most people feel victimized, out of control, blame others, etc. Accept responsibility for where you are (good and bad), take stock of your situation, determine where you want to go and take action on that. My personal turning point in life came when I finally realized I was responsible for my own success or failure. If I did not like my current result, I would have to make a change.

This is true for every area of life. If you are broke, it is a choice. It is a cumulative choice made up of hundreds and thousands of previous individual decisions. If you are spending more than you earn and not saving, where you are is up to you and in your control. Change is not immediate, but the course correction can be. If you are going the wrong direction on a trip while driving your car, when you realize your mistake you turn around at the nearest safe opportunity. Shouldn't it be the same if you are traveling down the wrong road with your personal decisions? To change your result you must change your decisions. Remember the old saying, "You can't dig yourself out of a hole."

Do not be a victim of circumstances. Take a look around you, gather your resources and take action to make a change. Only when we take control of our character, does the rest of our life follow suit. Decide for yourself what your life will be and what circumstances you want for yourself. If you abdicate, outside forces or other people and situations will decide for you. It takes a measure of self-discipline and sacrifice to accomplish what you set out to achieve, but the price of success is literally paid up front in one lump sum rather than on the lifetime installment plan that failure provides. Write down your goals and dwell on them in your mind to experience what it will be like when you have accomplished your objective.

Self-Discipline

An old adage I have heard many times states, "Successful people do what unsuccessful people cannot or are unwilling to do." The unwilling to do part involves self-discipline. It really comes down to choices. Would I rather watch TV or spend an hour growing my earning capability? Would I rather eat the rest of my sandwich, knowing that it will be converted to fat, or push it away feeling satisfied? Would I rather sleep in until 7:00 A.M. or get up early to exercise and start my day off right?

Napoleon Hill refers to self-discipline as the "Master Key to Riches." Within self-discipline is the engine of action. Self-discipline is a muscle that improves with use and with practice. Harry Truman remarked, "In regarding the lives of great men, I found that the first victory they won was over themselves…self-discipline with all of them came first." The ability to exert power to overcome your natural tendencies allows you to direct your strengths and weaknesses and marshal great resources, allowing you to master yourself. The habits we form create the ICE in our lives. Good habits produce a good life. To create habits that work for you rather than against you requires discipline of one's self.

General Douglas MacArthur once observed, "There is no security in this life. There is only opportunity." How ironic it is that the more people seek security, the further removed it becomes. Playing it safe ironically yields results far from safe. It is funny to me how people say they would never want to be in sales, not realizing everyone is in sales. We all sell ourselves, ideas, our personalities, etc. There is no job security. The only security is in your talents and your skills, abilities and adaptability to the situation around you. If you are looking for a job or another person to give you security, you will likely be disappointed.

One of the great weaknesses within our society today is the increasing attitude of victimization. Many people feel themselves victims from some outside force. Governments, jobs, current spouses, former spouses, weather, economy, coworkers, other people, immigrants, children, etc.—these are just some of the scapegoats for people to evade personal responsibility. When we are victims of circumstances, or as James Allen says, a "creature of outside conditions," we have no power. We have given over the power in our life to the circumstances or to other people. The longer we give power to our circumstances the worse we allow our current and future situation to become. Dr. Stephen Covey explains it like this: "Look at the word responsibility; 'response-ability,' the ability to choose your response. Highly proactive people recognize that responsibility. They do not blame circumstances, conditions or conditioning for their behavior. Their behavior is a product of their own conscious choice...."

Personal Responsibility—
The Glue of Your Character

We are responsible for what happens in our lives. We certainly cannot control every detail or every event that happens to us. We can control what happens in the larger context of our lives, in our choices and in how we utilize our skills, talents and abilities. Ultimately, we can control the meaning attached to events and our response. Our life happens in tiny seconds and minutes rather than months or years. Those seconds and minutes and the emotions and decisions create action that weaves a tapestry of our lives. Used purposefully, those incremental units of time can produce results seen and enjoyed over a longer period.

Only you can take responsibility for your actions and decisions. When you blame others, it takes you down the path of mediocrity. People who are successful in their lives take responsibility for everything they do as well as what happens to them. Our results are our reward, good or bad, positive or negative for what preceding actions we have taken.

People who are successful in life or specific endeavors do not make excuses or blame others or circumstances for their "luck." Circumstances and luck play no part in long-term success, because the underlying actions bring the results. If this is not so, how can some people be poor and others wealthy in virtually the same situation? Children raised in the near identical family circumstances turn out different. Some people in prison grow and develop while others atrophy and slowly die. Some children of extreme poverty continue the cycle and others break it.

Personal responsibility is essential to the foundation of your character and your integrity. It works the other way as well. Those who are deficient in integrity and character seem always to blame others and find scapegoats for issues of their own creation. If you continue the path you are currently on, your results will be along the same path or trend. There is an old saying: "If you continue to do what you always have done, you will continue to get what you always got." If you want to create a different future than the one that is laid out on your current path, you need to create a new path and begin to act differently. This change happens first in your belief structure, then in the planning of your mind to be carried out and is followed through in your actions. These actions over time will yield a result.

Whether consciously active or subconsciously passive, you are in control of your own choices. What happens in your life is up to you. Every choice you make carries with it a corresponding effect. Newton's third law explains this. Every decision made today will have an impact on how your life is in the future. A log put in the fire today provides fuel for the fire later. Success is a chain of decisions creating a solid foundation. This foundation is made through the individual bricks and mortar of our daily actions and habits.

"Accepting responsibility is the fulcrum point for succeeding at anything."
—Jeffrey Gitomer, *Power of Leverage*

How many times do you think you could lift your best friend 3 feet off the ground? At the park the other day, I noticed that my kids were doing it with each other numerous times. Of course they were using the power of leverage on a teeter-totter rather than attempting to dead-lift. Leverage in essence is simply added advantage. In the physical world, a lever is created using a rigid object over a fulcrum (immovable or stationary point) to create a force greater than the original force applied. In the example of the teeter-totter, the fulcrum point would balance if each of the children weighed the same amount. A small increase in force allows the movement across the fulcrum. The longer the lever, the more force can be applied. The Greek scientist and mathematician Archimedes lived more than 200 years before the birth of Christ. He studied the mechanical nature and mathematical advantage of the lever on which he famously remarked, "Give me a lever long enough and a fulcrum on which to place it, and I shall move the world."

Leverage allows you to do more with less. Big doors move on small hinges. Leverage may be applied to many areas outside of physics. There is financial leverage. You probably would not be able to own a home if not for the power of financial leverage balancing your monthly small payment with the large overall cost of the home. You can find an application of leverage in almost every one of your modern conveniences. Your car provides you leverage over walking. A computer provides leverage in several areas. A microwave oven has leverage over a conventional oven in regard to time.

In addition to all the other forms of leverage revolving around physical objects and financial concepts, there is an opportunity for significant leverage in human relationships. Leverage or achieving advantage in your life through people is in itself neither positive nor negative. Intent and application create the meaning in human leverage. Creating jobs and opportunities for others as they help you drive your business objective forward is usually positive. Sweatshops and child labor would be negative examples. When friendships, marriages, partnerships, teammates and other close relationships work in harmony, leverage is usually present. Leverage in human relations allows for the ability for people to play to their strengths and to provide value to each other. My wife Lisa is extremely strong in some areas I am not. She picks up my slack so I am able to concentrate on other important areas. My wife's willingness to assist me in some areas allows our family to benefit. I have business partners with skill sets in some areas far above mine. This allows me to focus on my strengths and them to focus on theirs, providing overall leverage to our company.

There is kind of a corny line in the movie, *Jerry Maguire* where the melodramatic delivery of the phrase "You complete me" is used. When used properly in relationships in families, in work, in teams and in organizations, people do complete other people. In this situation, advantage through others is achieved. The key for positive or negative is found in the benefit. When only one party or one side of the fulcrum receives benefit, there is inequity and opportunity for trouble. This is the root of marriages, partnerships and other groups seeking disillusion. When both parties are happy with the benefit being received there is positive leverage. Positive leverage to provide benefit to other people is at the heart of personal responsibility.

Leverage of Your Character

When you construct a magnificent character, the cornerstone upon which all will be built is personal responsibility. Without personal ownership of our own actions and attitudes, the foundation upon which all else is built will be weak. Perhaps you have witnessed people with lives falling apart, cracking under the strain of pressures not supported with a foundation of personal responsibility. The blame is spread like an exploding bomb with fragments of accusations and blame radiating out to everyone and everything in range. When you look at a bomb pattern after the fact through the lens of forensic science, all collateral damage and fragmentation can always be traced back to a single place at a single time. This may be a difficult reality, perhaps the most difficult thing you have ever faced, but the one thing in common with all your problems, with all those who wrong you, with all the times you have been cheated, stolen from or lied to, *the common denominator and the epicenter of all your problems is you*. This is not blame or letting everyone off the hook. It is an understanding that at the base of our lives, our situations, and our future course of action is personal responsibility.

Your success will be in proportion to your personal responsibility. No one will do it for you. Luck and serendipity do not just happen, they follow the law of cause and effect. The harder you work and the more personal responsibility you take for every situation in your life, the more the law of sowing and reaping and the law of cause and effect will work to your benefit. Personal responsibility is manufacturing your own luck.

"Leaders aren't born, they are made. They are made just like anything else, through hard work. That's the price we have to pay to achieve that goal, or any goal."
—Vince Lombardi

CHAPTER 17

Weather Your Storms and Come Through Stronger

Below is a quote from a man who was completely despondent. This man was so upset and melancholy that his friends were concerned about the possibility of his taking his own life. They removed all the sharp objects from his house and made sure he was not alone: "I am the most miserable man in the world. If my sadness were spread equally among the family of Earth, there would be not one smiling face on the planet. Whether I shall ever be better I cannot tell; I awfully forebode I shall not. To remain as I am is impossible. I must die or be better."

As you read this quote, you can feel the despair and depression. What would become of this person? Would he allow himself to wallow in self-pity and fade away? Would he take his bitter mood and infect all those with whom he came into contact? Would he choose to cease life or would he choose to turn around his experience and grow from it? A clue to the answer lies in the choice presented in the last two sentences.

We have already talked about this man earlier in Chapter 7. The quote is by a very young country lawyer in Illinois struggling with personal loss and disappointment in 1841. Abraham Lincoln chose the latter of his choices.

How did this change happen? Another quote by Mr. Lincoln later on in his life reflects a simple philosophy that turned his life around. He went on to profoundly say, "I've noticed that most people are about as happy as they make up their minds to be."

Even in the midst of tragedy, sorrow and adversity, successful people find a way to maintain their positive and optimistic qualities. They are able to find joy, humor, gratitude, beauty and sunshine even when the situation is dark and stormy. We all will have storms in our life of some sort. We will have hard times and rough patches. We will also have opportunities for reflection and the chance to benefit, improve and grow.

Hard times, loss, sorrow and disappointment are part of life. Helen Keller commented, "Character cannot be developed in ease and quiet. Only through experiences of trial and suffering can the soul be strengthened, vision cleared, ambition inspired and success achieved."

Forging Steel

Forging is the act of shaping, strengthening and hardening metal far beyond its natural characteristic. It is both art and science and dates back to far beyond medieval times. The process of forging steel is about changing the very nature of the metal. Through a systematic combination of extreme heating, beating with instruments and fast cooling in water, steel can be made extremely hard or very pliable. Strong forged tool steel contains more carbon than mild or regular steel. Regular steel is fibrous or stringy whereas forged steel is small and granular. The smaller the size of the grains in forged steel, the stronger and tougher it is. For steel to be forged properly, the steel is heated above a certain temperature, called the critical temperature. When this happens, the heat causes the grain size to increase. The critical temperature for forging steel is somewhere between 1,300 and 1,600 degrees Fahrenheit.

When the steel is hammered with hard blows from a forging hammer while it is just above the critical temperature, the grain size will greatly reduce. Since the smaller grain size creates the hardness, the steel can be refined and improved by repeating this process. Steel heated above critical temperature and cooled in water immediately will have a much larger grain size and different properties. Steel that is heated too hot (glowing white instead of glowing red) will have the grain size permanently enlarged and the metal will become brittle and most likely worthless.

It is a safe conclusion that a piece of steel can be strengthened and tremendously improved through the forging process. Conversely, the steel also can be damaged or permanently ruined through the process. Steel has no choice in this process. The resulting quality of steel, whether positive and valuable or a negative waste of metal is dependent largely on the skill of the blacksmith. You will have forging in your life and must be your own blacksmith. Your attitude and response to your circumstances will determine the strength of your mettle. Your example in the midst of your forging will show the world a representation of your character. Your example through adversity tells you who you are and shows it to the world.

. . . .

"When one door closes another one opens; but we often look so long and regretfully upon the closed door, that we do not see the ones which open for us."
—Alexander Graham Bell

. . . .

Find Blessings in Adversity

The late Norman Vincent Peale said, "When God wants to send you a gift, he wraps it up in a problem. The bigger the gift that God wants to send you, the bigger the problem he wraps it up in." To apply this principle to the future, begin by looking for the lessons to be learned and the hidden benefits within each difficult situation from your past. There is always something to be gained from adversity, setbacks and difficulties. We are just not always trained to see what they are. Once you realize how this works, it is easier to have faith that your current hardships and adversities will work out for the good in the end. It may not be what you want now, but chances are it will be better for you in the long run and after the perspective of time un-fogs the rearview mirror.

Our Family's Blessings in Frankie's Ordeal

Frankie's bout with leukemia and his struggle to survive was an ordeal and one I would never wish on any family. In the midst of this terrible storm, our family looked for and found so many blessings. As time adds perspective to the situation it is possible to look back and view the good in contrast with the bad. We made over a hundred new friends and acquaintances (patients, family, staff, etc.). We were humbled by the suffering and courage of others. We grew closer to God. We grew closer to each other. We learned to rely on other people. We found joy in simple things. We observed generosity, love and caring from hundreds of people. Our church family and our community rallied around Frankie and offered generous support in many areas.

My company grew and prospered during my absence. People within our organization developed new skills and confidence. I could easily list pages full of blessings and ways our life was impacted by our experience and our new family at St. Jude. Again, I would not wish the experience on anyone, nor would I trade it for anything. I learned optimism from my son and our family learned that blessings are always present, but you need to look for them. Looking for and distinguishing blessings in the midst of adversity is a major part of the skill of optimism.

Seeds of Greater or Equivalent Benefit

As a continuation of the blessings we received, we also found what Napoleon Hill called the "seed of greater or equivalent benefit." The entire experience provided me with insight I did not have before. I was presented with the time and opportunity to write this book. This book will raise money for St. Jude which will continue to help my son and will help other kids. Please don't misunderstand; I am not happy my son had cancer. I would have given everything I owned in a second to have lifted that burden from him. But once we realized the situation, our family made the choice that we would look for the good in the situation and look for blessings. I believe Frankie and our family's attitude played a part in his recovery. People who survive tremendous hardships do not overlook adversity, but neither do they dwell on it.

I have heard and read many inspiring stories of men who were imprisoned and faced the most severe and unimaginable pain and suffering. Most people gave up and died in those situations yet others were completely transformed and used the horrible for positive effect later in their lives. Men like Dr. Victor Frankl, who went on to write the groundbreaking *Man's Search for Meaning* after barely surviving the atrocities in a Nazi death camp.

During the war in Vietnam, many men were unfortunately captured ending up as American prisoners of war. Some courageous men did not make it through the ordeal. Others were broken by the process. In the face of an overwhelming personal storm, still others managed to not only survive, but grow through the ordeal. Admiral James Stockdale, Captain Gerald Coffee and Senator John McCain each spent many years in captivity during the Vietnam War. Each was starved, tortured, isolated and near death for years on end. How were these men able to not only survive, but go on to lead successful and productive lives? How did these men leverage their adversity into something positive while others died or were ruined by the same situation?

Each man decided he would do whatever was in his power to retain control of his emotions, and how he would respond to the situation. They each employed various techniques to maintain their sanity and their outlook on life. They had no control over what was done to them or what they were deprived of. The control they did have was in their ability to choose their response to the situation and the actions stemming from that response.

Dr. Frankl asserted in his post–concentration camp reflections that you cannot control what happens to you, but you can control your emotions. He felt he was able to survive by keeping this control. We can control how we feel by changing how we think and how we act. Emotions and attitudes do not come from events or outside circumstances, but rather the meaning we attach, give or are conditioned to give to the events. This is key as most people create their own negative reality out of situations that don't have to go that way.

Thoughts cause feelings. We can control our feelings by learning to control our thoughts. We can control our thoughts through practice, habit and conditioning. Our emotions are rooted in our thoughts. If you are feeling down and depressed or out of control of your own life, don't ask yourself how you feel or dwell on the feelings. This roots the emotions more securely. Instead change your approach and ask yourself what thoughts are making you have the feelings or emotions. Thoughts are the starting point so you must go there.

"The greater the difficulty, the greater the glory."
—Marcus T. Cicero

We all have negative thoughts, doubts and worry. Successful people are able to derail the train of negative emotion before it picks up any real steam. Successful people develop habits of optimism and learn to interrupt or stop negative patterns of thought. If you are lost, it makes no practical sense to dwell on being lost. It is more important to assess where you might have gone wrong and to get back to that place to resume going in the right direction.

"Smooth seas do not make skillful sailors."
—African Proverb

Unforeseen events will happen in our lives. People of decision will make choices of meaning and how to respond or proceed based on the meaning they attach. People of circumstance will be at the mercy of the situation. Brian Tracy observes, "The quality of your life is determined by how you feel at any given moment. How you feel is determined by how you interpret what is happening around you, not by the events themselves." There was certainly value for Frankie and our family through his battle with cancer. It is strange to say that, but adversity brings with it opportunity to learn about yourself and provides a growth experience. Our family grew stronger, our senses were heightened to value we might have otherwise taken for granted, our relationships grew and, although scary and trying, we would not change it for anything. In the same circumstances, we saw other parents who carried a "why me?" attitude about the situation.

"We who lived in concentration camps can remember the men who walked throughout the huts comforting others, giving away their last piece of bread. They may have been few in number, but they offer sufficient proof that everything can be taken away from a man but one thing: the last of the human freedoms—to choose one's attitude in any given set of circumstances, to choose one's own way....The last of the human freedoms is to choose one's attitudes."
–Victor Frankl

In the Bible in the book of James it is written, "Consider it pure joy, my brothers, whenever you face trials of many kinds, because you know that the testing of your faith develops perseverance. Perseverance must finish its work so that you may be mature and complete, not lacking in anything." Reflecting thoughtfully on our trials, challenges, defeats and hardships allows for the seed of situations to grow into a tree of experience that will ultimately bear the fruit of wisdom. Remember, a failure is only a failure based on the perspective. When two teams enter into a sporting contest, one team will win and one will lose. The success or failure of the contest lies completely with your interpretation based on your alliance. One team sees victory and the other sees defeat but the event itself is emotionally impartial.

When adversity presents itself to you as it most certainly will, it can be taken as either a blessing or a curse. A curse produces nothing positive; a blessing produces knowledge and understanding as well as wisdom. Probably the greatest separator in human progression is this moment of choice. You don't go looking for adversity as it knows where you live. Those who try to avoid it by refusing to challenge and grow still have adversity in the fear they live in.

Life is to be enjoyed and savored, but when hardship comes our way we need to choose to make the best out of what is presented to us. Sometimes the hidden blessing is being thankful for what we have left. Other times it is relationships or new beginnings or wisdom or being brought back down to earth with a gift of humility. Some people pay the equivalent of a new house or more for an education they are proud of and reflect on. Are the storms we have weathered in our lives any less valuable? All of our experience has brought us to this point and all can be profitable if we allow it to be and reflect with that intent.

A man died, leaving two small young boys without a father. Same home, same genetics, yet these two boys took divergent paths. This happened as a result of the attitudes and actions of each. The older son was bitter and resentful of the situation that left him without a father. His actions followed his thoughts and his life became a reflection of his feelings. His failed marriages and jobless periods mixed with his debt and drunkenness show a man whose life is in shambles. The other son, while equally sad for the loss, chose a path worthy of his father's admiration. His studies went well and led to professional opportunities. His marriage and his family are grounded in his faith. His work reflects his passion. His life is a work in progress, but he is happy for the journey.

Right now you fall into one of three categories or schools of thought. You either believe destiny and life happen and you deal with it as it comes, or you believe that you are the architect of your life largely controlling your destination and path to arrive there. The third category, and the one that most people fit into, is believing the second yet practicing the first. In this same way happiness is a choice. It is an inside issue rather than an external one. We are bombarded and brainwashed that we are unhappy and unfulfilled. An advertiser's number-one objective is to create discontentment…without their product. Every commercial you listen to or watch leaves you somewhat empty if you don't drive the new car, have the latest fashion, take the newest drug, etc. It is all shallow and superficial and nowhere does happiness come from what we own.

Happiness Is Choice

Here is a secret: Happiness is a game where you get to make your own rules. You may be living under some bad rules. I used to have a rule that I could only be happy when it was sunny. Some people can only be happy when others like them or when situations fall into place for them. The truth is you are in control. If you don't have rules working for you, change them! Set the game up to where you always win. Press your advantage. If your happiness is dependent upon or given up to others, chances are you will never be fully happy.

Count your reasons to be happy and take inventory of your blessings. Gratitude allows you to keep perspective, especially in hard times. It is important not to concentrate on what you lack, but rather what you have. This is fundamental and although contrary to what the network sponsors would have you believe, healthy. No one can make you happy or unhappy. People and events can certainly influence and work to direct you that way through normal stimulus-response behavior, but ultimately the choice is up to us.

Weather Your Storms

There are things in our life that we can't control or change. There may be times when we just can't be happy. Even so, we still have the choice at those times to maintain a cheerful disposition even if we cannot be happy. This is not "Fake it till you make it." Keeping a cheerful disposition allows you the ability to tread water in a situation rather than to drown. The best character example is provided to others through the opportunity brought by difficult times and adversity. Our adversities, once unburdened, serve only to make us stronger. It is like carrying a weight around and adapting to the weight. Once that weight is lifted you are stronger for the struggle.

"The harder the conflict, the more glorious the triumph."
—Thomas Payne

You Cannot Control the Weather

One day while driving to work in the pouring rain, I heard an upbeat song on the radio. I had gotten up early and refreshed, and just finished a great workout after a nice date with my wife the night before, so this song truly resonated with my mood for the day. It stayed in my head all morning and energized me. I would definitely have to classify that day as a success. Did the song verse that became my affirmation actually affect my day? In a very positive way the affirmation became a catalyst for me. A catalyst in scientific terms is a part of a chemical reaction that *affects* the reaction without being directly involved in it. My natural tendency is to allow myself to be affected by the weather. When it is sunny, I usually feel sunny. When the weather is dark and stormy, it is a struggle for my mood not to follow. This affirmation catalyst was a great reframe for me. It allowed me a new frame of reference for an old pattern of thinking.

Neither you nor I can control the weather. We cannot control what it will be today and we cannot affect in any way what it will be tomorrow. It is what it is and will be what it will be.

The same weather will make some people joyous and others miserable. When there is a snow day that shuts down everything, kids rejoice while parents who need to miss work or scramble for childcare do not. Rain is great when the farmers need it for the crops and devastating when the river peaks the levees. Hot sunny days are fantastic for people to enjoy a picnic yet miserable when you are in the field working. Weather in itself is neither good nor bad. Life reflects nature as good weather is broken up by periodic storms of varying intensities and make-ups. It is up to us and our decision how we choose to weather our personal storms and whether they leave us stronger and more resolute or weakened and cowering until the next one. Lou Holtz said, "Show me someone who has done something worthwhile, and I'll show you someone who has overcome adversity."

Adversity is a teacher instructing us through revealing our character and our true nature. If we do not like what is revealed, the good news is that we can change it. Our character and our constitution are not static. Challenge and adversity allow us the gift to choose our response and our action. We can change our character and grow into the person we wish to become if we take full advantage of the adversity that comes into our lives. It is different for each person, but adversity will find you. You cannot hide or run to avoid it. You must instead choose your response.

White contrasts black as dawn is contrasted by the darkness. Without the darkness there would be no dawn and without storms there would be diminished value in good weather. A man I used to work with always reminded me, "Without bad days, how would you know what a good one looked like?"

Your past is only alive if you allow it to remain that way in your thoughts. You cannot change what happened yesterday. Instead, build and work this day to benefit your tomorrow. Don't bind and shackle yourself with regrets or feel sorry for yourself. Don't hold the past so close that it prevents your future. Whatever you have gone through, whatever your previous circumstances, keep in mind that others have gotten through the same or worse. Learn from your past, but keep in mind the phraseology used in advertising investments: Past performance does not automatically guarantee future performance. Make this work in your favor as you recognize benefits from your past as applied to your future. Appreciate yourself and your situation as a survivor stronger for the trials and determined to make the best from every situation.

Theodore Roosevelt said, "The credit belongs to those people who are actually in the arena...who know the great enthusiasms, the great devotions to a worthy cause; who at best, know the triumph of high achievement; and who, at worst, fail while daring greatly, so that their place shall never be with those cold and timid souls who know neither victory or defeat."

Maintain positive perspective. A healthy sense of optimism and a cheerful disposition has tremendously more potential than a surly, negative outlook. Assess your situation honestly. See your adversity as a gift. Ask yourself what you can learn. Look for the seed of greater or equivalent benefit. Determine what action is necessary to change to a favorable outcome or to make the best of the situation. Take action as this helps birth optimism.

"Difficulties strengthen the mind, as well as labor does the body."
—Seneca

CHAPTER 18

Honesty and Integrity—The Twin Pillars of Your Support

. . . .

"Character is made up of those principles and values that give your life direction, meaning and depth. These constitute your inner sense of what's right and wrong based not on laws or rules of conduct but on who you are. They include such traits as integrity, honesty, courage, fairness and generosity—which arise from the hard choices we have to make in life."

—Stephen R. Covey

. . . .

Cornerstone

In building from ancient days to present, a cornerstone represents the one stone that all others will be laid from. A cornerstone is placed where two walls intersect. If this stone is set true, then the building can be built and all measurements taken from the cornerstone will result in proper alignment. But if the cornerstone is not set properly, all other measurements will be faulty and the building will not be structurally sound. Your integrity is your cornerstone and from it all other parts of your life will be based. It is tempting to take the easy way and shortcuts.

There can be no success in your life without integrity. Integrity is your internal wealth. It is knowledge that your life is transparent as you live out your values. The book of Proverbs (10:19) says, "The man of integrity walks securely, but he who takes crooked paths will be found out."

Integrity Defined

The American Heritage Dictionary defines integrity as "steadfast adherence to a strict moral or ethical code." You can lose everything else materially, your money, your job, etc., but the one thing to keep intact is your integrity. It would certainly be painful to lose everything, but as long as you maintain steadfastness to what you know is right, you maintain a positive ally in yourself. Honesty and integrity to others begin with personal honesty and integrity. William Shakespeare spoke the essence of this in *Hamlet*. The fatherly wisdom provided is the famous, "And this above all, to thine own self be true. And it must follow as the night the day—thou canst not then be false to any man." You need to be true to yourself. Keep promises to yourself and trust yourself.

Have Goals

Most of the modern success literature revolves around goal setting to obtain something or achieve something. Before you *have*, you must *do*. This concept revolves around the action principles we have discussed. Before you *do*, there is an extremely important aspect to take care of. Imagine a pyramid with three layers. At the top is the *have* or achievement level. This is the pinnacle of success with all that is important to you. The middle level is the *do* level in which you take action necessary to eventually achieve your goals. The most important thing is the base of the pyramid and the foundation for whatever your definition of success is. This is the *be* level. Who do you aspire to *be*? What kind of person do you want to *be*?

Your *be* goals reflect your character and what is important to you. Congruity with your major purpose in life provides the framework for integrity. You need to have internal congruity between who you think you are and the person you aspire to be. Don't get trapped by who you think you are, become instead who you want to be. If you want to be a person of integrity and character, but take action to cheat people to wealth, your actions are incongruent with your purpose and you will fail.

. . . .

"If I take care of my character, my reputation will take care of itself."
—D. L. Moody

. . . .

Understand yourself. If you could go back 10 years and counsel yourself, what would you suggest doing differently? Take a moment to reflect on how exactly you got to where you are. How did you end up in your career, relationship, financial condition, health situation, etc.? Develop for yourself who you are; don't conform to others' expectations of who you are. If you cannot be true to yourself and honest with yourself, how could you ever be honest with others?

None of us is perfect. We all make mistakes. Refuse to let this be an excuse or a safe harbor for what you know to be wrong. Look introspectively on your life and your journey. Reflect back from where you have been to get a better understanding of the road ahead. Are your goals aligned with the person you want to be? Are your action steps building a foundation of integrity for you to enjoy what you have built?

As just one example, wealth can be obtained by any number of methods. Methods built on service to others provide a rewarding sense of accomplishment. Methods built upon hurting or taking advantage of others are cheap and you will forever be forced to watch your back. Look at all the gangster stories in the past 100 years of America. From the Mafia to the drug trade to corporate felons, there is no honor among thieves. Many of the previous obtained short-term wealth only to lose their lives or the lives of those close to them. Who wants a retirement in the witness relocation program or constantly being paranoid? If you align with dishonest people or those whose lives are void of character, what will the law of the harvest bring back to you?

Most people are neither 100 percent honest nor dishonest. We all live somewhere in the gray, interpreting situations and making judgments based on our past and our knowledge base. Work to discern the lighter side of grey to build a solid foundation of "be" to support the rest of your life.

"Integrity is the most desired, demanded, and respected quality of leadership."
—Brian Tracy

Character

I read a *Successories* plaque in an office titled *The Essence of Destiny* that summed it all up nicely: "Watch your thoughts for they become words. Choose your words, for they become actions. Understand your actions, for they become habits. Study your habits, for they will become your character. Develop your character for it becomes your destiny."

Adversity, hardship or challenges in and of themselves do not necessarily build character, they reveal it. Your true character is revealed in your actions and in the choices you make. It is the promises you keep, the convictions you hold true to and the guiding principles of your life. What you say and do reveal who you are. The closer you are to the person you choose to be, the more people will observe you to be a person of character. We have all seen examples of, "Do as I say, not as I do." We have all seen people who live their lives in essence saying yes while nodding their head no. This incongruence is like a police officer breaking the law or a 300-pound weight-loss expert.

Value of a Name

Having the same name as your father and grandfather can be both a blessing and a curse. When I was eight years old, I am ashamed to admit, I shoplifted a candy bar from a local store. It is fair to assume that I was duly punished for my transgression. Although embarrassed, as I was forced to go back to the store and accept responsibility, I learned an indelible lesson through phase one of my punishment. Phase two was justice administered at home in a more private setting, which was also painful and memorable. In addition to the issue of right and wrong and stealing in general, I learned a powerful lesson from my father about the responsibility attached with carrying his name. Disappointing my father in my actions reflected poorly on him. His name and his reputation were very important to him, especially in a smaller town. Through his discipline he conveyed a message of the importance of a name and its billboard advertising of your reputation.

Your last name has a heritage and a lineage that long ago carried with it significance within the society that created it. You may not have the same full name as your parent, but you share a last name and hopefully it has value to you. Your name is your brand; what does it stand for? Think about your name for a moment. If it were brought up in a group of people you associate with, possibly at work, what do you think your name would represent? Do you take pride in your name and what it represents? I am not speaking about empty or boastful pride, but rather pride with recognition that your name has value. There once was a time that a person could go to the bank and get a loan on reputation alone. This is probably not likely to happen today, but your name still carries with it a value and your goal is to have your currency as high as you can.

Your name is your brand, representing you. Just like the high-profile consumer brands you instantly recognize, your name creates an association in the minds of people who know you. The association will be either positive or negative based on the impression others have of you. Your name is a (generally) two-word connotation for who you are to those who know you. That said, your word followed by your actions are your most important currency to value or devalue your brand. It may have evolved into a trite phrase, but it still remains very true. Your word is your bond! Jesus said, "By your words you are justified and by your words you are condemned." Your words set the tone for your actions. Walk your talk. Benjamin Franklin observed, "Well done, is better than well said." Honor your agreements with yourself and others. Certainly you are human. You will fall short, make mistakes and end up with your share of failures. With this acknowledgment, make sure you take responsibility, fail forward and increase the currency of your word.

One shortcoming I have had to focus on is working to not diminish the value of the currency of my word. I am naturally optimistic and tend to be very visual. As I started my career in sales and business, I would look to the future and see benefits I may not have been able to deliver on. On more than one occasion I have had to apologize for under-delivering on a promise. I certainly had good intentions and acted honorably yet the currency of my word was devalued each time this happened. My credibility bank account was diminished. I still struggle with this area and have learned to be more careful about what I promise versus what I hope and will work for. In these cases it is far better to under-promise and over-deliver. This is not only in business, but also in our interpersonal lives and relationships. I find it a constant battle to not over-promise, overextend or over-commit myself to my family and my friends. I can't think of a single time I purposefully did this, but the result is the same if you under-deliver on the expectations you set up for others. Just like a bank account, each promise kept is a deposit and each one missed is a withdrawal. Work to ensure you make consistent deposits or you will be overdrawn and your currency devalued.

When something does go badly, how do you respond and how do you correct to make the situation right? The actions you take when things go poorly are an insight into your character. Do you pass the buck, shift the blame and allow "it" to roll downhill? Or do you accept responsibility, find perspective and learn, going forward after dealing honestly with the people involved? When you make a mistake, admit it. Take action to correct it. Sometimes situations cannot be made right at the time. Do your best to make things right and then let it go as you progress forward.

Honesty and Integrity Are Building Blocks for Each Other

Integrity, like success is not a singular event. It is not an achievement to be hung upon the wall. Integrity is an accumulation built upon honesty to others but more importantly honesty to yourself. Honesty to yourself and to others can be as simple as keeping your word or as difficult as finding and honing your character in the midst of crisis and adversity. Honesty to oneself is the bedrock of integrity and integrity is the foundation of honesty. Does this sound like a circular argument? Look at integrity as your left foot and honesty as your right. You use your left foot to push off and gain distance at which your right foot can extend and hold the ground, while pulling the body past the center point to where it can then push for an extension opportunity for the left foot. Working in tandem, movement is accomplished and ground is gained. It is like this with honesty and integrity. They are similar yet different and both vital to a destination of character. Mark Twain suggests to, "Always do right—this will gratify some and astonish the rest."

Personal Responsibility to Develop Character—My Journey

Although completely different from my relationship with my grandfather four states away, my relationship with my dad early on was typical father and son. He appeared to me to have none of his father's patience. We always seemed to be up and down yet had a strong bond of love at the center. As I grew up, I found that my father and I were very much alike in many ways—something that often causes friction between people. As a young adult, the main point of contention between us was the fact I quit college in my junior year to chase after what he considered the "entrepreneurial pipedream." His feeling was that you needed to find a good company and a great boss and stay with that company until the very end. Although I did not disagree with him in principle, I did not see myself in this way.

I have always been an entrepreneur from as far back as my first lemonade stand to the candle-making business I started at eight that nearly burned down our house. Maybe that is part of the reason my dad resented my entrepreneurial leanings. I have always believed in myself and known that I wanted to be my own boss.

While in college, I joined ROTC and was commissioned as an officer in the army. I didn't initially want to be a soldier, but I love to learn and leadership is one of the most intriguing and exciting fields. I felt that the army would be a good opportunity to grow in this area. I figured I could just be a "weekend warrior" in the Reserves while I pursued my next great business adventure.

I had a great deal of selling success working for various companies, but I still had that itch for my own business. Seeing myself as the next "Zig Ziglar at 22," I attempted a business venture in the personal development industry, leveraging everything I had, and took the great risk. My father certainly didn't understand. I felt I had to show him and spite him with the millions I would soon make.

The millions did not happen. Ultimately, I had to fold up shop and get a real job. I vowed that I would never file bankruptcy and worked as hard as I could to juggle paying back loans, credit cards, vendors and investors. It couldn't have been any more depressing. I finally had to go, hat in hand, to Dad and ask him to co-sign a huge note at the bank for me. This loan was over $10,000, which seemed like $10 million. When coupled together, all of my other debts and obligations made it seem like an insurmountable obstacle. My father was gracious, even though he thought I would never pay it back. Nevertheless, he provided me the benefit of the opportunity to take responsibility for my actions.

Piece by piece, I started to dig myself out. I still had some army officer training to complete, so I set off to Fort Knox, Kentucky, for six more months to learn how to be an Armor Officer. As a matter of coincidence, my graduation date was in August of 1990, which happened to be the same time when Saddam decided to get frisky with his neighbors and a little war broke out. Within five months I was on the ground in a foreign country. One benefit of being in Saudi Arabia was that I could send all of my pay to my dad to apply systematically to my debts, as I had no real need for money. Prior to going to Desert Storm, I met and fell immediately in love with a young lady named Lisa. We became engaged before leaving for Saudi Arabia and were to be married the following year.

Now my dad loved Lisa right away because she could give as well as *he* gave. He was concerned about our starting a family in such a dismal financial condition; I still had a long way to go to dig myself out. Concerned yet supportive, he would encourage me and tell me to continue to, "Stack The Logs!" I understood yet really had no idea the depth of meaning in his words.

Several years of more ups and downs went by and brought the addition of a new son in our lives. Living in Chicago, working for a large convenience store chain and making very slow yet steady progress, my father's words were always consistent, "Keep Stacking the Logs and eventually the pile will be so high no one will be able to avoid it." I felt stymied at my job. I was discouraged. The more I tried to grow in my job and new career, the more my immediate supervisor became threatened by me, my enthusiasm and my willingness to contribute. She did everything she could to get in the way of my upward corporate mobility. My dad would just keep repeating, "Stack The Logs!"

Fast-forward again to my 30th birthday. All of the debts from the previous business were paid off, including that huge bank note. I had a wonderful wife in Lisa. We had a young son who was carrying the same name as my father, his father and grandfather, and we had another baby on the way. My father was working to teach me a life lesson that began when I was very young to the point of being a father myself. His message was consistent even though I did not see it or fully understand it at the time.

Success is not in your bank account, the car you drive or the house you own. Our society may portray this version of the American dream as success, but this is counterfeit. Success ultimately is in the character you develop and in what you give to others. Just as there is no real "get rich quick," there is no "instant character." Character is built and developed through the individual action steps resulting in ICE. It took me a while to really grasp my father's lesson to me. He could have rescued me any number of times, yet he cared enough about me to allow me to make my mistakes and most importantly to take responsibility for my own actions.

"Organize and execute around your priorities"
—Stephen R. Covey

Shortcuts Never Really Are

In my early days in business my goal was to be rich. I wanted to be a millionaire before I was 25. I created action yet my thought was about wealth for me rather than service for others. I found out the hard way that the only "quick" in get rich quick is in the quicksand. My situation did not turn around until I learned the lesson…service to others precedes wealth.

Have faith in yourself and what you believe. People may not always agree with you, but if you are true to your convictions, they will respect you. Know what you will fight for and what you will walk away from, but do not compromise what is right. Your decisions need to be made in alignment with your principles and values. Integrity is more than telling the truth. Sometimes integrity goes against self-interest, but this is where your value structure carries you. Keep your commitments and promises to yourself and others. Be honest, sincere and consistent in what you say and do. A hypocrite or one who is a "do as I say not as I do" person, weakens their value in the eyes of others. Your credibility with those around you comes not from what you say, but rather from your previous pattern of living up to what you have said.

Take the Long View and Practice Perspective

Develop a keen sense of humor. A hearty and natural laugh, a smile and a refreshing warm sense of humor are excellent bonding tools. A keen sense of humor adds a quality of magnetism and kinship to relationships. Be careful of a sarcastic wit and negative humor. Although usually funny, this is a skill to definitely keep in check as sarcasm can lead others to think you are negative in your thinking. Sarcasm has the potential to damage relationships. Be careful also to keep your sense of humor clean and without offense or malice. Contrary to the successful dirty and ribald comedians, your stock will be lowered to many with this type of humor. Use self-effacing humor without degrading yourself or reinforcing self-images you are attempting to change or improve.

Guard your reputation and character as if they were your most prized possessions. In most respects they really are. You will have situations arise where it will be easier to take shortcuts or do the more expedient thing rather than doing what is right. Stay the course. You may be slightly disadvantaged in the short-term, but your character will be developed and strengthened through any adversity or hardships. The news today is filled with corporate, political and personal scandal. We have all seen what happens when people as well as companies take the short view and compromise their ethics and integrity. The law of sowing and reaping will always work in your favor when you take the long view.

Abraham Lincoln was certainly tested and had ample opportunity to take a more expedient road. His adversity from early on, as we established previously, made up the building blocks of his character. Regarding the personality trait of character, Abraham Lincoln reflects, "I am not bound to win, but I am bound to be true. I am not bound to succeed, but I am bound to live by the light that I have. I must stand with anybody that stands right, and stand with him while he is right, and part with him when he goes wrong."

Develop Interpersonal Integrity

Act right now as the person you desire to be, a person with an excellent reputation and unquestionable character. How you talk, how you act, your dress, your facial expressions and body language all give off clues and are a reflection of your personality. Every day, realized or not, you give off signals to other people. They, in turn, process that information subconsciously, make decisions about you and respond to you. This is automatic and all under the radar, but it happens with every single personal transaction or interaction you have with others. Your current relationship with your family, acquaintances, coworkers, supervisors is based on the Incremental Cumulative Effect of every interaction you have had to this point. Occasionally there may be blips one way or the other. However, most relationships follow a trend having to do with the law of resonance we studied in Chapter 12.

There is connection and chemistry between people that is easy to detect. "We are definitely in sync with each other." "I have a good vibe about her." There is also the negative version. "I don't know, he just doesn't give me any warm fuzzies." "She really rubs me the wrong way." People watch you. When you are pleasant in demeanor, cheerful, smile, have good things to say about others, discuss solutions rather than problems, work hard, dress appropriately, etc., you give people a glimpse of who you really are. Conversely when you are pessimistic, carry a dark rain cloud with you, walk with a sad slouch letting your body language tell your Gloomy Gus tale, people will discount you and subconsciously treat you accordingly.

This happens all the time. People do it to you and you do it to others without even thinking. If you walked into a room with five other people you had never met before and spent five minutes with each, you would come out of there with your impression of each individual. They would also have an impression of you. Optimism and more directly, practical optimism applied to your actions has a direct bearing on your outcomes. Practical optimism is part of personal integrity. If you say you are happy but act sad and depressed with your body language, you are being incongruent. Make an effort to maintain a positive demeanor with your body as well as your language and your actions.

The Bedrock of Moral Character Is Personal Responsibility

George Washington Carver once observed, "Ninety-nine percent of failures come from people who have a habit of making excuses." It is certain you will make mistakes in your life. When you screw up, take responsibility as you practice the skills of failing forward. You will earn the trust and respect of others. Life is a team sport. In teams where there is blame and no responsibility, there is chaos. No one wants to be on a team with a person they in essence cannot trust. When others trust you as a person of your word, a person with integrity who will take personal responsibility, they will work with you through your shortcomings and missteps. Build your internal infrastructure around your congruence to values and the bedrock principle of personal responsibility.

. . . .

"Live your life in every way to earn and keep the respect of the people you respect."
—Brian Tracy

. . . .

Part VII

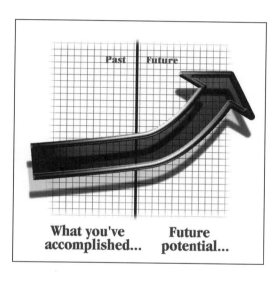

Past | Future

What you've
accomplished...

Future
potential...

KEEP ON STACKING THE LOGS!

CHAPTER 19

The Incredible Power of Continued Incremental Improvement™

"Success has nothing to do with what you gain in life or accomplish for yourself. It's what you do for others."

—Danny Thomas, entertainer and founder of St. Jude Children's Research Hospital

Applied Incremental Advantage

A young man named Amos Jacobs was born as the fifth child of nine to Lebanese immigrants on January 6, 1912. This young man had a dream to be in show business. He thought he had talent. Along with his brother Ray, he formed a burlesque duo and achieved some success until Ray decided to leave the business for a more traditional path. Amos wanted to be in show business. He had a dream and he had the passion to pursue his dreams. He worked hard and found some small success as a radio actor and singer in the Detroit area.

Amos, looking for a spark to his new career, changed his name by taking on the persona in the combination name of two of his brothers. At this time, he married his beautiful childhood sweetheart Rose Marie. Amos knew he had talent and knew his course.

His wife now pregnant, Amos was still a struggling entertainer and worried if he could support his new family as well as maintain a career in show business. His heart heavy with the responsibility, a troubled Amos visited a church in Detroit and earnestly prayed to St. Jude Thaddeus, the patron saint of hopeless causes. He beseeched the saint, "Show me my way in life and I will build you a shrine." Within a few weeks, Amos, now better known as Danny Thomas, secured a regular job at a Chicago nightclub. From that point, Danny Thomas's career as an entertainer skyrocketed. He set his course, took action, accepted his results as feedback, course corrected and kept Stacking the Logs! until he achieved the outcome he desired. Danny Thomas lived the STACK Strategy for his show business career; but he would not stop there.

The Success Story of St. Jude Children's Research Hospital

By all accounts, Danny Thomas was a Hollywood success. He was a nationally known entertainer who could have easily coasted through an enchanting life with all the perks and benefits of the glamour industry. But Danny Thomas was a man of great character and personal integrity and as such, he accepted personal responsibility for his life. Danny never forgot his promise to St. Jude Thaddeus. Danny created a trusted support structure to share in his dream and his passion. Danny Thomas and friends set out in the early 1950s to found St. Jude Children's Research Hospital, which unquestionably is his most lasting legacy.

In 1962, the first patients began their treatment. Today, St. Jude Children's Research Hospital, located in Memphis, Tennessee, is the world's premier institution for the study and treatment of catastrophic childhood diseases. When St. Jude officially opened the doors, the most common form of pediatric cancer, acute lymphocytic leukemia, was literally a death sentence as little more than 4 percent of children with this horrific disease survived. This was to be the starting point, knowing the destination lay far, far ahead. I would later learn through many other people and in our family's experience that the abysmal survival statistic was the motivation behind and the starting point of an ongoing journey.

Danny Thomas magnetized the conditions he sought. He attracted like-minded men and women as support structure dedicated to share his dream that, "No child should die in the dawn of life." Together this group knew their outcome and set their course accordingly. They took action on fronts from fundraising to breakthrough science to groundbreaking research and outstanding patient care. They achieved results as feedback. Some of the results were painful and heartbreaking as parents and families watched their loved ones die. They had break-throughs and they had setbacks, but each patient treated brought the St. Jude team closer to understanding and closer to the de-sired results. The course was corrected each time new information was learned or discovered. Each painstaking component of the process has been invented and reinvented with the end goal in mind. Most of all, Danny Thomas and his support structure with the St. Jude team never gave up.

Through more than 40 years of the highest highs and the lowest lows, St. Jude continued to make incremental improve-ment and incremental progress. Today, largely because of discoveries made at St. Jude, unbelievable advances have been made on many fronts with regard to childhood catastrophic dis-ease and illness. Each success was reinvested into the process. Each discovery shared with other institutions and other scien-tists expanded the information and knowledge base. Every victory has been reinvested for a compound cumulative incremental improvement. Now the survival rate for the initial leukemia enemy with the initial survival rate of 4 percent has increased to over 80 percent and is improving.

Close to Home

The success and humanitarian story of Danny Thomas and his dream could not hit any closer to home for me or my family. On Easter Sunday, March 31, 2002, our family became forever a part of the family of St. Jude Children's Research Hospital as

Frankie's treatment for acute myeloid leukemia began. When I first learned my son had leukemia, I was immediately numb, thinking he had just been handed a death sentence. We were reassured by many who were familiar with St. Jude that we were going to the best place available.

What I would observe over the next six months solidified all we were told. We were cared for by a very human organization that daily lived out the purpose of the man who founded it. In the past, I have worked with hundreds of corporations and organizations and have seen hundreds of mission statements adorning the walls or pages of company brochures. What I found in St. Jude was one of the finest organizations I have ever observed or been associated with in the daily demonstration of the mission and vision.

This incredible legacy and continuing living breathing organization began with a thought in Danny Thomas's mind. It began as a ripple spreading out from the center of Danny Thomas's being. This is in no way intended as a slight to the other fine institutions, but rather only what I witnessed as a critical observer.

Much of this book was written while Frankie was in his initial six months of treatment in Memphis. We lived in St. Jude–provided housing and all of our needs were met far beyond expectation. We were given a rare glimpse of not just a hospital, but also a family and community at work with complete alignment and singleness of purpose to the vision. I was able to talk to (and pester) and make some excellent friends while at St. Jude. As I look and review the material presented in this book, I can think of no better organization to share as a practical illustration of the principle of applied Incremental Advantage. Since I was writing this book during Frankie's treatment, my reticular activating system was on overdrive drawing me to observe and witness the very practical side of the material I was working on.

Practical Application

My father's letter of encouragement to me is what makes up the seven parts of this book. The components of his wisdom are evident to me in everything I witnessed while we were at St. Jude. As I reflect on what Danny Thomas began and his far-reaching legacy, I can clearly see the message my father shared with me at work in Danny Thomas and others' determined actions.

Plan Well

Danny Thomas began his journey as a tribute to St. Jude Thaddeus, the patron saint of lost or hopeless causes. What could be more of a lost cause than childhood catastrophic diseases? In addition to leukemia, there are a great number of other catastrophic and life-threatening pediatric maladies St. Jude treats. From the outset, the plan was simple and straightforward: to find treatments and cures to allow children to live far beyond the dawn of their lives. There is nothing more heartbreaking than the death of a child and no more motivating factor for the dedicated work of hundreds of staff and a legion of volunteers.

Not only was there a plan in place for the incremental improvement of medical care toward treatment and cures, but there was an incredible plan for the creating of a marketing and fundraising arm to provide support for families so that no child in need would ever be denied because of a lack of money. In this day and age, benevolence comes at a mighty cost. However, the creation of a dedicated marketing and fundraising organization working in complete alignment of the goals of St. Jude provides just that. ALSAC (American Lebanese Syrian Associated Charities) is an extraordinary organization that through its charter and existence allows the hospital the sole focus of its founder's intent.

Keep an Excellent Forward Thrust to Your Objectives

The lifesaving work at St. Jude Children's Research Hospital is far broader than what it might seem at the surface level. When you think of a hospital, you naturally think about a process to go from being sick to being well. With regard to the catastrophic childhood diseases St. Jude has targeted, there is ongoing focus and effort toward the task of finding effective therapies and cures. Much deeper at issue is the cause and understanding of why these diseases attack children. The focus drills down all the way to the molecular and biological level of the DNA blueprint. Without proper understanding of the causes, the cures will not be complete.

The clinical research at St. Jude includes study and focus on bone marrow transplantation, chemotherapy, radiation treatment and surgery as therapies. There is also an ongoing study of a wide variety of issues relating to the desired outcome. From understanding the biochemistry of normal versus cancerous cells, blood diseases, issues causing resistance to therapy, viruses, hereditary diseases, all facets from cause to cure are under the microscope. In addition, there is another ongoing biostatistical study on adults living cancer-free as St. Jude is blessed with positive results and the first considerable population of adults living cancer-free after having received chemotherapy and radiation treatments as children. The hospital maintains contact long after treatment with these former patients to conduct long-term studies on the history of their health. These studies have led to improvements in ongoing treatment to avoid potential additional problems related to the initial treatment. This has a positive effect to improve the life of future children diagnosed with cancer.

The dedicated team at St. Jude knows specifically what they want as an outcome and take focused consistent action toward that conclusion. The enemy in this work is not so much what is known or not known, but more so what is not known that is unknown. Each theory must be tested and proven and some effects or outcomes are not known until much later down the road. The effect of all this is a frustrating and many times dark journey. The team at St. Jude does a miraculous job focused on what they can do today while keeping an eye on where they desire to progress to tomorrow.

Deal with Your Disappointments and Setbacks

In the beginning, St. Jude was facing an amazing uphill battle. According to St. Jude's website information, in 1962, the survival rate for cancers and tumors affecting children were dramatically low. Below is just a sample as referenced by St. Jude faculty statistics (www.stjude.org) of the many types of cancers treated at St. Jude and their respective survival rates at the beginning of the hospital's existence compared to the progress made after 40 years of incremental improvement:

	SURVIVABILITY STATISTICS	
DISEASE TYPE	**1962**	**2002**
1. Acute Lymphocytic Leukemia (cancer of the blood)	4 percent	80 percent
2. Ewing Sarcoma (bone cancer type)	5 percent	75 percent
3. Hodgkin's Disease (cancer of the lymph nodes)	50 percent	90 percent
4. Neuroblastoma (cancer of the nervous system)	10 percent	59 percent
5. Non-Hodgkin's Lymphom (malignant tumor)	7 percent	80 percent
6. Osteosarcoma (bone cancer type)	20 percent	70 percent
7. Retinoblastoma (type of eye cancer)	75 percent	90 percent
8. Rhabdomyosarcoma (solid tumor affecting muscles)	30 percent	75 percent
9. Wilms Tumor (cancer in kidneys)	50 percent	90 percent

Behind the J-shape curve of these statistics hide two distinct stories. One is the amazing progress and the incredible life-saving advances made by St. Jude. The other side of the story is the amazing people who sadly are no longer with us today and the tragic loss for thousands of families. In 1962, 96 percent of childhood leukemia patients died. This is tragic.

Like all successes over time, St. Jude has had its share of heartache and disappointment in the past 40 years. Unfortunately, there is no success in this endeavor without the learning curve that must be traveled. The positive future cumulative effect and the value of lives saved through enduring this sometimes painful process can never truly be measured. This sorrow and frustration can only be contrasted by the priceless upside of children's lives saved.

Create a Positive Support Structure

Once Danny Thomas firmly had his vision in mind in the early 1950s, he began discussing with friends what this vision might look like. Over time, the idea of a children's hospital came about. In 1955, a group of Memphis businessmen agreed to help Danny. They would lend their support and leverage in the creation of a unique research hospital to be devoted to curing catastrophic diseases in children. The dream was to be more than just a treatment facility or regular hospital. The dream of Danny Thomas and his support structure would be to create a world-class research center to benefit the children of the world in treatment and a search for cures to catastrophic childhood diseases.

In the mid-1950s, Danny along with his wife, family and many supporters began raising significant money for Danny's vision of St. Jude. Tapping into Danny's entertainment friends as well as business leaders in the Memphis area, they created all of the necessary funds to build this great hospital and begin this worthy endeavor. Now built, they faced an even larger undertaking of funding the annual operation of the new hospital.

Danny looked to his fellow Americans of Arabic heritage. He deeply believed that Arabic-speaking Americans should, as a group, show respect and thanks to the United States for the gifts of freedom provided to their parents. Danny felt that supporting St. Jude would be a noble way of honoring his heritage and his immigrant forefathers who had come to America. Danny's commitment and passion for his cause struck a resonant chord. A hundred representatives of the Arab-American community met in Chicago in 1957 to form a fundraising arm dedicated to the support of St. Jude. ALSAC (American Lebanese Syrian Associated Charities), also founded by Danny Thomas, was created to be an ongoing positive support structure with the sole purpose of fundraising and generating support for St. Jude Children's Research Hospital.

Currently, ALSAC is the fourth largest not-for-profit health-related fundraising organization in America. Headquartered in Memphis adjacent to the hospital and with regional offices throughout the United States, ALSAC has 100 percent of the responsibility of the hospital's fundraising efforts. ALSAC is supported with the dedicated efforts of over one million volunteers across the nation and in many other countries. Together, this amazing support structure raises millions of dollars annually through a variety of creative methods. The fundraisers, benefits and solicitation drives involve Americans of all economic, religious, racial, cultural and ethnic backgrounds. In addition to the many millions of dollars raised is the education and awareness created for the ongoing mission of the hospital. Danny Thomas truly created a positive support structure to enable the dream to continue beyond his life.

Stay Positive, Stay Focused

Frankie was initially diagnosed by Dr. McAllister from the St. Jude Midwest Affiliate office in Peoria, Illinois. After the initial shock, I tearfully asked him, "How much time do I have with my son?" He looked me right in the eye and said something I will never forget. He said to me, "You cannot think that way. You have to think 100 percent that your son is going to live!" Those confident words started our journey on the right path and kept our mind-set where it needed to be.

Studies upon studies have proven a direct correlation between a patient's mental attitude and his or her progress in healing. With children as patients, the parent's attitudes and beliefs about their children are crucial as the children look to the parents for understanding. The response of the children mirrors the attitude of the adults. With this knowledge, St. Jude provided care far beyond the scope of treating the disease. With a dedicated child life team of employees and volunteers working with the doctors and nurses, St. Jude assisted parents and families to remain positive and focused on the desired outcome. It is difficult to measure how this affected patients and their recovery, but it was easy to observe. St. Jude is a hospital full of life and hope with practical optimism in practice daily.

Maintain Your Moral Character

St. Jude is a research hospital. What this means is that as a patient family, you are completely informed at the outset that with your consent, your child will be part of a treatment protocol. Some parts of the treatment are done differently with one group than with others to study the long-term effects. There were some parts of Frankie's treatment where a certain medicine's dosage was unknown to the doctors and to us. There were instances where another patient with the same diagnosis might have a slightly different treatment path to study different effects. Before Frankie started his treatment, we were given a complete briefing by his team of doctors and nurses. We were told the truth as were given the good, bad and ugly with regard to his prognosis and treatment plan. We were told what the negative outcomes could be for everything from different medicines to the possibility that he might not survive. All of this was presented to us in candor and with great humanity and sensitivity to our needs.

I am convinced that since St. Jude was founded, each patient has received the absolute best care, the best medical treatment and the best technology available at the time. The best decisions were made and the best course of treatment was put into place. All grouped together, this is called a protocol. Each disease has its individual protocol created by the best minds with the best information available. The treatment plan is carried out and a result for each patient and group of similar patients is studied over time. The results as feedback allow the scientists and doctors to make changes, modifications and course corrections in the treatment plan and a new protocol is established.

The treatment my son underwent without a shadow of a doubt saved his life. What is so sad is the understanding that many lives were lost prior to Frankie's treatment in order to build the knowledge base of the disease and the treatment. There is no other way to describe the process of treating cancer than trial and error. I am certain the process I witnessed by the team at St. Jude is similar to other hospitals and other treatments of catastrophic diseases.

As a research hospital, there are clearly opportunities for competing interests taking precedent over patient care. There is clinical research, drug testing, patents, grants, legislation, regulation and funding issues all at stake. In a research hospital, ethics are paramount. There is a gray area in need of constant balance to maintain service to present needs with integrity as well as pursuing the desired outcomes for future generations. I feel 100 percent confident and can say with total certainty that I witnessed an institution possessing moral character and living integrity throughout the entire process and organization. We never felt for a second anything but confidence in the process or the motives during any facet of Frankie's treatment.

In addition to the ethical side of the equation, St. Jude demonstrated a humanitarian side in how they dealt with the financial aspect of an exorbitant process. With treatment costs of healthcare nationwide skyrocketing and the daily operating cost of St. Jude edging up close to a $1 million per day, all St. Jude patients are treated regardless of their ability to pay. ALSAC covers all costs above what is reimbursed by third-party insurers. When there is no insurance, ALSAC generously covers all of the costs.

Keep on Stacking Those Logs!

As of this writing, St. Jude has treated nearly 20,000 children from the United States and more than 60 foreign countries. Research discoveries and patient care victories are freely shared with other institutions to add leverage and increase the collective medical community's advantage to the common goal. Unfortunately, every patient experience is filled with ups and downs and in some cases the patients do not survive. Even though there are still gut-wrenching heartbreaks, every patient is cared for as part of the St. Jude family with love and respect. Patients and families understand that every patient experience provides increased knowledge and insight toward finding the cause and the cure for these terrible diseases as a benefit for future patients. The progress continues!

Applied STACK Strategy of St. Jude Children's Research Hospital

The basis of this book is creating success through applied Incremental Advantage and utilizing the STACK Strategy as a framework or blueprint tool to assist in guiding and determining your outcome. As you look at the components below, it is clear that Danny Thomas and all of the dedicated team who created and funded St. Jude Children's Research Hospital used the major principles in their creation.

Although he did not know the STACK Strategy as a formal course of action, Danny Thomas certainly applied the principles. He used them effectively to create not only his entertainment success, but also success far beyond the scope any man could see in his founding of St. Jude and ALSAC. He knew his desired outcome and took action. He accepted his results as feedback and retooled his approach until he achieved the result he sought. He continued to Stack The Logs!, providing ongoing benefits for children and families today.

Achieving Incremental Advantage Through Persistence

Starting with Danny Thomas and carried through the doctors, nurses, scientists, fundraisers, volunteers, and everyone else associated with the hospital, St. Jude put into practice every important principle and natural law contained within this book. The practical application of applied Incremental Advantage for the St. Jude team created a results graph starting at the 4 percent in 1962, growing to over 80 percent survivability in 2002 and improving. The results graph of St. Jude Children's Research

Hospital is the personification of the J-shaped curve and I can think of no better illustration to demonstrate the effectiveness of the STACK Strategy. Creating leverage through information sharing and researching genetic root causes as well as searching for cures, St. Jude has ultimately helped save the lives of innumerable children everywhere in the world...including my son.

Danny Thomas began St. Jude as a commitment repaid to his prayer request. His initial pledge of, "Show me my way in life and I will build you a shrine" began a creation and a dream fulfillment that would outlive the creator. Sadly, but with no regrets, Danny Thomas passed away on February 6, 1991, only two days after celebrating the hospital's 29th anniversary. Laid to rest in a family crypt at the Danny Thomas/ALSAC Pavilion on the grounds of the hospital with his beloved wife, Rose Marie, his dream and his legacy will forever live on. Danny and Rose Marie's three children, Marlo, Terre and Tony, carry on the passion and important work of their parents. Together, along with an army of dedicated friends and supporters, they continue to be a driving force in fulfilling their father's mission.

"Never give in! Never give in! Never. Never. Never. Never..."
—Sir Winston Churchill

CHAPTER 20

Advanced STACK™ Action Plan

(A Success Strategy Guaranteed to Work 100 Percent of the Time)

. . . .

"Confidence doesn't come out of nowhere. It's a result of something…hours and days and weeks and years of constant work and dedication."
—Roger Staubach

. . . .

Strategy Versus Tactics

Strategy is defined as the overall planning and conduct of an operation or an overall plan of action. Tactics are the smaller scale securing of objectives of the overall strategy. Tactics are the methods used to bring about the achievement of the goal or objective. An example of this would be in war. A strategy would be created and set forth by the generals and commanders. This strategy would be accomplished by breaking everything down into smaller component parts into a tactical plan. This would continue to be passed on and the detail would grow the further down the chain of command the mission went.

In the Gulf War, General Norman Schwarzkopf and his brilliant team of military strategists, created an overall plan for how he intended to bring war to the Iraqis. This strategy was then divided into major subgroups or commands all working in coordination. In turn each major command had to communicate and create tactical sub-plans for their units as well as communicate with surrounding units. If the 82nd Airborne needed to parachute behind enemy lines at a certain time, assets of the Air Force needed their tactical planning to coincide. It was an amazing and extraordinary undertaking to take General Schwarzkopf's strategy and translate it all the way down to the smallest unit's tactical mission. Yet without the success of the tactical missions and the coordination, communication and support of every unit and sub-unit in his command, Norman Schwarzkopf could never have achieved his amazing success in the Gulf War.

As a young first lieutenant during the Gulf War, I was provided my own opportunities with strategies and tactics. My unit was the 685th Transportation Unit and we were assigned the offloading and reloading of all of the army's major equipment in the ships at the Port of Damam, south of Iraq. Our unit and our peer units were given our overall missions by our commander and we were responsible for getting the job accomplished. Resource allocation, personnel, logistics, etc., were all part of our tactical planning. Obstacles to overcome and challenges to face were our tactical issues. Like all of the other great units that comprised the thousands of servicemen and women from the different branches and even different countries and nationalities, our combined tactical execution of the strategic objectives provided to us was instrumental in the successful execution of the brilliant strategy utilized in this war.

Please do not misunderstand. I am not trying to maximize in any way my importance in the success of the Gulf War. I am proud of what we did and my role as a cog in the machinery. I also understand that had I been absent from duty, there is still a fairly good chance we would have won. Kidding aside, I could see that my tactical role was a part of many thousands of similar tactical components creating the success of the overall strategy ultimately winning the war in dramatic fashion.

Throughout recorded history military battles and campaigns show the relationship between tactics and strategy. Although a great strategy can sometimes overcome weaker tactics, rarely can a major campaign be won without a great strategy. In World War II, many battles were both won and lost by both sides. In the end, the strategy of the Allied Forces prevailed over the uncoordinated and changing objectives of the Axis powers. Adolph Hitler's increasing feeling of invincibility and his dementia created cracks in the strategic framework of what seemed to be an invincible military power. Many historians agree that had he maintained the course with regard to his strategy and his earlier successes, Adolph Hitler might have won World War II.

A recent example of strong tactics losing out to a poor overall strategy would be the war in Vietnam. The U.S. Army never lost a major tactical battle in the entire campaign, yet the strategy for victory in that war was never strong enough to allow for the major victory. How is it that you can win every battle and yet lose the war? In this case it might be a dramatic oversimplification, but there was no clear communication of objectives and no compelling vision of a strategy or endgame. With tremendous respect for those who served, it is a sad observation that thousands of men gave their lives to win victory in battles yet not achieve the overall success due to the weak strategy and absence of clear-cut military goals. General Schwarzkopf and many of his senior team were soldiers in Vietnam. They learned valuable lessons from that war and applied them brilliantly to their new situation. They vowed not to repeat the mistakes made in Vietnam with the soldiers under their care.

In pursuit of our goals and dreams, it is vital to have the large picture strategy for our compelling and dynamic destination. It is equally vital that we have "rubber meets the road" tactics and tools to get us to where we want to be. We have discussed goal setting previously, but I want to share a very simple understanding of this extremely powerful tactical tool.

Focus on Doing the Right Things—
Not Just Doing Things Right

People who focus on just doing things right are bound to come up short and lead lives of mediocrity. People who focus instead of doing the right things will find success. Prior to World War II, the Polish cavalry was the finest precision outfit of the day. They had the most focused and finely honed skills of any horseback unit around. They concentrated all their efforts in their strategy and tactics to doing things right. Unfortunately, they were wholesale annihilated in the first battle of World War II against the aggression of Adolph Hitler and the German tanks.

Who is the most successful executive in the vinyl record industry? How about the beta tape industry? It does not take much to see the importance of an overall strategy and how you fit in. It may seem a minor point of semantics to differentiate between doing the right things versus doing things right. In reality, there is a world of difference between the two. Too often we get trapped in the routine of our lives and focus all our efforts on doing things right. In this tunnel vision, we lose sight of the real question: Are we focused on the right things? In his book, *The 7 Habits of Highly Effective People*, Stephen Covey illustrates this phenomenon as putting forth tremendous effort to climb the ladder of success only to find out you had it up against the wrong wall.

Advanced STACK Action Plan—
Strategy and Tactics Applied

Strategic planning is a process leaders use to envision the future. Through this, they develop the necessary sub-strategies to achieve that future, and implement each strategy according to a specific timetable. Organizations use strategic planning and it is absolutely applicable in your personal life. It is an ongoing process. It is a systems approach to maneuvering yourself through a continually changing environment to fulfill your overall mission. At the start of this chapter, we defined strategy as the overall planning and conduct of an operation with tactics being the securing of objectives within the overall strategy. Strategy is the larger framework or the map with tactics being the action points to achieve your goal. As with the example of overwhelming success in Desert Storm, the overall strategy was determined first.

Once established, the individual components could be developed and allowed to work within the structure of the larger strategy. Not only is this important in winning a war, it is essential in your personal and business life as well. Without an overall framework for what you want to achieve in your life, you cannot determine or apply meaningful action steps. Most people wander in life as Newton's third law of motion works in their lives. This law basically states that for every action, there is an equal and opposite reaction. Most people are on a meandering walk without a clear destination and outside forces (action) change their path (reaction). They stay on this path until other outside force influence them and change their direction. A strategy for your life and your objectives is critical if you want to remain in control of your destiny rather than let it happen.

STACK Strategy: Five Steps to an Outcome

S – Set your destination and course
T – Take immediate action
A – Accept results simply as feedback
C – Correct your course based on feedback
K – Keep on Stacking the Logs!

The STACK Strategy for Success is a big-picture issue. It requires some thinking to determine what course you want to set. It is an operating strategy that provides you with an understanding of what to do in sequence, much like a computer's operating system. In a computer's operating system, there may be many types of programs. Some of them are completely different from one another. The only real commonality or thread running through all of the programming is how it works as part of the operating software. Microsoft became the absolute giant company it did creating wealth and billions for the shareholders not because of the individual programs, but because of the operating software. Microsoft's recent legal battles stem from the fact that their operating system was so successful, so prevalent and in use in the marketplace that competing programs and companies were forced to adapt and use Microsoft's platform (if they were allowed).

This strategic framework is designed to allow the various goals and objectives in different areas of your life to work in conjunction and harmony with each other. Each different goal you have can work within this operating system. None of us are the same and none of us are one dimensional. My definition of success may be different than yours. My priorities are most likely different than yours. There are many facets of our lives where it is important to have planned outcomes rather than just ending up somewhere. Your health, family, financial, social, educational, spiritual and other significant components of your life need to be part of a deliberate structure if they are important to you. There is no value in attaining wealth as your sole purpose, yet have no one to share it with or be in such poor health as to diminish your enjoyment of the rewards. This is true in all areas of our lives as we need to strive for balance.

Utilize this strategy to think about what you want for every area of your life and then as step 2 suggests, take action. The action you take will produce results from which you can determine if you are on track or if you need to vary your approach. If on track, stay the course. If not, make an adjustment to your action. Repeat the feedback process. If working, persist until you achieve your goal. If not, go back a step and repeat the process as many times as necessary to achieve your objective. This is a simple concept, yet does take effort as we are constantly distracted and pulled by the momentum of our lives and the issues and events we must respond to daily. A captain of a sailing vessel en route to the intended destination is also affected by currents, weather, crew and other outside forces. The job of the captain is to manage and deal with these factors to get to his destination.

Making Your Goals SMART

The SMART Method is another tool I learned from Brian Tracy and others. I am not sure where credit belongs for the original creation, but I certainly appreciate what I learned from Mr. Tracy in its very useful and practical application. In creating and writing your goals and objectives, it may help to utilize the mnemonic aid of SMART (Specific, Measurable, Attainable, Result-oriented, and Time-specific).

- *Specific*—What is my objective in one sentence? An objective must be specific with a single key result. If you seek more than one result, create additional written objectives. As you find clarity in knowing what you want to accomplish, you are a big step closer to achieving it.
- *Measurable*—Will I be able to tell when I have achieved my goal? An objective must be measurable. Hazy and vague goals produce hazy and vague results. Some objectives are difficult to measure creating problems for many people. You can't measure an emotion. It is important to benchmark otherwise, how will you know how and how much you have progressed?
- *Attainable*—Am I confident in my ability to achieve this goal? An objective must be realistic and attainable. It is realistic to lose 25 pounds in a year, but unrealistic to think you can do it naturally in a month without hurting yourself. What are the obstacles? Can they be overcome? How and in what time frame?
- *Result-oriented*—Is my objective meaningful? Will doing this make a difference? Does this help me with my other goals? Is it aligned with my values and my mission?
- *Time-specific*—Is there a deadline to achieve my objective? What about subgoals and benchmarks for tracking along the way? Can I break into phases with sub-deadlines?

Success Plan of Action (Tactical)

There is a big difference between a success plan and a success plan of action. Without action, there is no movement and without movement there is no progress toward your dreams. Persistence is continued action and effort toward an objective, even in light of hardships, difficulties, challenges and even failures. Each day brings with it opportunities for our defining choices. Each choice we make becomes part of the fabric of our character. Each choice is woven together with our other past choices to create a tapestry of our lives. Each decision and every action creates the cumulative effect of our lives.

A tactical plan of any kind revolves around action and accountability for the action in relationship to the overall objective. Take the example of getting out of debt. Using the STACK strategy, the outcome goal is determined to be a target of all debt except for the mortgage to be eliminated in three years. From this, a tactical plan can be put in place. Below is a dramatically simplified example:

1. Objective—total debt to be eliminated—$18,600 (car, credit cards, loans, etc.)
2. Date to be accomplished by—06/06—three years from now
3. Approximate total per month needed—$520
4. Current total net household income—$61,000
5. Create a budget
6. Amount to be applied monthly after debts—$350
7. Shortfall—approximately $170 per month
8. Create ideas to reduce current expenses
9. Create ideas to expand income
10. Family commitment to stop digging the debt hole

As this family works toward their objective over the next 36 months, they will have many opportunities for reevaluating and getting feedback for possible minor adjustments. A promotion at work or the refrigerator going on the fritz creates decision points. As the family progresses to their goal, perhaps they can pay off one bill and apply the entire payment to the other open balances, and repeat after they pay off the next. This practical plan is part of the strategy and at the same time is entirely tactical.

Take (Tactical) Action— The Absolute Master Principle

Go forth and have activity. Become a goal setter and a goal achiever. Start small and create little victories from which you can build. Your initial success in setting and achieving goals will give you amazing confidence to incrementally edge up your expectations. This is a cycle of success. Be what former Navy Seal, author, speaker and professional consultant to Fortune 500 corporations Michael A. Janke calls a "Goal Warrior." He challenges, "Begin setting daily, monthly, yearly and lifelong goals for yourself. Attack your goals and desires like a commando..." We need action to fuel our dreams. We must take action to break free of the path we are currently on. This action is incremental, piece by piece and decision by decision within each hour of each day. Benjamin Disraeli said, "The secret to success is constancy of purpose."

The STACK plan is an overall strategy. You can utilize it for any number of large or small objectives. It is a starting point, a protocol or framework to build upon; it is not the end. Within this strategy, steps 2 and 4 are your tactical components. Setting the course, receiving feedback and maintaining the corrected course are part of the overall strategy. The planning and the "rubber meets the road" tactician's job comes about in deciding what action to take initially as well as what additional, or change in, action needs to be taken after feedback is received.

Plan of Action

In keeping with the power of positive and empowering questions we discussed in Chapter 13, I have found it helpful to go through this series of 10 questions for any serious goal or objective I have. They don't always have to go in any particular sequence, but it is helpful to follow a process until the method becomes more familiar. I recommend you identify one area of your life that is important to you. Now answer the following 10 questions and see if it doesn't immediately begin to work on you. Follow this exercise all the way through. Fill in as much detail as you can. Put it down and come back to it later to add additional insights as your reticular activating system has now turned on your servomechanism. Your awareness surrounding every aspect of this goal is heightened. Do not be afraid. Your thermostat may try to act against you, but you have the power. You can change your beliefs and your attitudes. These will reflect in your actions, and your persistence will determine your outcome. Take action now and you will immediately see benefits.

Tactical Goal Plan of Action

1. Specifically what is my goal? (Write it down!)
2. Why is it important for me to achieve this goal? (What is my driving motivation?)
3. What are main benefits I will gain by successfully achieving this goal?
4. What losses will I avoid?
5. Am I currently set up with all necessary resources to achieve my goal? If not, what do I lack?
6. What are the main action steps I must take to accomplish my goal? (list out)
7. What obstacles are possibly in my way?
8. What is my specific plan for getting past each obstacle?
9. What other resources do I have at my disposal that I can utilize as leverage for successful completion of my goal?
10. Looking back *after* I have achieved this goal, how do I describe my process and successful goal accomplishment to someone else?

After going through this exercise, there is one final practical question for you to ask yourself and answer: *Knowing all of the above, am I 100 percent committed to take continued action and full responsibility for achieving my goal?* If your answer is a resounding yes, your path is clear. If it is no or any degree less than a 100 percent committed yes, you need to reevaluate. The reason people nearly always fail in New Year's Resolutions is they fail in this litmus test. If you can't answer affirmative, perhaps it is better to shelve the goal or file it somewhere in the wishes, hopes and dreams folder to perhaps come back to later.

This is not meant as a flippant observation. Not all of your goals are meant to be pursued. Maybe timing or other situations are not right. Better to recognize the issues honestly in advance rather than midway through the journey. When the realization comes too late, it breeds disappointment and takes away confidence from the entire process leaving you feeling "burnt." When you go through this process and answer "yes!" you can undertake the challenge with confidence and knowledge that you have already done most of the important work in the process. You have an overall strategy and a tactical plan to get you where you want to go.

10 Tactical Questions to Begin a Purposeful Day

In addition to the very tactical goal plan of action, here is a bonus tool you can apply to add purpose and clarity to your daily journey and the life destination of your choosing. This is something a friend of mine introduced me to a while back. I used it purposefully for a time and somehow got away from it. When I used this daily, I would go into every day with assured confidence and directed action toward my deliberate goals. I am glad I found this old friend. I am happy to put it back into use and to share it with you.

1. What will I absolutely do today without fail?
2. Do I have a passion for what I will do today?
3. Do I have belief in my abilities?
4. Is what I will do today planned and part of my strategy?

5. Do my actions planned support my goals and objectives?
6. Will I take personal responsibility for myself, my actions and my results?
7. Can I visualize my future and what I set out to accomplish?
8. Is my attitude reflective of what I seek to achieve?
9. Am I willing to do whatever is necessary today in pursuit of my dreams and goals?
10. Will I take sustained action in pursuit of my goals regardless of other people, criticism, setbacks or any other circumstances?

Your Success Bank Account

If you will apply what you have either learned or been reminded of in this book, you will see a dramatic change in your results. I am 100 percent convinced this is true. I am as convinced of this as I am convinced that if you fall off a ladder, you will achieve a result of hitting the ground. The principles are universal; they work every time without fail. Most people will read a book like this or many books like this and never put into practice what they learned. Knowledge is not power until it is applied. As you create opportunities for application into your situation, you will achieve a result. You will make progress in your endeavors. This is the critical first step.

Just like a bank account, you have a choice as to what to do with your gains. You certainly can pull out your interest income to use as you will, but that will stagnate your principal balance. The other choice you have is to reinvest your interest income. Doing this allows your initial principal and your interest income to earn new interest income on the first and second generations of your savings. Each choice to reinvest the new interest creates a bigger base. Each generation of subsequent interest opportunities is on a larger and larger base. As we learned in the first chapter, this successful increase may be extremely small at first. The reinvested gains make a growing difference as they are applied over time. Each reinvestment creates a larger future opportunity since the base is enlarged as the incremental interest in each cycle grows. Over a period of time and with consistency, the gains can far outstrip the initial investment.

Although not as controlled and highly more volatile, your life can have the exact same result. Your initial investment is wherever you are in your life today. Each improvement in your life, each clarifying and empowered question, each written goal supported with visualization and affirmations, each opportunity to give to others…each applied Incremental Advantage is your reinvested interest income. Every time you take a purposeful action step toward the direction of your dreams, you shorten the distance. Each gain reinvested changes who you are and enlarges your potential. Applied compound interest working on your money will ultimately yield significant monetary gains. As the principle of compound Incremental Advantage is applied in your life, you can harvest rewards far beyond the value of money and into the quality and substance of your life.

Force Multiplier

How do you take all of these concepts and make them pay off, put them into practice? How do you increase your results and achieve them faster? How do you magnify your results to allow for success geometry? Use the military concept of…Force Multiplier. This is a key strategic concept I learned during my officer training and was able to witness firsthand during Desert Storm. This is battlefield geometry in that the more directions and more methods of attacking your enemy, the better your chance for success. In Desert Storm, we saw the most massive coordinated air assault in modern history followed by a ground war using so many battlefield force multipliers, the war lasted only 100 hours before complete victory was achieved. The planned, coordinated and executed operation rewrote the textbook for force multiplier—air supremacy, assault from the sea, land forces, armor units, rangers, marines, Airborne soldiers dropping from the sky, special forces popping up out of the sand, artillery, psychological warfare assets, etc. All of the assets from multiple countries and multiple branches of the military put together as it was seen in the mind of General Norman Schwarzkopf and his leadership team.

The force multiplier strategy is employed to achieve victory and to decimate the enemy. The more you can utilize and employ your tools of success, the better your chance to achieve your objective and in the shortest amount of time. You can lose weight by dieting alone or you can lose weight by exercise alone. Put them together and you have a force multiplier; your results are compounded. Utilize the high leverage principles and the mental programming techniques in a coordinated effort and you will see your result tree bear fruit as it has never done before. You were born with and have developed over time your skills, talents and abilities. If you will commit to yourself to employ even a small portion of what you have learned, you will change the course of your ICE, redirecting it purposefully.

Your Role as Teacher

There is no better way to employ what you have learned than to immediately apply it. There is no better way to apply concepts than to share them with others. Chances are that everything you have read in this book you already knew or had heard a time or two in your past. Remember, knowledge is not power, but *applied* knowledge certainly can be. Success is available for you if you will only take and methodically apply the building blocks.

Each moment and each day are building blocks from which you will build your life. If your actions are random, without thought or planning, your ultimate structure will be flawed, lacking in utility and purpose. But if each activity and each goal is planned, a carefully laid brick upon a solid foundation, the resulting structure will be a mighty castle. Building blocks for your success come in manageable pieces as habits of success. Small achievements create larger achievements. Decisions in the minutes of the day create the effect for the day. Actions of the day compounded over weeks and months and years will produce results. The question is, will you be the architect of your actions and your future or will you allow yourself to be the laborer of someone else's castle?

Your desired future will not just happen, it will be created through the bricks of your activities and the mortar of your attitude. The enterprise of your life is an ongoing journey. Your destiny is not in the stars or in the tarot cards of a fortune teller, but in your own ability to envision your future and then act diligently upon it. You can certainly follow in trails blazed by others before you, but ultimately what you do and where you go is on your shoulders.

"Nothing can take the place of persistence. Talent will not; nothing is more common than unsuccessful people with talent. Genius will not; unrewarded genius is almost a proverb. Education will not; the world is full of educated derelicts. Persistence and determination alone are the omnipotent."
—Calvin Coolidge, former U.S. President

"Keep on Stacking Those Logs!"
—Frank F. Lunn III (words to his son
regarding sustained and determined effort)

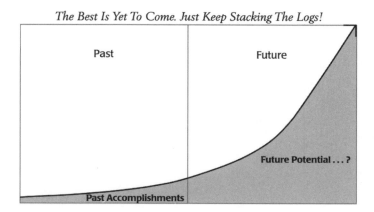

The Best Is Yet To Come. Just Keep Stacking The Logs!

Epilogue

Thank you for sharing this journey with me. My sincere hope is that you will be able to apply some of these principles to your life to increase your personal Incremental Advantage in every area.

For additional resources or to communicate with me directly, please visit our website www.stackthelogs.com.

For more information regarding St. Jude Children's Research Hospital, please contact them directly via www.stjude.org.

Best wishes for your future as you continue to "Stack The Logs!"

Sincerely,

Frank F. Lunn
Kahuna Business Group
www.kahunaworld.com
www.stackthelogs.com
Bloomington, Illinois

Further Reading to Gain an Incremental Advantage

Abraham, Jay. *Getting Everything You Can Out of All You've Got.* St. Martin's Griffin, 2001.

Allen, James. *As a Man Thinketh.* Camarillo, CA: DeVorss and Co., 2001.

Carnegie, Dale. *How to Win Friends and Influence People.* New York: Simon and Schuster, 1998.

Conwell, Russell. *Acres of Diamonds.* Old Tappan, NJ: Revell, 1975.

Covey, Stephen. *The 7 Habits of Highly Effective People.* New York; Fireside, 1990.

———. *First Things First.* New York: Simon and Schuster, 1994.

Frankl, Viktor. *Man's Search for Meaning.* New York: Washington Square Press, 1984.

Franklin, Benjamin. *The Art of Virtue.* Battle Creek, MI: Acorn Publishing, 1996.

Hill, Napoleon. *Think and Grow Rich!* New York: Fawcett Crest, 1969.

———. *Napoleon Hill's Keys to Success: The 17 Principles of Personal Achievement.* New York: Plume, 1997.

Mackay, Harvey. *Swim with the Sharks Without Being Eaten Alive.* New York: Fawcett, 1996.

Maltz, Maxwell. *Psycho-Cybernetics.* New York: Pocket Books, 1970.

Nightingale, Earl. *Lead the Field* (Audio Cassette Program). Chicago: Nightingale-Conant, 1997–2002.

Robbins, Anthony. *Unlimited Power.* New York: Fawcett, 1986.

———. *Awaken the Giant Within.* New York: Simon and Schuster, 1991.

Seligman, Martin. *Learned Optimism: How to Change Your Mind and Your Life.* New York: Pocket Books, 1998.

Staples, Walter D. *Think Like a Winner!* Gretna, LA: Pelican Publishing Company, 1991.

Tracy, Brian. *Focal Point.* New York: Amacom, 2002.

———. *Maximum Achievement.* New York: Simon and Schuster, 1993.

Ziglar, Zig. *See You at the Top.* Gretna, LA: Pelican, 1985.

———. *Top Performance.* Old Tappan, NJ: Revell, 1986.

For additional *Incremental Advantage*™ success resources, please visit www.stackthelogs.com.

Acknowledgments

Writing this book could never have been possible without the help from so many people. To my great friends and business partners, Tom Mortimer, Jason Sharpe and Ernie Beckman—your support, encouragement and stewardship of our business was inspirational and allowed me the freedom to make this happen. To our great Kahuna Team, thank you for your efforts day in and day out. You are the unsung heroes making it happen every day, and I am very appreciative. Nancy, my accountability and daily prayer partner, thank you for being the glue to hold it all together.

I had a special group of professional advisors, book reviewers and personal friends I would like to thank. Rick Galbreath, Phil Wegeng, Tom Jennings, Vance Rowland and Ron Schuldt provided me encouragement wrapped in candor in both the personal and professional realm. Dara Royer—not only did you significantly help me in the review process, but more importantly, you provided a gift of the "right words at the right time" for me to continue with this book when I was filled with self-doubt. The benefits St. Jude Children's Research Hospital will receive from this book are due in large part to your initial and sustained support. "Miss Penny," you were the face of encouragement and a constant source of inspiration; thank you for your smile and joy.

I would like to say thank-you to my mother, Mary Beth, for your encouragement, love and belief in me. I am thankful for my sister and good friend Cindy, her husband Scott and their family—Emily, Noah and Katie. Thanks for your unceasing support as well as your prayers. To my brother R. K., I just want to say that I believe in you and I know you have a great future. I know you will hear and apply Dad's words as they speak to your life as well. To my mother-in-law, Claudia, thank you for your unselfish support of our family. We could not have made it through Frankie's illness without your help, love and prayers. I am so thankful to have married into your family. To Joy and James, I appreciate you as in-laws yet even more so as true friends and a loving family.

This project would not have come together as it did without the significant help of my special project assistant and friend Kim Wohlwend. We both had to learn as we go on this first one, and I am sure the next one will be even better. Thanks to Michelle Higgerson for your help in the review and editing process. I would like to offer a special message of gratitude and thanks to the entire team at About Books, Inc. Your efforts to guide me through the intricacies of this project gave me confidence to just write and to allow you to do all the behind-the-scenes work to make it all seem easy. Thank you to my assistant Tammy Cook for all of your help to keep me on track.

I would like to provide special recognition for the following authors, teachers and practitioners of personal development: Zig Ziglar, Denis Waitley, Dan Kennedy, Brian Tracy, Larry Burkett, James Dobson, Paul J. Meyer, Tony Robbins, Stephen Covey, Earl Nightingale, Maxwell Maltz, Les Brown, Robert Allen, James Allen, Jim Rohn, Jay Abraham, Jay Conrad Levinson, Michael Gerber, Napoleon Hill, Norman Vincent Peal, Jack Canfield, Mark Victor Hansen, Kenneth Blanchard, Spencer Johnson, Warren Bennis, Doug Hall, John Maxwell, Chris Widener, Napoleon Hill, Og Mandino, Walter Doyle Staples, Robert Stuberg, Viktor Frankl, Benjamin Franklin and Stephen Covey. Although I do not know each of you personally and many of you are gone, we have taken many car rides and spent much time together in study. I *feel* like I know each of you personally as you have all left an imprint on my life. Your influence has contributed to this book both directly and indirectly. I hope to give back a portion of the gifts you have shared with me

When we first arrived at St. Jude our only thought was Frankie and his condition. Over the next several weeks and subsequent months we made friends with and got to know so many other little children fighting horrible diseases. Their courage and their friendship have touched us in a way that will never allow me to be the same. Here are a just few of our family's St. Jude buddies whose spirit inspired us: Maya, Bobby, Graham, Elijah, Kayla, Matthew, Haily, Ashleigh, Ashley, Hannah, Andrew, Alex, Dominick, Kisha, Ammunique, Kiesha, Kevin, Ana, Nicole, Makayla, Katelyn, Dylan, Donnie, Felicia, Danielle, Ethan, Mike, Danny, Nick, Miranda, Robbie, Will and Jason. You will always be in our prayers!

A special thank you to Dr. McAllister for setting our journey off with the right attitude and positive expectation as well as Dr. Hijiya, Gwen, Michelle, Karen, Martha and all of the other awesome nurses, doctors and caregivers who took such excellent care of Frankie and our family. To special new friends and blessings along the way, we thank the Wichlinski family for their love, friendship, support and wonderful southern hospitality! To Dr. John Wilkinson, Stacey Cloarc, Dara and Brent Royer, Lori Laird, Teri Watson—we thank you for sharing part of this life journey with us. There were certainly so many other patients, caregivers and friends. I certainly apologize for any omission.

To our church family at LeRoy Christian Church, thank you for your constant and unceasing prayer support during Frankie's illness and return. Above all, I give praise to the Lord God Almighty, creator of heaven and earth, and in Jesus Christ where I find my salvation. Thank you for loving me even as I am unworthy.

Index